Visual Studio 2015 Cookbook

Second Edition

Over 50 new and improved recipes to put Visual Studio
2015 to work in your crucial development projects

Jeff Martin

PUBLISHING

BIRMINGHAM - MUMBAI

Visual Studio 2015 Cookbook
Second Edition

First published: March 2014

Second edition: August 2016

Production reference: 1110816

Published by Packt Publishing Ltd.
Livery Place
35 Livery Street
Birmingham B3 2PB, UK.

ISBN 978-1-78588-726-0

www.packtpub.com

Credits

Author
Jeff Martin

Reviewer
Ahmed Ilyas

Commissioning Editor
Edward Gordon

Acquisition Editor
Denim Pinto

Content Development Editor
Anish Sukumaran

Technical Editor
Sunith Shetty

Copy Editor
Sonia Mathur

Project Coordinator
Izzat Contractor

Proofreader
Safis Editing

Indexer
Tejal Daruwale Soni

Graphics
Abhinash Sahu

Production Coordinator
Aparna Bhagat

Cover Work
Aparna Bhagat

About the Author

Jeff Martin has been a contributing writer for InfoQ (http://www.infoq.com) for over four years, focusing on .NET and Microsoft-based platforms. Experienced in writing, testing, and designing software, he enjoys learning about new technologies and explaining them to a broader audience. You can follow his work at InfoQ as .NET lead editor.

I would like to express my sincere gratitude to my wife, Carolyn, for her support and encouragement as I set out to write another book. Additionally, I would like to thank the team at Packt Publishing for their efforts to make this book a success.

About the Reviewer

Ahmed Ilyas has a BEng degree from Napier University in Edinburgh, Scotland. He has majored in software development and has 17 years of professional experience in the field.

After leaving Microsoft, he ventured into setting up his own consultancy company, which offers the best possible solutions for a multitude of industries and provides real-world answers to those problems. He uses the Microsoft stack to build these technologies and to bring in the best practices, patterns, and software to his client base to enable long-term stability and compliance in the ever-changing software industry, improve software developers around the globe, pushing the limits in technology, and to enable the developers to better themselves.

This has been awarded the MVP in C# by Microsoft thrice for providing excellence and independent real-world solutions to problems faced by developers.

With 90% of the world using at least one form of Microsoft technology, his motivation and inspiration come from the breadth and depth of knowledge he has obtained from his research and the valuable wealth of information and research at Microsoft.

He has worked for a number of clients and employers. The reputation that he has earned has resulted in him having a large client base for his consultancy company, Sandler Ltd (UK) and Sandler Software (USA). His client base includes clients from different industries, ranging from digital media to medical and beyond. Some of his clients have included him on their approved contractors/consultants list; these include ICS Solution Ltd, who have placed him on their "DreamTeam" portal, and CODE Consulting/EPS Software (www.codemag.com) based in the USA.

Previously, he has contributed as a reviewer to books by Packt Publishing and wishes to thank them once again for this great opportunity.

I would like to thank the author and publisher of this book for giving me the great honor and privilege of reviewing this book. I would also like to thank my client base and, especially, Microsoft Corporation and my colleagues over there for enabling me to become a reputable leader as a software developer in the industry, which is my joy, passion, and pride.

---

www.PacktPub.com

eBooks, discount offers, and more

Did you know that Packt offers eBook versions of every book published, with PDF and ePub files available? You can upgrade to the eBook version at www.PacktPub.com and as a print book customer, you are entitled to a discount on the eBook copy. Get in touch with us at customercare@packtpub.com for more details.

At www.PacktPub.com, you can also read a collection of free technical articles, sign up for a range of free newsletters and receive exclusive discounts and offers on Packt books and eBooks.

https://www2.packtpub.com/books/subscription/packtlib

Do you need instant solutions to your IT questions? PacktLib is Packt's online digital book library. Here, you can search, access, and read Packt's entire library of books.

Why subscribe?

- ▶ Fully searchable across every book published by Packt
- ▶ Copy and paste, print, and bookmark content
- ▶ On demand and accessible via a web browser

Table of Contents

Preface

The release of the *Visual Studio 2015 Cookbook* marks the third edition of a book series devoted to provide the reader with an informative tour of how Visual Studio 2015 (VS2015) can make your development work easier. This newest release of Visual Studio demonstrates Microsoft's renewed drive to make the best programming tools it can, regardless of the device and platforms that a developer is targeting. If that target happens to run Windows, then all the better—but it is no longer a hindrance if it does not.

This book is significantly updated and rewritten so that the reader can make use of the incredible array of new tools and devices supported by VS2015. With the greater number of platforms supported, it can be easy to overlook the new features offered in VS2015. One of the main goals of this book is to show developers the new ways in which they can put VS2015 to work in their daily development.

This book will begin by providing a guided tour of the main editor windows used in VS2015, which should be of interest to all users regardless of their desired language. After that, the book will show how different platforms can get work done faster with VS2015, whether it is for web programming, .NET, or classic C++ application development.

VS2015 lets you use the languages you are comfortable with while you target the platforms needed to support your customers. Taking advantage of the information provided in this book will help you maximize the tools VS2015 provides.

Choosing the right version of Visual Studio 2015

With V2015, Microsoft has greatly simplified the different offerings it provides. If you work on open source projects or independent developers, Visual Studio Community 2015 is free of charge and probably your best choice. Professional developers working in corporate settings or larger software companies should choose between Visual Studio Professional and Visual Studio Enterprise. If the price is of no concern, then Enterprise is a better choice as it includes all the available features. Note that Visual Studio Premium is no longer available for VS2015.

Different editions of VS2015 can be installed side by side, so feel free to install any/all of the above as needed for your work.

What this book covers

Chapter 1, Exploring Visual Studio 2015, starts us off by taking a tour of the new features found in the editor itself. VS2015 makes some key refinements, and this chapter covers them all, ranging from logging in to project navigation.

Chapter 2, Getting Started with Universal Windows Platform Apps, examines the development process for UWP apps for Windows 10 powered systems. The full process of obtaining a developer license to build, test, and publish an app is covered here.

Chapter 3, Web Development, covers several areas of web development and how VS2015 can assist you. Here, we'll cover the multi-browser preview, as well as editor enhancements that can benefit HTML5, CSS, and JavaScript programmers.

Chapter 4, .NET Framework Development, focuses on developing applications that run on .NET. Desktop application development is still a key market, and this chapter shows different ways in which VS2015 can help.

Chapter 5, Debugging Your .NET Application, profiles the various ways to debug your .NET-based code. This includes dealing with troubleshooting the code running on a device other than your development workstation.

Chapter 6, Asynchrony in .NET, deals with the use of asynchronous code to provide more responsive applications and discusses how it may benefit your applications.

Chapter 7, Unwrapping C++ Development, tackles the elder statesman of languages served by VS2015. Several recipes are provided to benefit your C++ usage—some of the areas covered include unit testing, DirectX, and the Visual Studio Graphics Debugger.

Chapter 8, Working with Team Foundation Server 2015, describes how Team Foundation Server can benefit your productivity. As modern source control continues to evolve, information on using Git is included.

Chapter 9, Languages, takes a moment to look at some languages other than .NET and C++, which include TypeScript and Python. Python has a long and successful history, and it is now a first-class citizen of Visual Studio. A new capability for VS2015 is Linux-based targets, and this is also explored here.

Chapter 10, Final Polish, in this final chapter, we will cover some ways to extend Visual Studio's abilities, and we will get your app ready for consumption by end users.

What you need for this book

To follow the recipes in this book, you will need a copy of Visual Studio 2015. Some of the features covered in the recipes may only be available in specific editions of Visual Studio. Thanks to Microsoft's new product lineup, most of the recipes are compatible with the freely available Visual Studio Community. It will be noted if a given recipe has additional requirements.

If you wish to follow one of these recipes, and you do not have the right edition, trial versions for premium versions can be downloaded from the Microsoft website, which enables you to check whether a particular feature will benefit your project.

For any of the recipes that deal with Universal Windows Platform (UWP) applications, you will need to use Windows 10 as your operating system.

Who this book is for

If you already know your way around the previous versions of Visual Studio, if you are familiar with Microsoft development, and if you're looking to quickly get up to speed with the latest improvements in the 2015 edition of Microsoft's number one development tool, this book is for you.

If you are an experienced developer who has used Eclipse or XCode, you should also be able to find this book useful to explore the differences between your tools and the latest ones that Microsoft has to offer.

Sections

In this book, you will find several headings that appear frequently (Getting ready, How to do it, How it works, There's more, and See also).

To give clear instructions on how to complete a recipe, we use these sections as follows:

Getting ready

This section tells you what to expect in the recipe, and describes how to set up any software or any preliminary settings required for the recipe.

How to do it...

This section contains the steps required to follow the recipe.

How it works...

This section usually consists of a detailed explanation of what happened in the previous section.

There's more...

This section consists of additional information about the recipe in order to make the reader more knowledgeable about the recipe.

See also

This section provides helpful links to other useful information for the recipe.

Conventions

In this book, you will find a number of text styles that distinguish between different kinds of information. Here are some examples of these styles and an explanation of their meaning.

Code words in text, database table names, folder names, filenames, file extensions, pathnames, dummy URLs, user input, and Twitter handles are shown as follows: "We can include other contexts through the use of the `include` directive."

A block of code is set as follows:

```
var http = require('http')
var finalhandler = require('finalhandler')
var serveStatic = require('serve-static')
```

When we wish to draw your attention to a particular part of a code block, the relevant lines or items are set in bold:

```
class BankVault
{
  public:
  BankVault();
  ~BankVault();
  int AddFunds(int amount);
  void StageHeist();
  int CurrentFunds();
};
```

Any command-line input or output is written as follows:

```
print('Hello World')
a=32
b=64
print("Results: " + (b+a))
```

New terms and **important words** are shown in bold. Words that you see on the screen, for example, in menus or dialog boxes, appear in the text like this: "The arrow in the following screenshot indicates where the **Sign in** option is located."

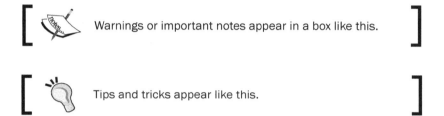

Warnings or important notes appear in a box like this.

Tips and tricks appear like this.

Reader feedback

Feedback from our readers is always welcome. Let us know what you think about this book—what you liked or disliked. Reader feedback is important for us as it helps us develop titles that you will really get the most out of.

To send us general feedback, simply e-mail feedback@packtpub.com, and mention the book's title in the subject of your message.

If there is a topic that you have expertise in and you are interested in either writing or contributing to a book, see our author guide at www.packtpub.com/authors.

Customer support

Now that you are the proud owner of a Packt book, we have a number of things to help you to get the most from your purchase.

Downloading the color images of this book

We also provide you with a PDF file that has color images of the screenshots/diagrams used in this book. The color images will help you better understand the changes in the output. You can download this file from https://www.packtpub.com/sites/default/files/downloads/VisualStudio2015CookbookSecondEdition_ColorImages.pdf.

Errata

Although we have taken every care to ensure the accuracy of our content, mistakes do happen. If you find a mistake in one of our books—maybe a mistake in the text or the code—we would be grateful if you could report this to us. By doing so, you can save other readers from frustration and help us improve subsequent versions of this book. If you find any errata, please report them by visiting http://www.packtpub.com/submit-errata, selecting your book, clicking on the **Errata Submission Form** link, and entering the details of your errata. Once your errata are verified, your submission will be accepted and the errata will be uploaded to our website or added to any list of existing errata under the Errata section of that title.

To view the previously submitted errata, go to https://www.packtpub.com/books/content/support and enter the name of the book in the search field. The required information will appear under the **Errata** section.

Piracy

Piracy of copyrighted material on the Internet is an ongoing problem across all media. At Packt, we take the protection of our copyright and licenses very seriously. If you come across any illegal copies of our works in any form on the Internet, please provide us with the location address or website name immediately so that we can pursue a remedy.

Please contact us at copyright@packtpub.com with a link to the suspected pirated material.

We appreciate your help in protecting our authors and our ability to bring you valuable content.

Questions

If you have a problem with any aspect of this book, you can contact us at questions@packtpub.com, and we will do our best to address the problem.

1
Exploring Visual Studio 2015

In this chapter, we will cover the following topics:

- ▶ Synchronizing settings
- ▶ Touring the VS2015 IDE
- ▶ Managing the editor windows
- ▶ Finding Visual Studio commands
- ▶ Searching and navigating
- ▶ Navigating in depth

Introduction

The user interface in **Visual Studio 2015** (**VS2015**) is very similar to that of **Visual Studio 2013** (**VS2013**) from an appearance standpoint. However, existing users will still want to browse this chapter to make sure they don't overlook subtle changes. New users will want to read this chapter carefully so that they are able to easily navigate the Integrated Development Environment (IDE).

The goal of this chapter is to provide all users of VS2015 with the various tools that will benefit developers working on any project type. Having an in-depth familiarity with the IDE will make learning the language-specific functionality much easier.

Synchronizing settings

Given the prevalence of cloud computing, and the central role the Internet has in daily life, it should be no surprise that nearly all Microsoft products utilize some form of an online account, and VS2015 is no exception. If you have an MSDN account, Microsoft recommends that you use it to log in to Visual Studio. If you don't have one, or would prefer to use a new account, you can create one at `https://login.live.com/`. A new account can be useful if you wish to separate your personal and professional settings.

Settings synchronized under Visual Studio are shared by all applicable product types, so if changes are made in the Visual Studio Community edition, they would replicate to Visual Studio Enterprise edition when synchronized. Similarly, if changes were made in Visual Studio Express for Web, they would propagate to Visual Studio Community if so enabled.

Settings receive a one-time migration from VS2013 to VS2015. Any subsequent changes made under VS2015 will not propagate back to VS2013 products.

New to VS2015 is the implementation of single sign-on. Now from the moment a user first authenticates with an account on one of Microsoft's cloud services (VS2015, Azure, Visual Studio Team Services, and others), additional log-in requests will be reduced or eliminated where possible.

In this recipe, we will look at how this synchronization works, and what it will coordinate on your behalf.

Getting ready

To explore, launch your copy of Visual Studio 2015.

How to do it...

If you are not prompted to sign in at start-up, you can always sign in from within Visual Studio. The arrow in the following screenshot indicates where the **Sign in** option is located:

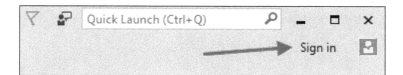

VS2015 will synchronize the following settings for you:

- ▶ **Environment**: This section consists of several sub-items.

- ▶ **General**: This includes settings for the chosen color theme (blue, dark, light, and so on), and case styling for the menu bar (whether VS2015 should use title case styling or all capital letters).

- ▶ **Fonts and Colors**: This includes preferences for the display text used throughout the editor.

- ▶ **Keyboard**: This includes user-defined keyboard shortcuts and the selected keyboard-mapping scheme.

- ▶ **Startup**: This indicates what should display when VS2015 opens (startup page, last solution, nothing, and so on).

- ▶ **Tabs and Windows**: All settings shown here are for tool windows and editor tabs.

- ▶ **Text Editor**: A multitude of settings, including whether to use tabs versus spaces, word wrap, scroll bar placement, and so on.

- ▶ **XAML Designer**: Not seen in the screenshot that follows Document view, orientation, and other settings used with XAML Designer.

- ▶ **Environment Aliases**: Not seen in the screenshot that follows; applies to premium versions only. Commands defined in the command window (*Ctrl + Alt + A*).

Custom-defined window layouts defined under **Window | Manage Window Layouts** are also synchronized. The following screenshot highlights the synchronized categories as shown under **Tools | Options**:

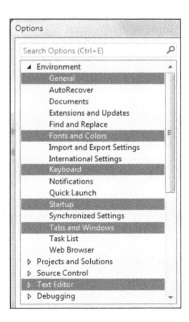

Take advantage of the usability enhancements in the **Options** dialog. Use the integrated search box (once **Options** is opened, the hotkey is *Ctrl + E*) for specifically searching within the **Options** dialog box. Also note that the dialog is now resizable, making it much more useful for viewing settings that have lengthy configuration options.

How it works...

Microsoft stores a copy of your settings on their servers. A constant Internet connection is not required to use Visual Studio, but your settings will not synchronize until you are reconnected. If a connection is not available, you cannot log in until Internet access is restored, but Visual Studio will still be usable. Taking it one step further, VS2015 remembers if you were logged in the last time when you closed the program, so your last known settings will be available, as they are stored locally.

There's more...

All synchronization options are configurable by navigating to **Options** | **Environment** | **Synchronized Settings**, and you may opt to have any combination of the preceding categories synced. Choosing what to sync is specific to each machine, and is not transferred. By default, VS2015 will attempt to synchronize all settings if you are logged in with a Microsoft account.

Touring the VS2015 IDE

It is a great idea to familiarize yourself with the main components of the VS2015 IDE, since that is where you will spend most of your time. Users coming from VS2013 will see many similarities, but there some new details that you will find useful to review. Let's take a look at what is available in this recipe.

Getting ready

All you will need for this recipe is a copy of VS2015 so that you can follow the location of the different options. The next screenshot provides an overview of what will be covered:

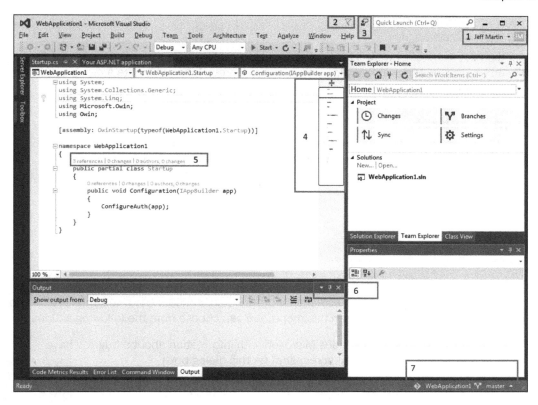

The legend for the highlighted items in the preceding screenshot is as follows:

- ▶ The user's account entry/selection is indicated by **1**
- ▶ The notification center is indicated by **2**
- ▶ The Send Feedback menu is indicated by **3**
- ▶ The scrollbar thumbnail is indicated by **4**
- ▶ **CodeLens** (Professional and Enterprise editions only) is indicated by **5**
- ▶ The editor window controls are indicated by **6**
- ▶ Git version control indicators (for Git-based projects; not available on Community) are represented by **7**

How to do it...

Over the next few pages, we will take a first-hand look at how these areas of the Visual Studio IDE can be used. You may follow along with your own project, or just create a new project using one of the templates provided with VS2015.

Send Feedback

This screenshot shows the choices available when the Send Feedback menu is accessed by clicking on the Send Feedback icon (represented by a person with a chat balloon):

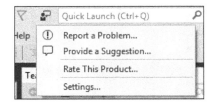

The menu shown in the preceding screenshot provides an immediate way to send feedback to Microsoft from within VS2015. From this menu, you can choose from the following actions:

▶ **Report a Problem...**: Provides Microsoft with information about a bug you have experienced. (See the next screenshot for this dialog box.)

▶ **Provide a Suggestion...**: Uses your current web browser to navigate to the VS2015 area on Microsoft's **UserVoice** site to request a new feature or change to V2015.

▶ **Rate This Product...**: Uses your current web browser to navigate to a web-based product survey for VS2015.

▶ **Settings...**: Allows you to view and change whether or not you will send information to Microsoft as part of the Visual Studio Experience Improvement Program.

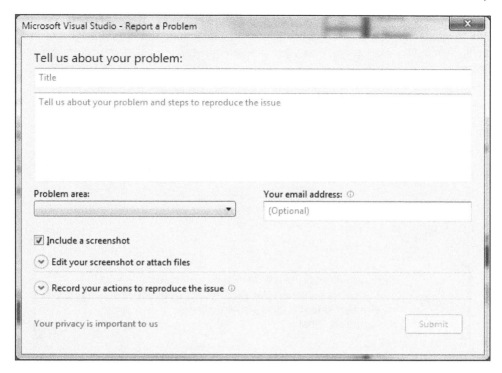

Notifications

On the far left of the **Quick Launch** field is a flag icon that indicates product notifications (if any):

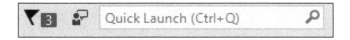

In the preceding screenshot, you can see that three updates are pending. The notification flag is designed to provide an unobtrusive alert when updates are available to VS2015 and its installed packages. Notifications listed in the sidebar are color-coded with yellow and red, which are used to indicate medium and high priority respectively.

Examples of notifications that could appear include the presence of Visual Studio updates, updates to installed extensions or samples, or notice indicating that the VS2015 product license is invalid. Notifications may be dismissed en masse, and once dismissed, they do not reappear:

 If you would like to review dismissed Notifications, navigate to **Tools | Extensions and Updates**. Select **Updates** and review the **Product Updates** that are available, as shown in the preceding screenshot.

User account

If you have already signed in to VS2015 with a Microsoft account (refer to the *Synchronizing settings* recipe), this area displays the graphical avatar, along with your account's display name. The following screenshot shows the difference in the display that occurs when you log in:

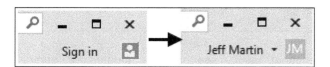

The **Sign in** command provides a way to sign in if you have not done so, or if you wish to change the active account being used. In the preceding screenshot, the left-hand side has the text **Sign in**, and a grey icon indicates that the user has yet to log in. On the right-hand side, you can see the difference after the user has logged in, as the user's name and avatar has replaced the **Sign in** text.

Scroll bar thumbnail

Similar to other code editors that you may be familiar with, VS2015 has a configurable scroll bar in its main editor window. It can be customized to show your overall position in a source file, and provide a tool tip that lets you examine code elsewhere in your current file without changing your current location. The new option is called map mode, as opposed to the historical behavior, which is called bar mode (which follows the traditional scrollbar appearance and behavior). All aspects of map mode are customizable, including whether it appears at all, its width (narrow, medium, or wide), and the ability to show the preview tool tip.

The following screenshot shows these features in action:

The preceding screenshot shows the scroll bar configured to be in map mode. The first arrow (marked as **2**) indicates what is being displayed in the editor relative to the overall source file. The second arrow (marked as **3**) points to the preview tool tip that appears when your mouse cursor hovers over the scroll bar.

The scroll bar's pull-down feature (marked as **1**) remains, and when used to split the main window, it allows for two independent viewing panes of the same file, each of which can have its own independent vertical scroll bar. In split view mode, both the vertical scroll bars share the same options (width, bar mode versus map mode, and so on).

The following screenshot lists all the options available for configuring the scroll bar's functionality. It can be accessed directly by right-clicking on the vertical scroll bar and selecting **Scroll Bar Options...**. Alternatively, it is accessible in the main **Options** dialog box of VS2015 by navigating to **Tools | Options** with the scroll bar settings listed under **Text Editor | All Languages | Scroll Bars**. For additional customizations, you may set language-specific settings (**C/C++**, **C#**, and so on) for the scroll bar in the **Options** dialog box if desired:

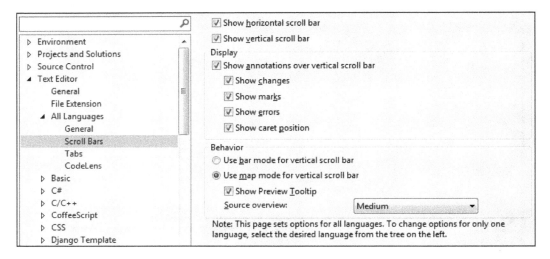

Peek Definition

Visual Studio has had the **Go To Definition** (*F12*) option for several versions now. When we right-click on a method or move the cursor to it, selecting the **Go To Definition** option will automatically bring you directly to the file with the corresponding definition. While you can easily navigate back and forth with (*Ctrl + -*) and (*Ctrl + Shift + -*), sometimes changing the open file is not what you would like to do.

Enter **Peek Definition** (*Alt + F12*). This allows you to select a method and look it up, but instead of switching to the appropriate file, VS2015 will create a mini window within your current editor. The following screenshot shows the results of using the **Peek Definition** option on the `PasswordSignInAsync()` method:

Sequential peeks can be performed, each opening via a tabbed interface. Navigation between these tabs (represented by circles / marked by the arrow in the preceding screenshot) can be done via the mouse or keyboard: peek forward (*Ctrl + Alt + =*) and peek backward (*Ctrl + Alt + -*). The **Peek Definition** window uses the same scroll bar behavior as that of the parent editing window, and this behavior can be changed in either window by right-clicking on the scroll bar and selecting **Scroll Bar Options...**

CodeLens (Visual Studio Professional and Enterprise only)

CodeLens, also known as code information indicators, debuted in VS2013 but was limited to the Ultimate edition. In response to user feedback, Microsoft has made it available to both VS2015 Professional and Enterprise. Activated by default, CodeLens provides real-time meta-information about the file you open in your main editor window:

```
// Models returned by MeController actions.
2 references | Jeff Martin, Less than 5 minutes ago | 1 author, 1 change
public class GetViewModel
{
    // Formerly hometown
    1 reference | Jeff Martin, Less than 5 minutes ago | 1 author, 1 change
    public string PlaceOfBirth { get; set; }
}
```

As illustrated in the preceding screenshot, shown in line with your code will be light-colored term references, and the name of the developer with the time since the most recent commit. The references term indicates the number of places a method is used, and can also display a pop-up window upon hovering the mouse over the term that shows where it has been used. If unit testing is part of the project, the number of passing and failing tests can be shown.

VS2015 provides additional functionality using either the source control provided by **Team Foundation Server** (**TFS**) or Git. This enables CodeLens to display the most recent author of the method in question, and clicking on that name will pop up a details window listing the change history.

If you would prefer to keep your hands on the keyboard, holding down *Alt* will bring up hotkeys that can be used to select among the features discussed earlier. The following screenshot illustrates these options, with *Alt + 2* opening a pop-up dialog box listing references for the selected method, and *Alt + 5* displaying information about who last modified the code. *Alt + 7* provides the revision history:

```
// 2dels returned b 5 MeController acti 7 .
2 references | Jeff Martin, Less than 5 minutes ago | 1 author, 1 change
public class GetViewModel
```

New in VS2015 is the addition of file-level indicators for supported file types. When Visual Studio isn't able to offer details at the code element level, file-level indicators provide similar (although, not identical) functionality. A file-level indicator is shown at the bottom of the editor window when available, as indicated by the arrow in the following screenshot:

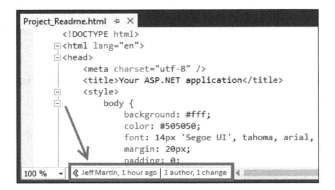

 CodeLens provides code element-level indicators for C# and Visual Basic files. All other source file types receive file-level indicators.

The display options for **CodeLens** are labeled as **Code Information Indicators** in the **Options** dialog box, and can be found under **Text Editor | All Languages | Code Information Indicators**. Alternatively, you may simply right-click on the indicator line, and choose the **CodeLens** options:

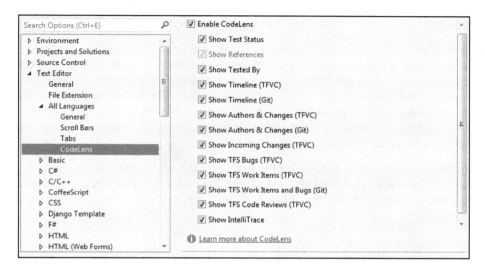

Code Maps (Visual Studio Enterprise only)

VS2015 Enterprise provides the ability to generate and use a code visualization tool, which Microsoft calls Code Maps, to provide a representation of the open project. The following screenshot shows Code Maps in action:

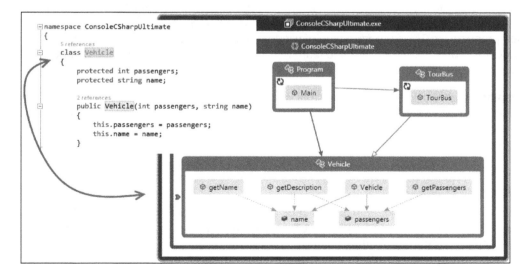

Code Maps can be created and used in VS2015 Enterprise, but VS2015 Professional and VS2015 Community can only consume them. This means that users of Professional and Community can interact with the maps, and add comments/flags as they are reviewed. Code Maps can be activated in an editor window via *Ctrl + `*, which is *Ctrl* plus the back quote key (typically found sharing a key with tilde). It may be also called by right-clicking in the editor window on a particular method or class that you want to map.

Once generated, the map may be manipulated in several ways, including zooming and the ability to expand to show related elements. Individual elements may be double-clicked so that they are brought up in the code editor for closer analysis. An element may also be right-clicked when in the Code Map for further navigation options (**Go To Definition**, **Show Base Types**, and so on) or to be commented on. This is particularly helpful for large or complex code bases where a map can assist in comprehension by visualizing the relationships and adding commentary external to the source code.

The Code Map indicates your position on the map from the active editor window with a green arrow icon. In the preceding example's screenshot, the editor is in the Vehicle class, which is pointed to on the Code Map by the green chevron (relationship marked in the preceding screenshot).

See also

▸   Refer to the *Choosing the right version of Visual Studio 2015* section in the *Preface*

Managing the editor windows

One of the advantages of using a graphical IDE is the ability to have multiple windows open, so learning how to customize their size and layout in Visual Studio is important for maximizing their productivity. Given the multitude of windows (editors, debugger output, and so on) Visual Studio has open, it can be helpful to learn how to place them where you want so that you can focus on your work without being slowed down by clutter.

Tab pinning allows you to mark individual windows so that they stay open while you navigate through the editor. **Previewing documents** is a useful way to navigate across several files without cluttering your tabs with several open documents. This recipe will explore both options.

Getting ready

To follow along, open a solution of your choice. The following walkthrough uses a brand new **Single Page Application ASP.NET 4.6.1 Template,** but the concepts apply to any project. Ensure that the **Solution Explorer** window is open.

How to do it...

The following steps will show how the position of open windows can be changed to your liking. Let's get started:

1. In the **Solution Explorer** window, locate the `AccountViewModels.cs` file in the project folder (under `Models`), and double-click on it. The source file will open in the main window area, as in the previous versions of Visual Studio; however, you will now notice that the document tab features a pin icon next to the tab name, as you can see in the following screenshot. You'll use that pin in just a few steps:

2. Using the **Solution Explorer** window, open both the `IdentityModels.cs` and `ManageViewModels.cs` files by double-clicking on them. You should now have three documents open with their tabs showing in the tab well (this refers to the row of tabs for each open document in the editor), as shown in the following screenshot:

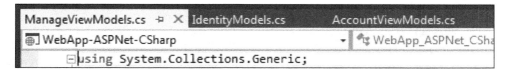

3. Click on the `ManageViewModels.cs` tab to select it, and then click on the pin. The pin will change to point downwards, indicating that the document is now pinned. Visual Studio will always keep pinned tabs visible in the tab well. These pinned tabs will remain visible, even when Visual Studio has to start hiding unpinned tabs to save screen display space. The pinned document tab will be moved to the left next to any other pinned documents you may have open:

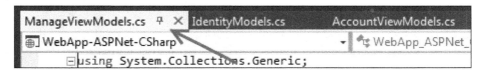

4. Right-click on the `AccountViewModels.cs` document tab, and click on the **Close All But This** option to close all open documents except for the one currently selected. This will include closing any pinned documents, which are shown in the following screenshot:

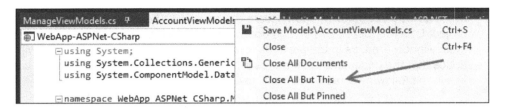

 There is a related option **Close All But Pinned**, which is useful when you would like to only keep pinned files open.

5. Reopen both files, `ManageViewModels.cs` and `IdentityModels.cs` by double-clicking on them in **Solution Explorer**.

6. Notice that in VS2015, like in VS2013, double-clicking on a document tab of your choice gives that tab focus, the same as single-clicking on it. Previously, double-clicking on a document tab would cause it to float.

7. Now lets see how the preview window works in conjunction with the tabs we already have open. Press *Ctrl + Shift + F* to open the *Find in Files* dialog box. Enter some search text (we will use `login`) in the **Find what** field, and ensure that **Look in** is set to solution; then click on the **Find All** button.

8. In the **Find Results 1** window, select a result from a file that is not already open; we will use `AccountController.cs`.

9. The file will open in the preview tab located on the right-hand side of the tab well.

10. The preview tab shows the contents of the currently selected document if it is not already open. In the **Find Results 1** window, select a different file. This new file will now appear in the preview tab, rather than clutter your tab well with open files as you search for the exact file that you want.

11. Assuming you now have found what you are looking for, and want to keep the current file in the preview tab open, either click on the Keep Open icon on the preview tab, or start making changes to the contents of the file. Any document that is changed in the preview tab is automatically promoted to a normal tab. The following screenshot illustrates using the Keep Open icon to promote a document in the preview tab:

Visual Studio will move the document from the preview tab area into the main tab area. The color of the tab will also be changed from blue to yellow (exact colors depend on the theme that you have selected) indicating that the tab is now a normal document tab.

How it works...

Pinning documents works much like pinning does in any other part of Visual Studio, and is very handy for keeping the documents that you are working on regularly within easy reach, especially when you have many documents open at once.

The preview document tab is a great way to prevent tab clutter, and is very useful while debugging deeply-nested code. You may recall that **Go To Definition** is one function that uses the preview document tab. For example, multiple source files may be opened as you trace a program's operation across methods and classes. The preview document tab helps you cycle quickly through these files, while preventing the tab well from filling up with documents that aren't needed for more than a few moments.

There's more...

As you may expect, there are more ways to use and customize the behavior of the document tabs in Visual Studio.

Single-click preview in Solution Explorer

The preview tab isn't restricted to just the **Find Results** window. It can also be used from within **Solution Explorer**. If you activate the **Preview Selected Items** button in the **Solution Explorer** toolbar, then every item you click on will be opened in the preview tab automatically. The **Preview Selected Items** button is a toggle button. If you want to disable the behavior, then you only need to click on the button to deselect it, and the preview behavior will be turned off:

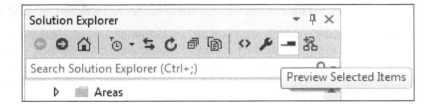

Customizing tab and window behavior

Navigating to **Tools** | **Options** | **Tabs and Windows** in Visual Studio will show the following dialog box:

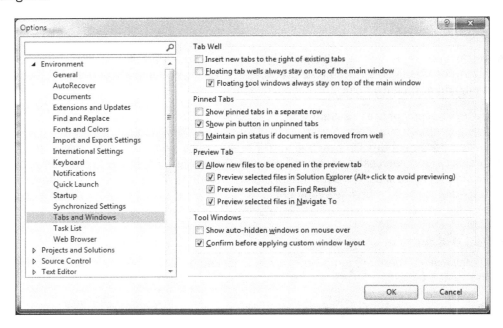

There are a number of options here that let you control how the tabs behave. Choices like **Show pinned tabs in a separate row** or **Insert new tabs to the right of existing tabs** may be helpful to you. Feel free to experiment with the **Tabs and Windows** settings to get Visual Studio working the way you like it most.

Finding Visual Studio commands

The goal of the **Quick Launch** box is to provide a keyboard-friendly way of accessing the extended features of Visual Studio without having to clutter the central interface. Keyboard shortcuts are a great way to speed up tasks, but it can be difficult to learn and remember while first starting out or while exploring a new area of Visual Studio. The **Quick Launch** option addresses this by providing a way to locate different areas of the program and learn keyboard shortcuts, and providing a keyboard-centric way to access commands.

Getting ready

Simply start VS2015.

How to do it...

To try it out, start with pressing *Ctrl + Q*, then begin typing the topic/subject that you are looking for, as shown in the following screenshot:

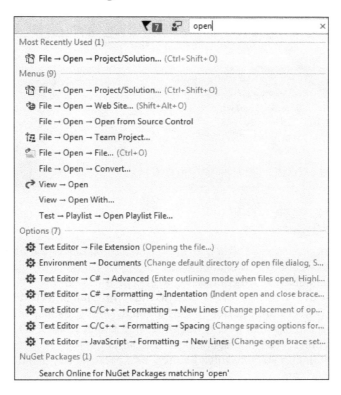

What is important to notice is that **Quick Launch** can do even more than what may be obvious at first glance. In this example, notice that open was the term entered as a search term. **Quick Launch** produces a list of results to this query, grouped by the following categories: **Most Recently Used**, **Menus**, **Options**, and **NuGet Packages**. As you can see, this list of results is more than just commands; it includes various areas in the **Options** dialog as well as **NuGet Packages**.

You can immediately navigate through the search results with the arrow keys on the keyboard if the desired result is immediately available. You can access a command directly from this list, and where available, the accompanying keyboard hotkey for a command will be listed. In this way, you can learn new shortcuts while doing your daily work.

In the next example, `jquery` was entered into **Quick Launch**, producing a list of results that includes context-specific file menu commands (Save and Save As), the option to switch to an open editor window with `jquery` in the file name (`jquery-1.10.2.js`), or to search NuGet for packages using `jquery` as the search term.

The following screenshot shows the availability of these various options:

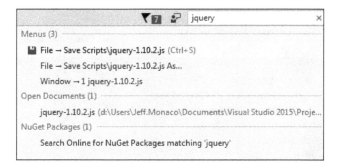

There's more...

The **Quick Launch** option can go further; let's return to the results of the open term. Note that at the bottom, the **Quick Launch** option indicates that *Ctrl + Q* can index through additional views. Additional presses of *Ctrl + Q* will toggle the list of results to show only results from an individual category, in this case **Menus**, **Options**, or **NuGet Packages**. A final press of *Ctrl + Q* will return to displaying all of the available results. This ability to toggle through categories is of particular usefulness when your **Quick Launch** list is lengthy, and you would like to ignore unnecessary categories that are cluttering the list of results. Pressing *Esc* once will clear the search results in **Quick Launch**, and pressing *Esc* again will return you to the open file in your editor.

Using the Command Window / Command Aliases

The **Command Window** (accessible via *Ctrl + Alt + A*, and available on premium editions of VS2015) in the preceding screenshot, allows you to keep your hands on the keyboard while quickly accessing commands via an integrated command prompt window. As Microsoft ships Visual Studio preloaded with command definitions, entering an alias will display all of the currently defined commands, and the `alias cmd` action (where `cmd` is the desired name of your alias, and action defines what should happen) will allow you to define your own. You can see from the following screenshot that typing `bl` is much faster than typing `Debug.Breakpoints`. Note that, by default, command aliases are stored as part of your synchronized profile.

```
Command Window
>alias
alias ? Debug.Print
alias ?? Debug.QuickWatch
alias AddProj File.AddNewProject
alias alias Tools.Alias
alias autos Debug.Autos
alias bl Debug.Breakpoints
alias bp Debug.ToggleBreakpoint
alias callstack Debug.CallStack
alias ClearBook Edit.ClearBookmarks

  Code Metrics Results   Error List   Command Window
```

Searching and navigating

Visual Studio provides many ways to make maneuvering through your code easier and more efficient. Let's take a look at a few of them.

Getting ready

To best see this in action, open a project that has multiple files available for editing. This can be the sample project or one of your own choice. Once it is open, simply open a couple of source files.

How to do it...

Pressing *Ctrl + Tab* provides easy access to a couple of different ways to navigate around Visual Studio. If *Ctrl + Tab* is pressed and immediately released, Visual Studio will alternate between the two most recent files that you have opened in the editor window, providing a quick way to move back and forth. If *Ctrl + Tab* is pressed and *Tab* is released, a pop-up window will appear. Continue to hold down *Ctrl* when it appears, and then arrow keys can be used to maneuver around the list of all active files and windows. To make a selection, either release *Ctrl* while highlighting the desired target, or while holding *Ctrl*, press *Enter*.

This is shown in the following example screenshot, where active files currently open in Visual Studio are shown in the right-hand side column, while open tool windows are shown in the left-hand side column:

There's more...

If you would rather use a keyboard mouse hybrid approach, the window *Ctrl + Tab* produces, and also supports, selection by mouse. Start in the same manner as done earlier in this recipe, holding down *Ctrl + Tab* to bring up the window. Release *Tab* while holding down the *Ctrl* key, and then use your mouse to left-click directly on the file you would like to switch to.

Quickly searching your code

Searching a project file to find specific strings of text is a common task regularly performed by developers. Visual Studio tries to make this easy by offering specific tools to find and replace text at various levels of your code base. Several options are available under **Edit | Find and Replace**, including **Quick Find**, **Quick Replace**, **Find In Files**, and **Replace In Files**.

The **Incremental Search** option (*Ctrl + I*) is a quick way to search within the file you are currently editing. When activated, a **Find** dialog box appears in your active editor window, allowing you to enter search terms.

The **Quick Find** (*Ctrl + F*) and **Quick Replace** (*Ctrl + H*) options share a common dialog box. Both provide the ability to search the current code block, the current project, all open documents, or the entire solution. If your search options include the currently open file, the vertical scroll bar will highlight any matches found. This provides quick visual feedback on the frequency of a search item:

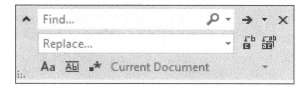

Another feature that **Quick Find** and **Quick Replace** share is the ability to set the following search options: match case, match whole word, and whether or not regular expressions can be used. The use of regular expressions allows for more complex queries to be used, allowing users to extract more detailed information from their searches.

The **Find In Files** (*Ctrl + Shift + F*) and **Replace In Files** (*Ctrl + Shift + H*) options provide a more advanced method of conducting searches across a code base. They expand on the functionality offered by the quick tools by allowing you to specify the file types that should be searched (for example, all HTML and JavaScript files), and provide the ability to display the results of an operation in a separate window.

 When using **Quick Find/Replace** or **Find/Replace in Files**, Visual Studio will automatically prefill the word or character nearest your cursor into the search box.

Find Results 1

```
⊟lution, "*.cs;*.resx;*.resw;*.xsd;*.wsdl;*.xaml;*.xml;*.htm;*.html;*.css"
 -CSharp\WebApp-ASPNet-CSharp\App_Start\IdentityConfig.cs(45):          var manager = new ApplicationUserMa
 -CSharp\WebApp-ASPNet-CSharp\App_Start\IdentityConfig.cs(81):          var dataProtectionProvider = option
 -CSharp\WebApp-ASPNet-CSharp\Areas\HelpPage\HelpPageConfigurationExtensions.cs(313):
 -CSharp\WebApp-ASPNet-CSharp\Areas\HelpPage\HelpPageConfigurationExtensions.cs(393):     foreach
 -CSharp\WebApp-ASPNet-CSharp\Areas\HelpPage\HelpPageConfigurationExtensions.cs(399):     foreach
 -CSharp\WebApp-ASPNet-CSharp\Areas\HelpPage\ModelDescriptions\ModelNameHelper.cs(30):     modelNa
 -CSharp\WebApp-ASPNet-CSharp\Areas\HelpPage\SampleGeneration\HelpPageSampleGenerator.cs(101):    vai
```

Code Metrics Results Error List Command Window Output Find Results 1 Find Symbol Results

In the preceding example screenshot, a text string was used to search the entire solution using the specified file mask. The results were outputted to **Find Results 1**, which is a live window. This means that you can click on a line with a particular search result, and you will go directly to that file where the match was made. Notice that some of the details provided in the results include the line number and context of the value being searched for.

Navigating in depth

Solution Explorer in VS2015 provides a range of features intended to make navigating and searching within your solution effective without overcomplication. Knowing how to efficiently move among solution files will only help your productivity, so let's take a look at what is available.

Getting ready

Open the same web application solution that we have been using for the other recipes in this chapter, or choose a solution of your own. The concepts here will be of use in any project type.

How to do it...

1. We'll begin by navigating through our solution. Locate the `Global.asax` file in the web app solution, and click on the arrow next to it so that its contents are displayed. As you would expect, there is a code-behind file:

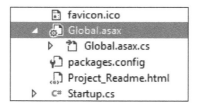

2. Look at the `Global.asax.cs` file. You can see that there is a small arrow next to it, just as there was for the `Global.asax` page. Click on the arrow:

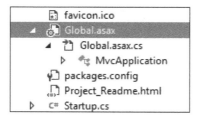

3. VS2015 expands the file to show its contents, and in the case of a code-behind file, these contents are the class definitions it contains. Classes have methods and properties in them, so click on the arrow next to the `MvcApplication` class to see the methods inside it. In this case, there is a method called `Application_Start()`, as shown in the following screenshot:

4. Now select the `AccountController.cs` file from the project, and expand it to see its contents. You will see that there is a class definition (`AccountController`), as shown in the following screenshot:

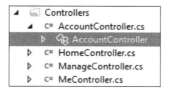

5. Right-click on the `AccountController` class, and click on the **Base Types** option to see what class this is based on:

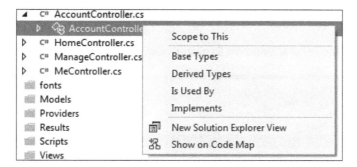

6. The **Solution Explorer** window will change views to show you the classes that `AccountController` is derived from, as shown in the following screenshot (with class hierarchy fully expanded). Click on the back button (as marked by the arrow) to return to the standard **Solution Explorer** view:

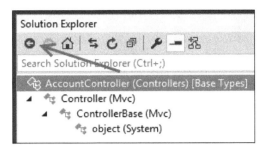

7. Right-click on the `AccountController` class, and choose the **Is Used By** option to see where the interface is currently being used. As with the **Base Types** or **Derived Types** options, you will see **Solution Explorer** change its context to only show the interface and where that interface is used in the solution, including line and column numbers:

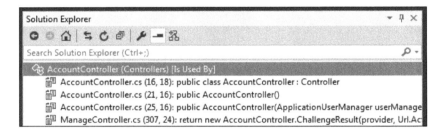

8. Return to the regular **Solution Explorer** view by clicking on the home button:

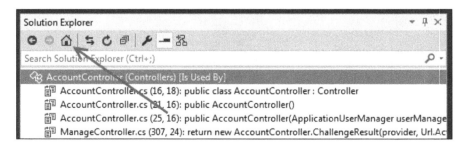

9. At this point, you know how to navigate using **Solution Explorer**, and you have already used the existing **Navigate To** feature in the *Finding Visual Studio commands* recipe while opening a file. With the enhancements to **Solution Explorer**, you can locate files in much the same way as with the **Navigate To** command, albeit with a slightly different user experience. Click on the **Search Solution Explorer** textbox at the top of the **Solution Explorer** window, or use the default shortcut key: *Ctrl + ; (Ctrl +* semicolon).

10. Enter models in the textbox, and wait a moment for the search results to display. The results should look similar to the following screenshot if you are using the sample project. You can see, not only the filenames that match the search term, but also any matching references, classes, and methods:

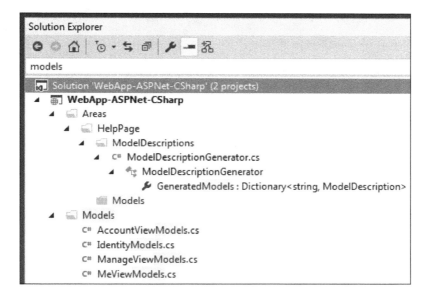

How it works...

The **Solution Explorer** search tool provides similar results to the **Navigate To** feature, but having the location of a match represented in the tree view makes it very easy to quickly identify the specific match you are interested in.

There's more...

It's worth mentioning a few other things about searching within your solution.

Navigation behavior

Assuming you have the Preview icon enabled for **Solution Explorer**, as you navigate using **Solution Explorer** to various classes and methods, you may have noticed that the document preview tab updates and shows exactly where the selected class, method, or property was declared. This makes it easy to see what the code is doing without the need to specifically open the file, or scroll through a source file to see the code which is actually inside a method, class, or property. The Preview icon's location in the **Solution Explorer window** is shown in the following screenshot:

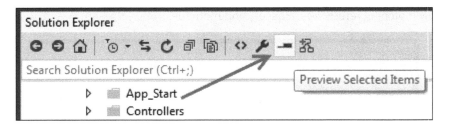

CSS, HTML, and JavaScript files

Even though it's possible to extract the structure from CSS, HTML, and JavaScript files, **Solution Explorer** doesn't show the internal structure of these files. You can navigate to the source file, but not to any of its contents.

2
Getting Started with Universal Windows Platform Apps

In this chapter, we will cover the following topics:

- ▸ Enabling UWP app development on Windows 10
- ▸ Creating a UWP app
- ▸ Customizing your UWP app
- ▸ Using the UWP app simulator
- ▸ Defining capabilities and contracts
- ▸ Analyzing your app's performance
- ▸ Packaging your UWP app
- ▸ Validating your Windows Store app
- ▸ Submitting your app to the Windows Store
- ▸ Distributing your UWP app through sideloading

Introduction

Windows 10 marks the second radical departure from the traditional Windows desktop applications in as many releases. Whereas Windows 8.x saw the introduction of the modern interface and major support for touch-based apps through **Windows Runtime (WinRT)**, Windows 10 has introduced the **Universal Windows Platform (UWP)**. An evolutionary change from the Windows 8 apps, UWP apps run on any device that runs Windows 10. This includes tablets, desktop PCs, hybrid systems, and phones. Taking advantage of UWP will let you focus on writing solid code while having your app automatically benefit from the multitude of hardware devices that exist.

The UWP approach works by targeting one or more device families rather than a specific operating system. Your app can elect to only use the base APIs provided by UWP that are found on all devices, or it can augment those with the additional device-specific APIs. Choosing which APIs to use can be a decision made during design (such as targeting the Xbox specifically), or it can be done at runtime, adjusting functionality to suit the device that your app is currently running on. This means that a single UWP app could be run across the desktop, phone, and tablet environments, and dynamically adjust its user interface to its current host device.

By targeting the UWP, developing an app that can be used across multiple device families is easier. And providing this flexibility makes it more valuable to your users, who can access the app on the device that they prefer. When you decide to support a new device family, core functionality can be used as is, shortening your development time as only APIs specific to that platform have to be considered for implementation.

The UWP supports several device families. That includes the following:
- ▸ Traditional Windows PC (laptop, desktop, touch-enabled devices, and the like)
- ▸ Mobile (Windows Phone)
- ▸ Xbox
- ▸ Internet of Things (IoT)
- ▸ Microsoft HoloLens
- ▸ Raspberry Pi 2 (via Windows 10 IoT Core)

Developing UWP apps is rather straightforward: install Windows 10 on your development machine (or VM), and then install VS2015. Both VS Community and VS Express for Windows 10 support UWP app development, so a paid edition of VS2015 is not required. What's more, UWP supports several languages so that you can get started using what you already know: C#, Visual Basic, C++, or JavaScript.

The net result is that Microsoft has positioned UWP both as their response to the shortcomings of their Windows 8.X app strategy, and as a proactive attempt at allowing developers a streamlined way to support the wide variety of devices that end-users have at their disposal. As a developer, you should benefit from the ability to support a number of different devices from a single code base using a language that you are already comfortable with.

 While Microsoft strongly encourages developers to distribute their UWP apps through Microsoft's app store, keep in mind this is not required. You target the devices you want through UWP, and deploy the finished app the way you want.

In this chapter, we will explore the world of UWP apps from top to bottom. By the end of this chapter, you should have a solid understanding of the major UWP concepts, and how to get started with UWP app creation, whether you are building them from scratch or from an existing codebase.

Enabling UWP app development on Windows 10

To get started with UWP app development, you must first enable app development for your Windows 10 device. If you are familiar with app development on Windows 8.X, you will recall the need to possess a developer license that had to be periodically renewed with Microsoft. That is no longer the case for UWP apps—once you have enabled development support, you are good to go. Let's look at how to do that.

Getting ready

Have Windows 10 installed on your computer. VS Express for Windows 10 will install all the necessary tools for you by default, so if you are running a different version of VS2015, make sure you have opted to install the Universal Windows App Development Tools for your particular installation of VS2015. You can rerun the VS2015 installer, if needed, to install them.

The following screenshot shows the items that should be installed. Note that specific version numbers may change between the time of writing this and when you read it, but that is okay. You will want the latest of the following:

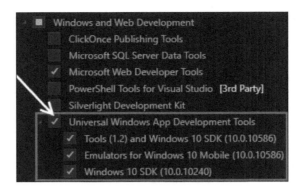

How to do it...

Now that we have successfully installed a version of VS2015 suitable for UWP development, we will enable **Developer Mode** on our computer running Windows 10. If you are using VS Express for Windows 10, you will be prompted to do this when you start Visual Studio. If running Community Edition or one of the premium editions, you will be prompted to do so when you begin a UWP project. The following screenshot provides an example of this prompt:

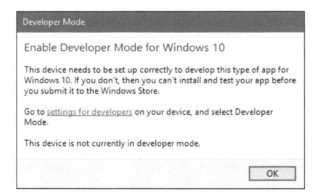

To enable **Developer mode**, you will actually need to make some changes in your system settings (formerly known as the Control Panel). You can get there by clicking the **settings for developers** link shown in the preceding screenshot, or look for **Update & Security** in your Windows 10 settings page, and then click on **For developers**. Once there, you will want to select **Developer mode**, as shown in the following screenshot:

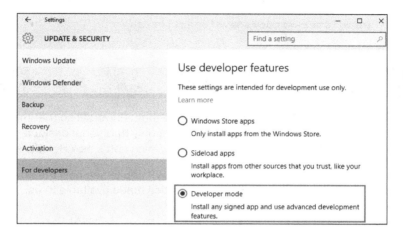

For security purposes, Windows 10 will present a confirmation box when you make the selection, so confirm your intent and proceed.

How it works...

UWP app development simply requires the host device to be in **Developer mode**. This greatly simplifies a process that was needlessly convoluted when developing apps for Windows 8.X, whereby a specific Developer License had to be obtained and renewed. Now a single set-and-forget setting change can be made, and your system is ready for UWP app development. Besides your day-to-day development, this makes testing your app easier, as you can easily enable this setting on test machines (including tablets, virtual machines, and others) without having to get (and renew) developer licenses for those environments too.

There's more...

When you publish your UWP app to the Windows Store, a user can download and use it without any system modification. Distributing your UWP app outside of the Windows Store is possible via the method described in this recipe or via **sideloading**.

In some Windows upgrade scenarios, upgrading a developer machine from Windows 8.1 to Windows 10 can result in a situation where the now-unnecessary Windows Developer License remains. To ensure your Windows 10 development is hassle free, open a PowerShell command prompt with Administrator privileges, and run the following command:

`unregister-windowsdeveloperlicense`

Creating a UWP app

One of Microsoft's goals for UWP apps is to truly make them universal so that they run on any system based on the core Windows 10 technology—not only traditional desktop computers, but devices ranging from Raspberry Pi, to Xbox One, to Microsoft's new HoloLens.

In this recipe, we will begin by creating a brand new UWP app to see how the process differs from Windows 8.X app creation, and the new capabilities made available to us.

Getting ready

Windows 10 is required for this recipe. Visual Studio Community will be used to provide the example screenshots, but of course, a premium edition or VS Express for Windows 10 would also be suitable.

How to do it...

The types of app templates available has changed with VS2015 and Windows 10. Let's begin by creating a **Blank App**. For our example, we will use C#:

1. From Visual Studio's **File** menu, navigate to **New | Project...**
2. A dialog showing the available project templates will appear. From the **Installed** templates category, navigate to the **Visual C# | Windows | Universal | Blank App** template:

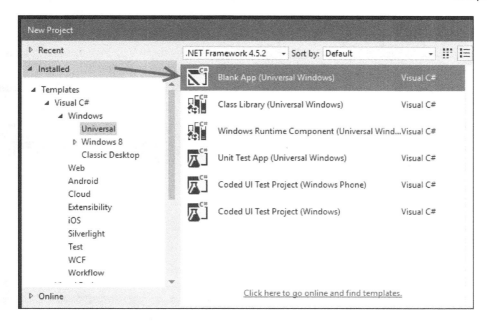

3. You may leave the default project name or change it to one of your choosing, and click on **OK** to create the app.

4. If you chose to use a source control system, make your selection now. (We will cover this in greater detail in a later chapter.)

5. The newly created project will appear in **Solution Explorer**, and `App.xaml.cs` will open in the document area.

6. Press *F5* to run the application in the **Debug** mode. Visual Studio will package and launch the app for you. As you might expect, we are presented with a blank app window (marked by **1** in the next screenshot). However, note that in VS2015, executing an app under debugging mode also runs **Diagnostic Tools** (marked by the **2**):

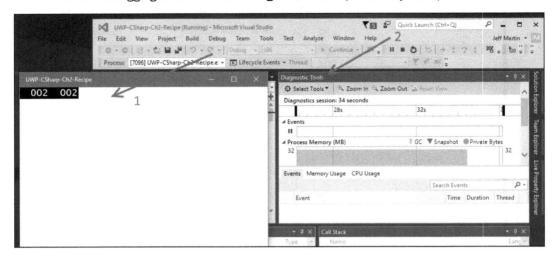

7. When you have finished exploring the app, you can use *Shift + F5* as a direct command to stop debugging. However, you may find that the best approach is to use *Alt + Tab* to switch back to Visual Studio, and stop debugging from there.

How it works...

Those familiar with app development under Windows 8.X and VS2013 are no doubt wondering what happened to the usual templates. Those of you new to UWP app creation are wondering why the app is blank. In VS2015, the various types of templates with predefined GUI elements have been removed, in favor of some key starting points to which different layouts and GUI elements can be added. Different templates are available, based on the language you wish to develop with.

There's more...

Let's take a look at the available project templates, and what they can provide us. JavaScript developers will find only the **Blank App** template provided to them, while C#, Visual Basic, and C++ developers find a larger selection to choose from.

Choosing the right project type...

There are several Universal Windows app templates available. We are going to provide a brief overview so that you can decide what template would make a good starting point for your next project.

Blank App

The **Blank App** template is exactly what we have seen in this recipe—an empty shell ready for your customizations. It is available for JavaScript, C#, C++, and Visual Basic.

Class Library

The **Class Library** project creates a DLL for use with UWP apps, which is automatically set to use the .NET Framework. This promotes code reuse, and allows you to separate business logic from app-specific code. This is available for C# and Visual Basic.

Windows Runtime Component

The **Windows Runtime Component** is a project template for creating code in one language that can be shared or consumed in other languages. C#/VB/C++ can all create and consume these components for UWP apps. JavaScript can only consume these components. Components let you take advantage of the features of each language, and then combine them into a single application.

For example, code requiring high performance can be written into a C++ component, and consumed by a JavaScript app. Or perhaps you have existing business logic written in Visual Basic, but want to use it in a brand new C++ app written to take advantage of the UWP features. These types of scenarios are facilitated with this project type, which uses exposed **Windows Metadata** (`.winmd` file) information to facilitate this interoperability. This is available for C#, C++, and Visual Basic.

Unit Test App

The **Unit Test App** project template creates a Unit Test Framework or a test assembly based on **CppUnit** for unit testing your code. It is available for C#, C++, and Visual Basic.

Coded UI Test Project (Windows Phone)

The **Coded UI Test Project (Windows Phone)** template allows you to test your Windows Phone-targeted app via the GUI, rather than underneath the hood as in the **Unit Test App**. It is available for C# and Visual Basic.

Coded UI Test Project (Windows)

The **Coded UI Test Project (Windows)** template allows you to test your app via the GUI, rather than underneath the hood as in the **Unit Test App**. Unlike the preceding template, this is not Windows Phone-specific. This is available for C# and Visual Basic.

C++ specific UWP templates

Developers using C++ have several unique UWP templates available for their use. They focus on DirectX, but also include some key infrastructure components:

  ▶ **DirextX11 App and DirectX 12 App**: Used to create a new project that uses the indicated DirectX features. Perfect for games or applications requiring high-performance graphics.

- ▶ **DirectX11 and XAML App**: A template that provides DirectX 11 support along with XAML. This allows XAML controls to be used for controlling your app, while using DirectX to provide rendering.

- ▶ **DLL**: Lets you write a DLL using C++, and then makes it available to other UWP apps.

- ▶ **Static Library**: Similar to a DLL, with the notable exception that this is for static linking. Can be consumed by other UWP-based apps.

 Veterans of Windows 8.X app development will notice that Portable Class Libraries are not part of the UWP, but those templates remain available for use with other projects.

Language interoperability

UWP apps written in JavaScript can call Windows Runtime Components written in either C++ or .NET when that function is contained in libraries or DLLs that expose **Windows Metadata (WinMD)** information. Unfortunately, the reverse is not the case—.NET and C++ apps cannot call a function contained in JavaScript libraries. C++ UWP apps can, however, call a function in .NET WinMD files (which are created using the Windows Runtime Component project type), and .NET code can call C++.

Customizing your UWP app

We saw in the previous recipe that creating a new UWP app is pretty simple, but in VS2015, the choices are limited to some basic types. Rather than provide some pre-made templates around common design themes (such as Hub, Split, Items, and so on) as was done previously in VS2013, Microsoft has instead decided to provide us with a blank canvas with which to work. Let's see how we can spruce it up a bit.

Getting ready

Windows 10 is required for this recipe. Visual Studio Community will be used to provide the example screenshots, but of course, a premium edition or VS Express for Windows 10 would also be suitable. If you still have the UWP app created in the previous recipe, open that solution file.

How to do it...

We are going to start with a brand new UWP app, so create a **Blank App** template. For our example, we will use C#:

1. Create a new UWP app using the **Blank App** template.

2. Once the project has opened, open the file `MainPage.xaml`, as shown in the following screenshot:

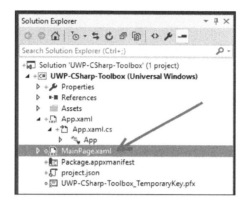

3. Once that file opens, your display should resemble the following screenshot. Next, click on the **Toolbox** label, indicated by the arrow:

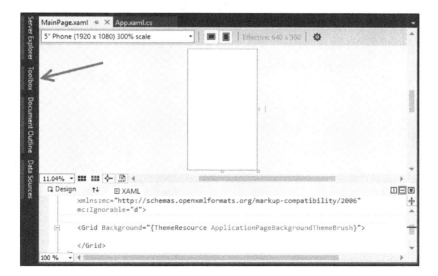

4. After opening the **Toolbox**, you will observe that the items previously separated into distinct templates are available in addition to several more XAML controls that can be used to implement your app's design. The following screenshot provides an excerpt:

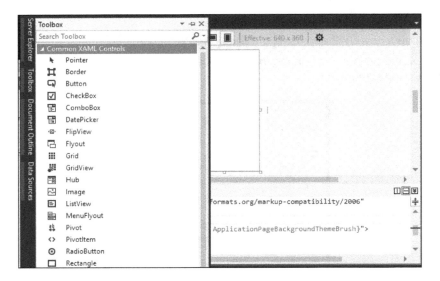

5. In our example, we will add a **Button** control and proceed. The following screenshot shows this addition:

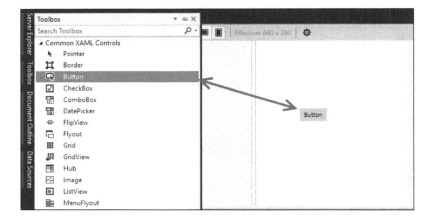

6. Now that we have a control added (or more, if you choose to do so), let's see what other design tools are available to us. The following screenshot illustrates the different sections that we will examine:

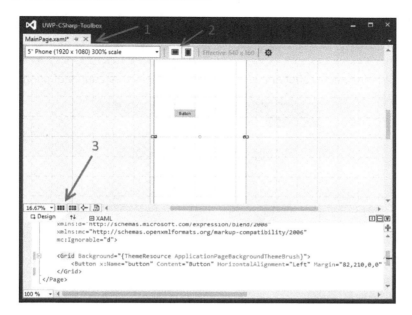

The following is the legend for the highlighted items in the preceding screenshot:

1. This drop-down menu allows you to set the display for a particular device form factor. In this preceding screenshot, it is set to a 5" screen running at a 1920x1080 resolution. Options include various tablets, phone, desktop, Xbox, Surface Hub, and IoT style devices.

2. The next two options allow you to toggle between portrait and landscape layout. In this screenshot, portrait has been chosen.

3. There are several options in this section. Starting from the left, the drop-down menu allows you to set the zoom. The screenshot shows a zoom of **16.67%**—several more are available, including Fit All. Next is the option to toggle the grid (for aligning controls), a toggle as to whether controls should be snapped to the grid, a toggle as to whether controls should align to snap lines, and whether or not the project code should be disabled.

[

Snap lines are the red guidelines that appear when aligning controls in a similar region (left margin, top margin, and so on).
]

4. After you have set the preview settings that you want, and possibly added some more design elements, you can view the changes by pressing *F5* (debugging mode).

 If you lose track of the **Toolbox** palette, you can return it to view via *Ctrl + Alt + X*, or through **View | Toolbox**.

5. The following screenshot shows a running sample with a couple of controls:

How it works...

With VS2015, UWP app development has been streamlined so that creating a user-facing project (as opposed to a **Class Library** or **Windows Runtime Component**) is started with a **Blank App** template. Then you can add the components needed for your app, and select the layout that best fits the device(s) you are targeting:

The **Toolbox** can be put to work for your needs. Right-clicking within the **Toolbox** lets you **Sort Items Alphabetically**. If you would like to make the list of controls more manageable to fit your particular workflow, you can create a new tab with a unique name (**Example Toolbox** was used here), as shown in the preceding screenshot. Controls can then be dragged from the existing tabs to your new grouping.

There's more...

As you have probably noticed from the tool box, there are numerous XAML controls available for use in your app. This includes the expected button and checkbox controls similar to those introduced with Windows 8.X app development, including Flyout and Hub controls.

Let's take a look at the some of the new controls added with Windows 10 for UWP apps.

SplitView

This is used to define a main content area for the most common presentation/interaction with your app, while also creating a work area for controls that can display on demand (if desired). Typically, this lets controls to be available as needed without clogging the view when they are not:

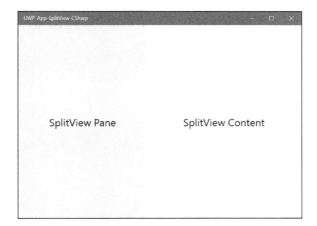

 As of VS2015 Update 1, when using SplitView, be sure to wrap the content with <SplitView.Content> the same way as the pane content is wrapped with <SplitView.Pane>.

RelativePanel

RelativePanel is a more flexible layout, which can be used when the app's style isn't compatible with more linear layouts like Grid or StackPanel. With a RelativePanel, relative alignments of XAML controls can be specified so that they maintain the desired positioning during resizing or different device form factors. The following screenshot demonstrates an example of this panel:

In the RelativePanel shown in the preceding screenshot, the Left button anchors the design, and is placed in the top-left corner. The Right button is located on its right, and its position is defined to be to the right of the Left button, wherever that will be. Then the text block below is defined to be below the Left button, aligned with that button's left edge, while its right edge is aligned with that of the Right button. This allows the TextBlock (containing the *lorem ipsum* text) position to be dynamic based on the positioning of the buttons.

CalendarView

CalendarView is a calendar control that provides data picking for the user while allowing the developer to specify various options to configure blackout dates, acceptable date ranges, and how the dates are formatted. Unlike the CalendarDatePicker, the calendar is always displayed. The following screenshot illustrates this control:

February 2016					$\wedge$	$\vee$
Su	Mo	Tu	We	Th	Fr	Sa
31	1	2	3	4	5	6
7	8	9	10	11	12	13
14	15	16	17	18	19	20
21	22	23	24	25	26	27
28	29	1	2	3	4	5
6	7	8	9	10	11	12

CalendarDatePicker

`CalendarDatePicker` is similar to the `CalendarView` in that it lets a user select a date; the difference is that this control is used to choose a specific date rather than a range. Unlike the `DatePicker`, a familiar calendar display is used for date selection. The following screenshot illustrates this control:

MediaTransportControls

`MediaTransportControls` provides the ability to give your app the traditional media file playback controls: play/pause, seek bar, stop, rewind, and so on. Developers can customize which of these various components are displayed:

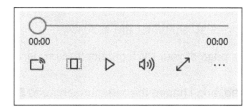

See also

▸ *Creating a UWP app* recipe

▸ Microsoft MSDN documentation on XAML controls at `https://msdn.microsoft.com/en-us/library/windows/apps/windows.ui.xaml.controls.aspx`

Using the UWP app simulator

The design behind the UWP architecture has been established so that your app can easily be deployed to any device that runs Windows 10. There may be some minor customizations needed depending on the capabilities that various platforms offer, but UWP will not limit you unnecessarily. As a reader of this book though, you are probably developing your UWP on a traditional computer that most likely has a keyboard and a mouse. While this is great for development (and usually, a keyboard is a needed component), this means that your workstation doesn't always match what is available to your app's users. Enter the Windows 10 simulator.

The Windows 10 simulator, available under VS2015, provides the ability to run your UWP app in your choice of Debug or Release builds, so that you can see how it runs and appears on a machine outside of your regular development machine configuration.

This recipe will show how to use the simulator to assist in developing your own apps.

Getting ready

For this recipe, you may use a project of your choosing if you have one available, but we are going to use one of Microsoft's publicly provided sample UWP apps for the examples. Specifically, we are going to use the RSSReader app listed at `http://microsoft.github.io/windows/`. If you are familiar with Git, you may clone the repo, but for brevity, we will just download the project's ZIP file to our machine and open the solution file.

How to do it...

The steps for using the Windows 10 simulator are as follows:

1. Go to the properties page of your UWP project (the properties page is available under the **Project** menu).

2. Select the **Debug** tab, and change the target machine to **Simulator**, as shown in the following screenshot:

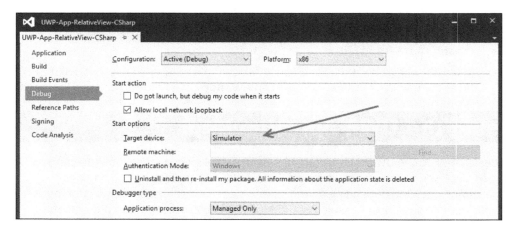

3. Start debugging the app by either pressing *F5* or navigating to the **Debug | Start Debugging** menu option.

4. Visual Studio will start the Windows 10 simulator and launch the app for you, as shown in the following screenshot:

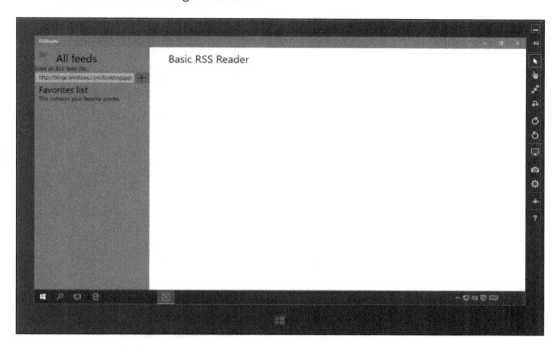

5. On the right-hand side of the simulator are a number of icons that control the simulator's behavior. By default, the simulator starts in the mouse mode so that you can navigate within the app using the keyboard and mouse. However, you aren't limited to those methods of input—touch is also available regardless of whether your physical PC supports it.

 For reference, the toolbar icon functions are, from top to bottom: Minimize, Always on top, Mouse mode, Basic touch mode, Pinch/ Zoom touch mode, Rotation touch mode, Rotate clockwise, Rotate counterclockwise, Change resolution, Copy screenshot, Screenshot settings, Change network properties, and Help.

6. With the initial defaults, you can interact directly with the UWP app running. For our example, click on the plus icon to add the default feed. This will add it to this app's **favorites**, making the article headlines available for reading. Clicking on the **hamburger** icon (three horizontal lines) in the top-left corner lets you experiment with closing and opening the navigation pane:

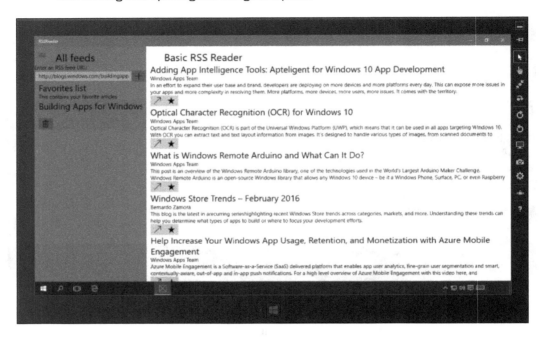

7. Switch to the basic touch mode by selecting the icon on the simulator toolbar.

8. As you move your mouse over the simulator, you will see that the cursor has now changed to a small crosshair in a circle icon.

9. You can simulate scroll with touch by left-clicking and dragging upward or downward with your mouse to scroll the content pane. The cursor will change form while you are holding the mouse button to reflect that touch input is being simulated.

10. Touch mode is very similar to receiving mouse input, so let's now try some simulator-specific functionality. Click on the Rotate clockwise (90 degrees) icon.

11. The simulator will now reflect a change in orientation, as if you had physically turned your tablet clockwise. The following screenshot illustrates this change:

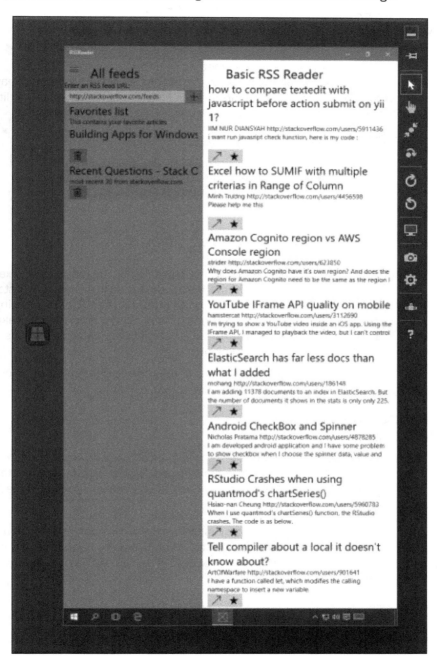

12. When the simulator has focus, it will capture the keyboard and handle key combinations such as *Alt + Tab* or *Alt + F4*. Close the simulator using *Ctrl + Alt + F4*. You can stop the debugging process with *Shift + F5*.

13. Now let's see how the simulator works with the debugger. Open the `FeedsArticlesViewModel.cs` file, and locate the `AddRssFeed` method.

14. Set a breakpoint in the `AddRssFeed` method by either pressing *F9* on the declaration, or by clicking in the gutter to the left of the code. This method may be found easily by searching for its name in Quick Find (found approximately at line 229). Once located, set a breakpoint, as shown in the following screenshot:

```csharp
private async Task AddRssFeed(string url)
{
    try
    {
        SyndicationClient client = new SyndicationClient();

        Uri myUri;
        if (Uri.TryCreate(url, UriKind.Absolute, out myUri))
        {
```

15. Restart the simulator and debug this app by pressing *F5*. The program will execute until it has two add feeds—so if you have previously added two feeds, it will stop at the breakpoint twice. Resume by clicking on **Continue** in the IDE or by pressing *F5*. After the app is fully loaded, try adding another feed, at which point the breakpoint will be immediately hit. Deleting an existing feed and then re-adding it will also demonstrate the effects of the breakpoint.

16. Feel free to add breakpoints in other areas of the code to experiment with how the debugger will operate in conjunction with your app.

How it works...

The Windows 10 app simulator actually connects to your local machine via a remote desktop connection, and this is why the start screen in the simulator looks the same as the start screen on your Windows 10 development machine, and the reason why you are signed in automatically.

Since it's simply a remote desktop connection running on the local machine, the debugger is simply connecting to a local process running in a different session. If you open the **Attach to Process** window via the **Debug | Attach to Process** menu, you can see the details of the process that Visual Studio has connected to.

The following screenshot highlights the details of the running `RSSReader.exe` executable, and shows that it is in session **2**, which is the Windows 10 app simulator session:

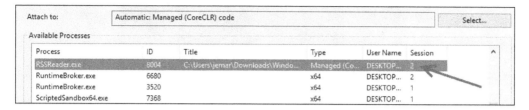

There's more...

There are a few more things to note about the simulator that we didn't touch upon in the recipe, including some items that will make using it much more useful.

Resolution and resizing

You can adjust the resolution the simulator is running at, allowing you to experience your app at different predefined resolutions and device sizes, as shown in the following screenshot:

Along with changing the resolution, you can also change the onscreen display size of the simulator by dragging the bottom-right corner of the simulator just like a normal desktop window. This can help if you are simulating a device on a high-resolution desktop, and you have the screen real estate to spare. It may also point out areas that are just too small for the end user and require a rework.

Change network properties

This dialog lets you set the simulator to use different network settings than what is actually being used by your development machine. This lets your app react to events such as roaming, data limits, and the cost of the network so that it behaves appropriately if the user is not on a no-limit network connection. A user near their wireless plan limits would be very upset if your app improperly used up all of their bandwidth, or causes them to incur unexpected charges.

Note that the icon on the simulator is titled **Change network properties**, while the dialog is labeled **Set Network Properties**.

Remote debugging

You may have noticed that when you set the **Debug** option for using the simulator, there was also an option to use a **Remote Machine** as the target device. Remote debugging is straightforward under Visual Studio 2015 when developing UWP apps. For the **Remote Machine** option to work, you need to have **Remote Debugging Monitor** running on the remote machine; the firewall needs to allow connections, and you need a reasonable network connection between the two machines.

On your development machine, you simply specify the machine name of the remote machine you are targeting, and start debugging. Visual Studio connects to the remote machine, prompts for credentials if required, deploys the app, and connects the remote debugging monitor for you.

From that point forward, the debug experience is almost the same as if it were a local process. As long as you have a stable network connection, you should find the experience very useful.

Taking screenshots

When you want to take screenshots of your Windows Store apps for creating your store listing, for example, then you can do so via the simulator. Simply click on the copy screenshot button on the toolbar (represented by a camera icon), and the screenshot will be placed on the clipboard, and optionally, in a file on your hard drive. You can control this behavior using the screenshot settings button (represented by a gear icon below the camera icon) on the toolbar.

Fresh app install

When a UWP app is running on your development workstation or the simulator, it will of course be saving files and settings on your system in its local storage area. While this is very useful to maintain state between app sessions, while debugging you may find it necessary to run your app as though it has been freshly installed, without any existing settings.

The following start option under the project's properties lets you do this. As a reminder, properties for your project are found in the **Properties** window located under the **Project** menu:

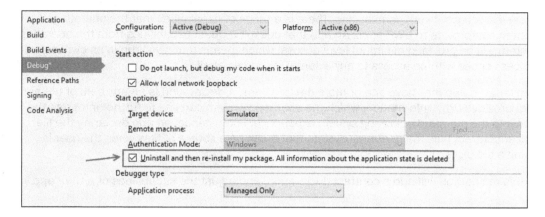

How to find locally stored app data:

When your app uses a `StorageFolder` object as `RSSReader` does, it is storing data on the system for which the app is installed. For a Windows 10 system, this information is typically stored under the directory `C:\Users\USERNAME\AppData\Local\Packages`, where each installed app will have its own subdirectory that is based on its official package name. The app's package name is defined in `Package.appxmanifest`, and additionally, viewable under the **Packaging** tab in the manifest editor.

See also

▸   The *Creating a UWP app* recipe

▸   The *Defining capabilities and contracts* recipe

Defining capabilities and contracts

Windows 10 provides UWP apps the ability to communicate with any other app on the computer, without prior knowledge of what those apps might be, through a concept called **contracts**. A contract is an operating system level interface that is implemented by consumers or providers of information. The operating system then keeps track of which apps support which contracts, and coordinates the information between apps using those contracts.

Windows 10, as part of its focus on maintaining a trust level in the apps it runs, expects UWP apps to communicate the capabilities they need. A **capability** is a permission or access right that a UWP app requires for it to run correctly, for example, an app that requires Internet access or local network permissions. There is a range of capabilities that the operating system can provide to UWP apps. An app that doesn't request capabilities from the operating system will be provided minimum level access, which means that it will run in its own isolated process space with no access to any external resources at all.

Similarly, an app may have one or more **declarations**. A declaration is an attribute of the app that provides extra information, which the operating system can use to further integrate the app into the standard operating system experience. For instance, an app declaring the file picker contract tells the operating system that it can be a source of files when the user is using a file picker.

In this recipe, you will add a contract declaration, and adjust the capabilities of a UWP app.

Getting ready

For our example, we will continue to use the RSSReader app that was exhibited in the *Using the UWP app simulator* recipe. Feel free to substitute a UWP app of your choosing if you prefer.

How to do it...

In order to add a contract declaration and adjust the capabilities of a UWP app, perform the following steps:

1. Open the Package.appxmanifest file shown in **Solution Explorer** (found at the top level of your app's project folder). This manifest file will open up in the manifest designer within VS2015, as shown in the following screenshot:

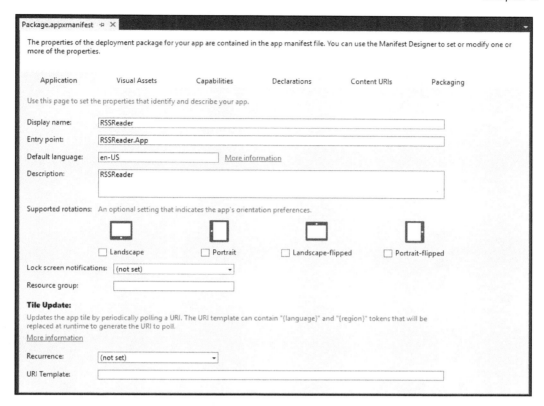

 If you want to look at the raw XML that is manipulated by the manifest designer, right-click on the `Package.appxmanifest` file in **Solution Explorer,** and then select **View Code**. Using XML for this file has the added benefit that it is easily storable in source control.

2. Select the **Capabilities** tab, as shown in the following screenshot:

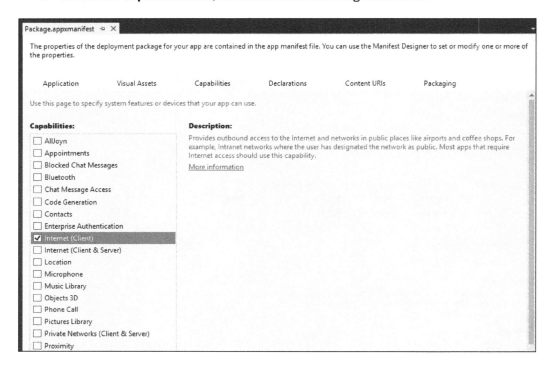

3. In the preceding screenshot, you can see that our app has **Internet (Client)** capability, as you might expect from an app that needs to use the Internet to read RSS feeds. Additional capabilities can be added or removed here—but your app should only specify those it actually needs to do its job.

4. Next let's visit the **Declarations** tab. In the following screenshot, you will see the various functions that your app can offer. For this example, please select **File Type Associations**:

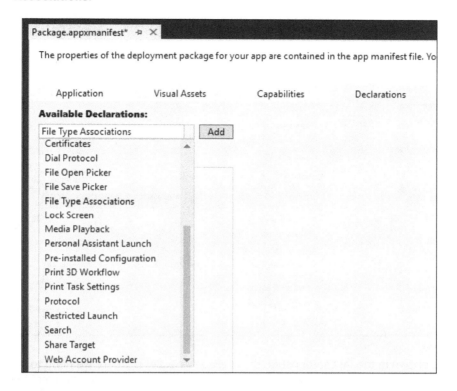

 Declarations are also referred to as extensions. Microsoft describes an Extension as an agreement between your app and Windows.

5. Now we will demonstrate how to register `RSSReader` to handle and be available for opening XML files. In order for our app to do so, make the changes shown in the following screenshot:

6. As shown in the last screenshot, there are several fields where we need to provide details. The **Display name** property is used to identify the app making the declaration. **Logo** can be used to specify a custom logo for this file association to easily identify your app—if left blank, the app logo will be used. **Name** is a lower-case identifier for a group of files that share the same characteristics (logo, info, tip, edit flags, and so on). The **Edit flags** are used to regulate how files opened from an untrusted source are handled. Since we are dealing with XML, the preceding example specifies that content should be treated as **Always unsafe**. Finally, we have set up this declaration to address XML files ending in `.xml`.

7. You're not going to implement a full app as part of this recipe; so, for now, just click on the **Remove** button next to **File Type Associations** in the **Supported Declarations** section.

How it works...

One of the design goals for UWP apps is, of course, that they should be universal, which means that it should be easy to download them from the Windows Store, and run them on any computer the user desires without needing any special permissions. By requiring an App Manifest to be bundled with every app, Windows itself can manage the app's installation without allowing the user to unknowingly compromise their system's security.

The App Manifest is a critical file for any Windows Store app, and you need to pay attention to it. It contains all the declarative information for informing Windows of the capabilities it needs, as well as the contracts that it satisfies. This lets Windows enforce the app's behavior on behalf of the user, and prevent it from overstepping its boundaries.

There's more...

There are numerous capabilities and contracts you can declare, but instead of describing all of the possible contracts that you can implement, let's have a look at the more interesting ones that you are most likely to consider for your apps.

Declarations

As noted earlier, declarations provide a way for an app to inform the system of how it intends to operate.

Background tasks

This is a very useful declaration that allows your app to run code, and react to events when it is suspended. This declaration may be used multiple times in your app, and will let it perform actions that include playing audio in the background, operating on a timer, or responding to a change in the device's physical location. There are eight tasks available in total, so this is worth reviewing as you write your app.

Update task

Most likely, your app will support updates, and your user's will want to ensure they always receive the latest features that your app has to offer. This task lets your app react to being updated, and make any configuration changes it needs to provide its new features. This differs from a preinstalled config task, which is code designated to execute immediately after your app has been installed.

Search contract

The Search contract allows the end user to search for information from within your program. Any program that implements the Search contract item template will be listed as a search source when the system's Search tool is used—which means that in order for your app to search, it must also agree to share searchable information with other apps. Note that in Windows 8.1, an app using the Search contract will only show on the Search charm from within that app. For example, as shown in the following screenshot, the **Wikipedia** app implements the Search contract:

File Type Associations

This declaration allows you to specify one or more file types that your app will work with. For example, a photo app may specify types such as `.jpg` or `.png`, while a music app may specify `.mp3` (This is also known as **File activation**).

 Certain file types are prohibited, because they are reserved, or for security reasons. For a list of prohibited file types, refer to: `http://msdn.microsoft.com/en-us/library/windows/apps/hh452684.aspx`. Forbidden filename extensions include system files and executables, to reduce security risks.

Certificates

This declaration provides the ability to package a digital certificate with your app. This is useful when your app intends to use communications over SSL. It is also known as **SSL/Certificates**.

Capabilities

As with the contracts, not all capabilities are of interest for most developers. The following are some of the more important ones that you should be aware of.

Internet (Client)

The `internetClient` capability lets Windows know that your app will be making requests to Internet-based resources, but it will not be receiving any connections. It is for outbound connections on public networks only.

Given that most Windows Store apps are expected to have some level of Internet connectivity, this is enabled by default in the project templates.

Internet (Client & Server)

The `internetClientServer` capability informs Windows that your app will not only request data but will also be serving data, and can accept inbound connections. Even if you specify this capability, you cannot accept inbound connections on critical ports. Specifying this capability means you do not need to specify the `internetClient` capability, and if you do, it will have no effect.

Home or work networking

The home and work networks are considered to be private networks with separate security profiles from the public Internet. The `privateNetworkClientServer` capability allows you to make both inbound and outbound connections on these trusted networks.

As with the `internetClientServer` capability, you cannot accept connections on critical ports.

Library access

UWP apps have limited access to the underlying file system, and must request access as part of their capabilities. The `musicLibrary`, `picturesLibrary`, and `videosLibrary` capabilities must be selected in order to access files programmatically in each of those locations.

When accessing a library, only files with the appropriate extensions for the content will be available. For example, the `picturesLibrary` capability will provide access to files in that library with common image file extensions (`.jpg`, `.gif`, and the like), but not to videos, music, or system files even if files with those extensions are in the library.

For a complete list of app contracts, refer to the MSDN article, *App contracts and extensions* (Windows Store apps) at the following link: `http://msdn.microsoft.com/en-us/library/windows/apps/hh464906.aspx`.

See also

▶ This recipe provides an introduction to using Visual Studio's tools for editing an `.appxmanifest` file. As previously noted, this can also be edited directly within Visual Studio outside of the GUI-based editor. Indeed, there are certain situations where specific capabilities may need to be specified manually. For more information, consult this link: `http://msdn.microsoft.com/en-us/library/windows/apps/br211476.aspx`.

Analyzing your app's performance

Given the wide variety of devices that your UWP app can run on, it is important to track performance to ensure you are not being wasteful. Users appreciate improved battery life, and a responsive app is always appreciated by users. VS2015 has several app performance and diagnostic tools available that can help you measure and review its performance to ensure it is as efficient as needed.

The **Diagnostic Tools** menu provides the following tools:

▶ **Application Timeline**: See where your app spends most of its time.

▶ **CPU Sampling**: Analyze which of the functions being used by your app are using the most CPU time.

▶ **CPU Usage**: Examine where the CPU is spending its time. Helpful when the CPU is the limiting factor.

▶ **GPU Usage**: Review and monitor GPU usage. Helpful when the GPU is the limiting factor.

▶ **Memory Usage**: Used to help find memory leaks, and examine how your app is using memory.

▶ **Network**: Provides for the monitoring of all network traffic used by your app.

▶ **Energy Consumption**: Information about an app's energy usage. Helpful when writing an app whose primary platform is battery-dependent.

▶ **HTML UI Responsiveness**: Helpful when dealing with apps or websites that use HTML to provide their user interface, so that inefficient areas can be identified.

▶ **JavaScript Memory**: Focuses on the JavaScript heap, and how it is being used.

Getting ready

For this recipe, we will continue to use the `RSSReader` app referenced in the *Using the UWP app simulator* recipe. Feel free to substitute an app of your choice if you have one available.

How to do it...

The following steps will demonstrate how to examine your app's performance:

1. Open the RSSReader project. Then, open the **Diagnostic Tools** window via **Debug | Start Diagnostic Tools Without Debugging** (or use the keyboard shortcut *Alt + F2*).

2. On the next screen labelled **Analysis Target**, you will be able to select from the different diagnostic tools that are available for use with your app. These tools are shown in the following screenshot:

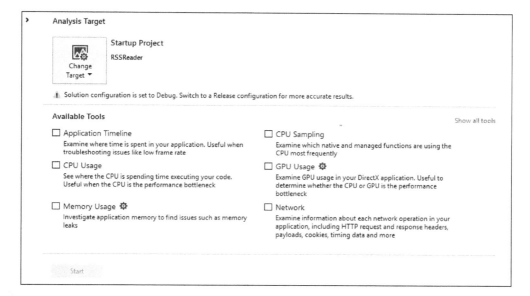

3. You will notice that VS2015 alerts you when you are about to run the app in the **Debug** mode. Switch your app configuration from **Debug** to **Release** if it is not already in the **Release** mode. (You can do this without leaving the **Analysis Target** page.)

4. While on the Analysis Tools screen, select **Application Timeline**, **CPU Usage**, and **Network**. Then click on **Start**.

5. You may be prompted by Windows to let `VsStandardCollector.exe` make changes to your computer. Be sure to click **Yes** so that the data collection process can continue, as shown in the following screenshot:

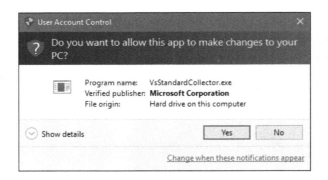

6. The `RSSReader` app will now launch, and VS2015 will monitor its performance via the selected tools. Operate it as you expect a typical user would if you would like an overall report, or focus on a specific area if you feel something is especially draining. When you are done, close your app as usual (*Ctrl + Alt + F4*).

7. VS2015 will then collect the performance information and prepare the results for your review, as shown in the following screenshot:

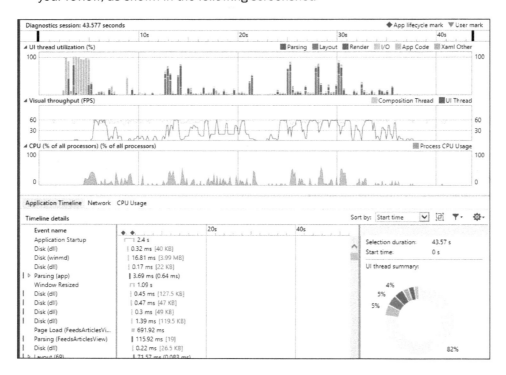

How it works...

Visual Studio attaches to your app's process, and is able to track the performance details that you've selected during its operation. These tools let you focus on the areas of your app that you wish to improve, and also bring to light areas that you may not have previously realized need attention.

There's more...

While the **Application Timeline** tool is selected in the previous screenshot, the other two tools are also available for review. Given that RSSReader relies on a network connection to obtain data, the **Network** tab is very helpful, as it shows exactly what is being sent and received by the app. Each network request can be reviewed, as you can see in the next screenshot:

Similarly, the **CPU Usage** tab will provide information on the various methods used by the app, and how much CPU activity they utilized.

Packaging your UWP app

Similar to the apps distributed for Windows 8, UWP apps are packaged and distributed in a specific format. Once packaged, they can be uploaded to the Windows Store, or distributed to a non-developer workstation. The information contained in the package includes the capabilities and contracts that your app uses as well as information on the app user tile, the splash screen, and more.

This recipe will show you what you need to do to package your UWP app so that it is ready for the outside world to use.

Getting ready

As before, we will continue to use the RSSReader app referenced in the *Using the UWP app simulator* recipe. Feel free to substitute an app of your choice if you have one available.

How to do it...

Perform the following steps to package your UWP app:

1. Open the `Package.appxmanifest` file from **Solution Explorer**.

2. Examine the fields in the **Application** tab. Add a space in the **Display name** field so that it reads as `RSS Reader` instead of `SplitApp`.

3. Add a useful description in the **Description** field. For example, `A simple but useful RSS feed reader`.

4. Moving to the **Visual Assets** tab, under the **Tile** section, confirm that the **Show name** field is set to **Square 150x150 Logo** as shown in the following screenshot. This setting will make the name of the app appear on the **Tile** on the Windows Start screen:

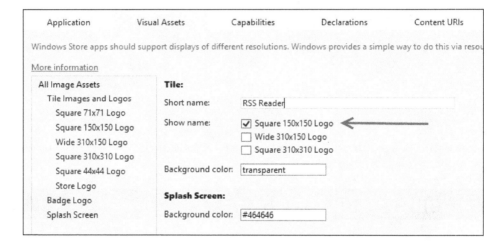

5. In the **Packaging** tab, adjust the Package **Display name** to include a space so that the package name is `Split App`, matching your earlier entry on the **Application** tab.

6. Save your changes to the manifest file.

7. Build the solution via **Build | Build Solution**, or press *F7*.

8. In Visual Studio, right-click on the solution in **Solution Explorer**, and select **Deploy Solution**. This will deploy the Split App template to your local machine ready for use.

9. In **Solution Explorer**, select the RSSReader project (not solution), and then click on the Show All Files icon, as shown in the following screenshot:

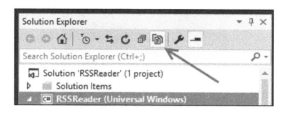

10. Navigate to the bin\Debug folder so that you can see the output from the build. This is the output that will be uploaded to the Windows Store when you publish your app. It should look something like the following screenshot:

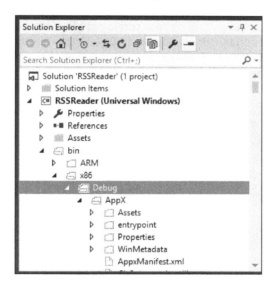

11. Press the Windows key to bring up the Start menu, and scroll as needed to locate your new app under **All apps**. (Alternatively, you can start typing the app's name in the Start menu to search for it.) You should see an icon for the RSS Reader template, as shown in the following screenshot:

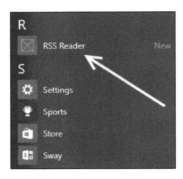

12. Deploying locally is fine for what it is, but if you want to test your app on another machine, you will need to create a package. Right-click on the RSSReader project in **Solution Explorer**, and navigate to the **Store | Create App Packages...** option from the context menu. Depending on your version of Visual Studio, you may have to be signed in for this option to be available, and you may also find it directly on the main menu **Store | Create App Packages...**. It may also be found under **Project | Store | Create App Pacakges...**. If you choose the context menu route, it will look similar to the following:

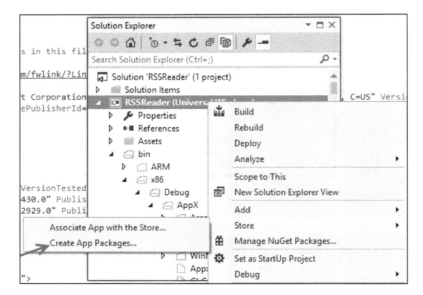

13. Select **No** when asked to build packages for the Windows Store, as shown in the following screenshot, and click on **Next**. Packaging and submitting your app for the Windows Store is discussed in the recipe *Submitting your app to the Windows Store*:

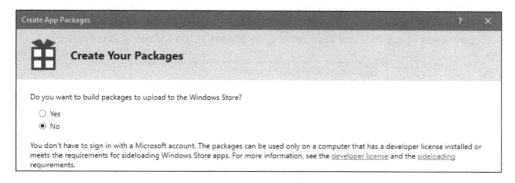

14. For the **Create App Packages** dialog box, the default settings are OK with the exception of the **Solution Configuration**—ensure that all are set to **Release**. (If you like, you can only choose the architectures supported by your specific workstation to save time.) After you have reviewed the screen, click on the **Create** button, as shown in the following screenshot:

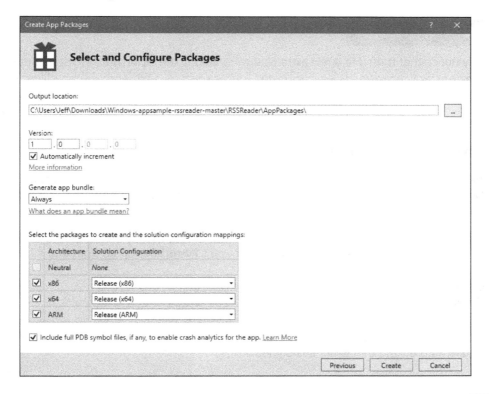

15. The build and packaging process may take a few minutes. When it is complete, you can verify the location of the packages by clicking on the **Output location** hyperlink. At this point, you can close the dialog, as we will cover certification in the next recipe.

16. You can also see that packages were created from within VS2015 if you refresh **Solution Explorer**—you will now see an `AppPackages` folder that contains the packages ready for local deployment, as shown in the following screenshot:

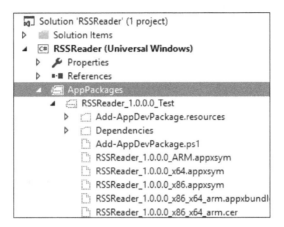

How it works...

You may notice that there are a few extra files generated in the `bin\Debug` folder, namely the `resources.pri`, `AppxManifest.xml`, and `RSSReader.build.appxrecipe` files. The `AppxManifest.xml` file is simply a renamed copy of the `package.appxmanifest` file.

The `resources.pri` file contains the app resources in a binary format, and the `RSSReader.build.appxrecipe` file is used for incremental builds of the package. So, each time the package is rebuilt, the package version number is automatically incremented.

Moving to the `AppPackages` folder, there is a file with an `.appxbundle` extension, which is a ZIP archive containing the app and any debug symbols, and there is a layout folder with a name based on the app, the CPU type, and so on.

Deploying an app to a test machine is simply a matter of copying this layout folder to the test machine, and running the `Add-AppDevPackage.ps1` PowerShell script from that folder.

There's more...

Packages need to be signed in order to be uploaded to the Windows Store. When developing locally, Visual Studio uses a temporary certificate. However, deploying to the Windows Store will require a certificate that is not self-signed.

See also

▸ The *Submitting your app to the Windows Store* recipe

Validating your Windows Store app

Every UWP app submitted to the Windows Store will be validated by Microsoft before being listed for the general public. Part of that validation process involves running the app through an automatic certification tool that Microsoft has included with Visual Studio. You should verify that your app passes the certification tool before beginning the Windows Store submission process.

Getting ready

You will need a packable UWP app to complete this recipe. You may either reuse the `RSSReader` app described in the *Packaging your UWP app* recipe, or use a UWP app of your own choice. Either way, ensure that you have a UWP app that is working correctly and deployable in **Release** mode.

How to do it...

The following steps need to be performed in order to validate your app for the Windows Store:

1. From the Windows Start screen, launch the **Windows App Cert Kit**. (If you are following directly from the *Packaging your UWP app* recipe, you can launch the kit from the **Package Creation Completed** dialog.) The following screenshot shows the app as found in the Start menu:

2. Once executed, the app will prompt for privilege elevation. Click on **Yes**; at this point, the application wizard will appear, as shown in the following screenshot:

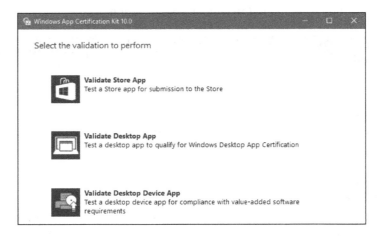

3. Select the **Validate Store App** option. The tool will search for Windows Store apps installed on your machine and list them.

4. Packages are listed by display name listed in each app's manifest file (manifest files have the extension `.appxmanifest`). Microsoft has added the option to browse for your app directly, but you should be able to find it in the app list. Locate your app and highlight it, then click on **Next** as shown in the following screenshot:

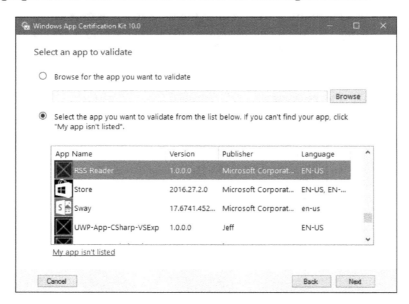

5. The kit will then allow you to select the tests you would like to run. The default technique to test everything is what we will use here, so click on **Next**.

6. The certification process will then proceed by running your app multiple times to test its various characteristics. You may notice that your system opens and closes your app during the validation process, so it is best to not try and do other activities while it is operating.

7. When the certification process completes, you will be immediately prompted to save an XML file containing the report. Choose a location to save the file to, and once the file is saved, you will see the completion dialog.

8. Click on the link in the dialog to view the report. Windows will prompt for a program with which to view the report; pick an editor of your choice, or use Internet Explorer. Scan the file for warnings and errors.

9. In this case, since `RSSReader` began life as a UWP app, it does have a few errors that will need to be addressed before it can be submitted. Your specific errors may vary depending on any changes you may have made, but our results include some simple ones (for instance, the lack of the app's logo for branding) to using a Windows API that is not supported in the Windows SDK for Windows Store apps. Validation can be rerun as many times as needed until your app has passed all the tests.

How it works...

The certification kit runs your app in order to verify that it follows the rules defined for each of the selected tests. It does not perform tests of your app's functionality, but validates how well the app behaves within the context of the Windows operating system, and whether the rules for listing the app in the store are satisfied. This is intended to prevent apps using a capability that they haven't defined, and to identify any possible weaknesses in the package that may allow it to be used as an attack vector for malicious code.

When your app passes the certification kit tests with no warnings or errors, it is ready for submission to the Windows Store, where Microsoft will perform additional content and behavioral checks.

See also

▸ The *Submitting your app to the Windows Store* recipe

▸ The *Packaging your UWP app* recipe

▸ The *Defining capabilities and contracts* recipe

▸ Microsoft's official guide, *Windows Store Policies*, is available online at `https://msdn.microsoft.com/en-us/library/windows/apps/dn764944.aspx`

▸ Further background on *The app certification process* and tips for a successful distribution are available at `https://msdn.microsoft.com/library/windows/apps/mt148554.aspx`

Submitting your app to the Windows Store

Similar to other vendors (Google, Apple, and others), Microsoft has designated their Windows Store to the preferred method of distributing apps to their users. Corporate developers can utilize company-specific areas, and sideloading is available in special circumstances, but the typical way the average user will obtain your app is through the Windows Store.

Certification is the process by which Microsoft ensures that the apps available in the Windows Store meet certain performance and quality standards. As a developer, the Windows Store makes it easy for customers to obtain and install your app. A user obtaining an app from the Windows Store can be reasonably confident that anything they download will behave according to the capabilities it has declared, and can be easily installed or uninstalled as desired without unexpected consequences.

In this recipe, we'll look at how the certification process works. We will take a look at how your candidate UWP app can be submitted to the Windows Store, and made available to your potential customers.

Getting ready

To start, you need to be using Windows 10, and either VS Express for Windows 10, or the Community Edition or higher of VS2015. If you have been following along in this chapter, you may continue to use the `RSSReader` app. Otherwise, feel free to use one of your own choice. Since we are focusing on the registration process, a blank UWP app is used for this recipe.

How to do it...

To submit an app to the Windows Store, we will perform the following steps:

1. Start a new **Visual C# | Windows | Universal | Blank App (Universal Windows)** project.

2. From the menu, select **Project | Store | Open Developer Account**. (For VS Express, the menu is **Store | Open Developer Account**.)

There are two types of Developer Accounts—individual and company. If you are an independent developer or just experimenting, the individual account will work fine. Before registering, be sure to sign in with the Microsoft account that you intend to associate with your Windows Store submissions. You can find more information in the article *Account types, locations, and fees* located at `https://msdn.microsoft.com/en-us/library/windows/apps/jj863494.aspx`.

3. A browser window opens, and you can apply for a developer account using the process as outlined on the page. Windows Store accounts may require a payment of a small license fee, so have a credit card handy when you perform this step.

4. From the Visual Studio menu, select **Project | Store | Edit App Manifest**, and use the information from the app name reservation to populate the appropriate fields. Take particular note of the fields in the **Packaging** tab.

5. Then select **Project | Store | Associate App with the Store**, and follow the steps of the wizard to automatically populate the **Packaging** tab with the appropriate values. This option will let you choose from a reserved app name, as well as reserve a new name if needed:

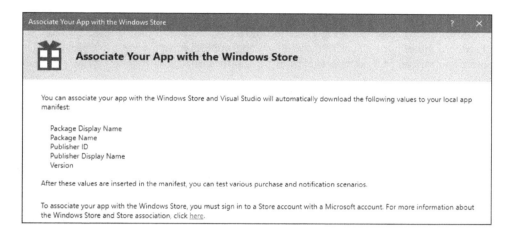

6. At this point, you are ready to write your application.

 Current Microsoft guidelines will allow an app name to be reserved for a year. If your app is not submitted by this deadline, the reservation will expire.

7. Package your application for uploading to the store by choosing **Project | Store | Create App Package...**

8. Verify your application using the Windows App Certification Kit. Refer to the *Validating your Windows Store app* recipe to learn how to do this.

9. Then upload the resulting package to the store by selecting **Project | Store | Upload App Package** from the menu, and following the steps presented in the ensuing upload wizard. Note that your packages have to pass validation before they can be uploaded.

10. Once the upload completes, you can monitor the progress of your package through the approval process using the tools provided by the store. (Your Developer Dashboard available through your Microsoft Developer account is a good place to do this.)

How it works...

The **Store** submenu is only available when running Visual Studio on Windows 10, and when you have opened the solution for a UWP app. When you upload a package to the store, there are a number of basic sanity checks to verify your package is acceptable, and meets the requirements of the Windows Store. These checks include running the certification toolkit on your app and verifying the manifest information against the information you supplied when you registered the app name. Using Visual Studio's Associate app with the store wizard is an easy way to make sure you don't have any typographical errors in your manifest, and it improves the chances of a successful first time submission.

There's more...

Earning money with Windows Store apps is not limited solely to upfront purchase revenues. You may also distribute your app using a trial mode that encourages a try-before-you-buy approach. Apps may include the ability to support in-app purchases, in-app advertising using your choice of ad platforms, and it may implement a custom transaction system if you so desire.

 For in-app purchases and trial versions of your product, Microsoft bundles supporting functionality in the `Windows.ApplicationModel.Store` namespace to make it easier for you to build applications with these features, as well as to simulate the Windows Store functions prior to official submission. A sample app using these features is available here: `https://github.com/Microsoft/Windows-universalsamples/tree/master/Samples/Store`.

If you want to confirm the details of the *Windows Store Policies*, refer to the Microsoft documentation on the subject at `https://msdn.microsoft.com/en-us/library/windows/apps/dn764944.aspx`.

See also

▸ The *Packaging your UWP app* recipe
▸ The *Validating your Windows Store app* recipe

Distributing your UWP app through sideloading

With Windows 8.X, Microsoft heavily promoted the idea of app distribution through their Windows Store. Indeed, we have covered this concept, because it is an easy way to sell and/or distribute your app to new and existing users. However, longtime Windows developers are used to the idea of controlling their application's distribution from start to finish. Additionally, there may be business reasons that make it impractical, if not impossible, to distribute a program through an outside vendor.

To address these and other concerns, Windows 10 supports the concept of **sideloading** apps. This term refers to the concept of taking a properly packaged UWP app and distributing it to end users outside of the Windows Store. While this capability existed to some extent in Windows 8.1, it is no longer so obscure in Windows 10. Outside of business and privacy concerns, how you distribute your app is entirely up to you.

 Even if you intend to ultimately distribute your app through the Windows Store, sideloading provides the ability to distribute your app to a select group of users for testing or demo purposes, if so desired.

Getting ready

You will need to be running Windows 10 for this recipe, as we are dealing with UWP apps.

How to do it...

There are a few different areas to review when employing app sideloading. We will discuss them all in the following steps:

1. To review your current system settings as they apply to app sideloading, visit your system's **All settings** screen. From there, select **Update & security**, then click on **For developers**.

2. This is the same screen where **Developer mode** is enabled for our UWP app development. You will want to verify that this is enabled, as shown in the following screenshot:

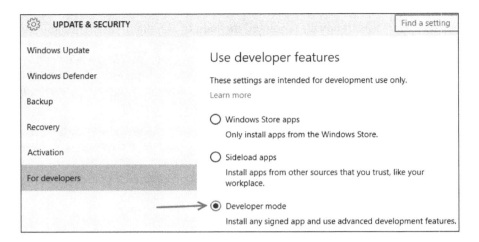

 System administrators can set this via Group Policy and using the setting **ApplicationManagement/AllowAllTrustedApps**. The value of 0 is an explicit denial of this ability, whereas a value of 1 is an explicit allow.

3. You will need a packaged app to continue, so if you haven't got one already, you can create one by following the recipe *Packaging your UWP app*.

4. The resulting files can be distributed to your users for installation on their own machine. You can make them available via network file share, or USB stick, or any other traditional distribution method.

5. The following screenshot provides an example of the app package distribution files:

Add-AppDevPackage.resources	2/27/2016 18:31	File folder	
Dependencies	2/27/2016 18:31	File folder	
☑ Add-AppDevPackage	7/7/2015 01:51	Windows PowerS...	61 KB
RSSReader_1.0.1.0_x86.appxbundle	2/27/2016 18:31	APPXBUNDLE File	601 KB
RSSReader_1.0.1.0_x86.appxsym	2/27/2016 18:31	APPXSYM File	2,279 KB
RSSReader_1.0.1.0_x86	2/27/2016 18:31	Security Certificate	1 KB

6. To install the app, you should execute the `Add-AppDevPackage` PowerShell script highlighted in the previous screenshot.

How it works...

Since your application has been packaged, all of the metadata needed for its installation and operation is available. The PowerShell script that Microsoft provides enables your app to be easily installed. Thanks to this script, you can use the app package on the target machines that you want.

There's more...

Users can avoid security warnings that may occur during app installation by first installing the certificate generated by the packaging process, which is included with your app package. To do this, right-click on the certificate, and select **Install Certificate**. This will present the **Certificate Import Wizard**, as shown in the following screenshot:

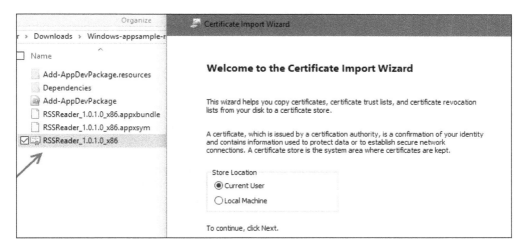

You can have the certificate stored in the current user location (specific to the user that is currently logged in to the machine), or the local machine location, which would grant it recognition to all the users using that specific Windows 10 machine. For a one-off installation, it may make sense to just install it as current user.

In a corporate setting, you will probably have an existing certificate infrastructure for your app distribution to be a part of. While creating the infrastructure is outside the scope of this book, you can specify that your app uses a specific certificate (as opposed to the default Microsoft created one) by editing your app's `Package.appxmanifest`, and selecting a specific certificate to sign your app's package, as shown in the following screenshot:

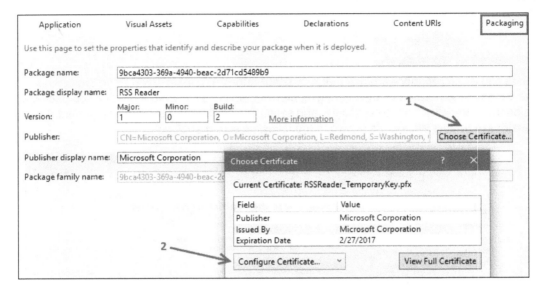

From here, you can choose a certificate that already exists in your machine's certificate store, or pick a certificate stored in a PFX file. Thus, if your corporate users already recognize a corporate certificate, you can use that to sign your app so that their machines recognize its legitimacy.

See also

- Distributing line-of-business apps through the Windows Store for Business. Refer to `https://msdn.microsoft.com/library/windows/apps/mt608995.aspx`.
- Generating Personal Information Exchange certificates. Refer to `https://technet.microsoft.com/en-us/library/dd261744.aspx`.

3
Web Development

In this chapter, we will cover the following topics:

- ▶ Getting started with a Bootstrap-based SPA
- ▶ Making the most of Browser Link
- ▶ Adding bundling and minification to JavaScript and CSS files
- ▶ Managing packages with NuGet
- ▶ Fortifying JavaScript applications with TypeScript
- ▶ Using Visual Studio for Node.js development

Introduction

The Internet remains a critical focus for modern application development. When its popularity began to skyrocket in the 1990s, the focus was on users who usually accessed the Internet via their web browsers and e-mail clients. The proliferation of devices beyond a traditional desktop computer (smart phones, tablets, dedicated gaming consoles, and more) in the 21st century has brought about the current situation where users expect to be able to access their data from anywhere on any device.

As developers, we need to support as many of these devices as we can to provide the best user experience. Users on a desktop expect a full-featured application that takes advantage of the larger screen and the typical peripherals (keyboard, mouse, and so on), whereas mobile users expect a touch-centric application that is sensitive to bandwidth limitations.

Web development in VS2015 has been further improved to support all of these use cases. Whether you are writing client-facing code or the server technology to support them, VS2015 has improved the tools available to you. And while the focus of this chapter is that of Internet-facing applications, many familiar languages that originated for the Web (HTML5 and JavaScript) have found a place across the full spectrum of application development, so you will be able to use them to write code for websites, UWP apps, or desktop applications.

In this chapter, we will look at different areas where VS2015 can help make your web development tasks easier for wherever you are putting these technologies to use.

Getting started with a Bootstrap-based SPA

VS2015 ships with numerous templates and project types available for creating web applications. Since the rest of the chapter will be much more useful with a sample project available, we will use this recipe to create a new **ASP.NET Single Page Application** using C# and Bootstrap.

Bootstrap is a popular open source framework for frontend web development. It provides a dynamic, mobile-first design, which automatically reacts in a useful way to the resizing of browser windows, thus lending itself to easily accommodate the wide range of phones and tablets in use today.

A default Bootstrap-themed web application will look similar to the following screenshot:

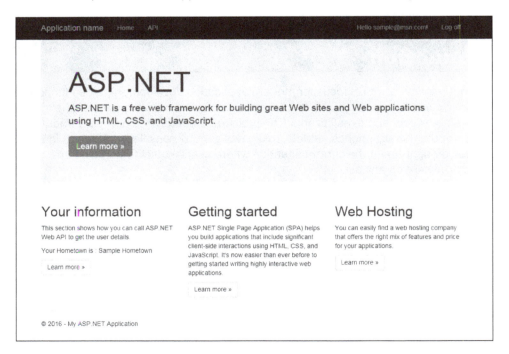

In this recipe, we will create a new ASP.NET single page application to see Bootstrap in action.

Getting ready

You can use Visual Studio Express 2015 for Web, Visual Studio 2015 Community Edition, or any of the premium editions for this recipe.

How to do it...

We'll start off by creating a new project to see what is provided out of the box, and then look at the options available for customization. This is performed with the following steps:

1. Start your copy of VS2015.

2. Create a new project by navigating to the template for **Visual C# | Web | ASP.NET Web Application**, and either accept the default project name, or enter one of your own.

3. In the next dialog box, choose the **Single Page Application** template, as shown in the following screenshot:

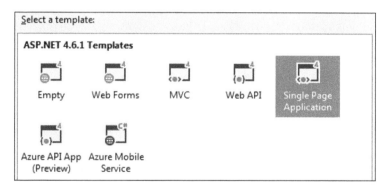

4. After Visual Studio finishes creating the project files, you may be prompted to select a source control system: **Team Foundation Version Control** or **Git**. For the purposes of this recipe, we will just click on the **Cancel** button, but if you have a preference, feel free to make your choice.

5. At this point, you can preview your application if you want to see what you are starting with. Pressing *F5* or navigating to **Debug | Start Debugging** will bring up the default Bootstrap template, as shown in the introduction to this recipe. If you decide to review/debug the app, please stop debugging before continuing.

6. The default MVC application that we've created uses the default Bootstrap theme. It's not a bad theme, but you will probably want to customize it a bit so that your site obtains some personality. The CSS files that define your site's theme are located in the `Content` directory, as shown in the following image:

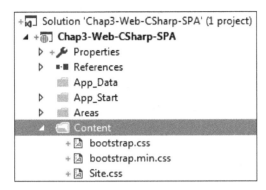

7. As you may surmise from the filenames, the `bootstrap.css` file contains a more human-friendly definition of the site, while the `bootstrap.min.css` file is the minimized version intended to reduce loading time when used in production.

8. Before replacing the `bootstrap.css` file, it is always good to make a backup. Rename it to avoid overwriting it, by right-clicking on the file in the **Solution Explorer** window and clicking on the **Rename** option. Feel free to use a name of your choice.

9. Let's find a new theme from **Bootswatch** to personalize our site. Navigate to `http://bootswatch.com/`.

10. You can review the themes there, and pick one that appeals to you. For this recipe, we'll choose Journal. The CSS file is found at `http://bootswatch.com/journal/bootstrap.css`.

11. Download this new theme file to the `Content` directory of your Visual Studio project. (If you are using the defaults, your project will be in the `Documents\Visual Studio 2015\Projects\directory`, where Documents should be adjusted depending on your version of Windows.)

 An easy way to navigate directly to your `Content` folder and to determine its location is to simply right-click on `Content` in the **Solution Explorer**, and select **Open Folder in File Explorer**, as shown in the following screenshot:

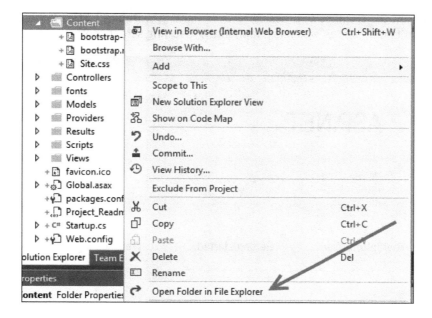

12. Once downloaded, it will have to be added to your project. Right-click on the `Content` directory in **Solution Explorer**, and navigate to **Add | Existing Item...**, as shown in the following screenshot:

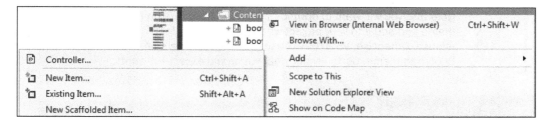

13. Locate your newly downloaded file, and add it to the project.

14. Preview the changes by pressing *F5* or navigating to **Debug | Start Debugging** as described in *Step 5*, which is shown in the following screenshot:

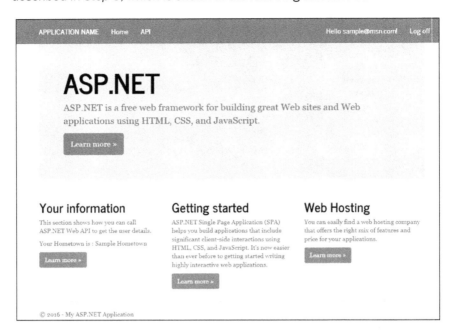

 Note that you will want to download the minimized version of your chosen theme and add it to your project when you are ready for a production release. Otherwise, VS2015 will use the minimized version of the original Bootstrap theme. Certainly not what you would expect—or want!

There's more...

You will notice that templates based on older ASP.NET versions (such as ASP.NET MVC 4) are no longer available with VS2015. As part of the price of progress, older templates have been removed—but this doesn't mean that VS2015 cannot help you. Any projects started in VS2013 can, of course, be opened and continued under VS2015. Even better, as long you do not invoke newer ASP.NET features, you can continue to work in VS2015 while a colleague still uses VS2013. This is due to **project round-tripping**, which lets you use your tools independent of your source code.

See also

▸ For more information on the Bootstrap framework, and to examine the source code, visit the project's home page at `http://getbootstrap.com/`. Specifically, customization is described at `http://getbootstrap.com/customize/`.

▸ See the *Adding bundling and minification to JavaScript and CSS files* recipe later in this chapter.

Making the most of Browser Link

A common task faced by web designers is dealing with the constant workflow of editing web pages and reviewing their changes. With the large number of web browsers in the market, it can be tedious to keep them all in sync as changes are made. VS2015 seeks to address this with the advent of the **Browser Link** feature. The Browser Link feature allows you to select any number of browsers available on your development machine, and have them refreshed after making changes to your web pages. This feature makes it very easy to make changes to your website, and to preview them across your site's supported browsers in a streamlined way.

In this recipe, we will look at how to set up Browser Link, and how it can help you with your projects.

Getting ready

You can use Visual Studio Express 2015 for Web, Visual Studio 2015 Community Edition, or any of the premium editions for this recipe. You should also make available all of the web browsers you plan to use (Google Chrome, Mozilla Firefox, and so on) before we start. If you would like to just see how the feature works first, Internet Explorer will work fine.

How to do it...

We will start this recipe by enabling support for Browser Link, and then we will see it in action by performing the following steps:

1. Open up a web-based project in Visual Studio. (The one created in this chapter's *Getting started with a Bootstrap-based SPA* recipe will work great.)

2. Browser Link should be supported by default in a new project if you are running in the **Debug** (not **Release**) mode. If this is not set in your `Web.config` file, you will see the following error message on your **Browser Link Dashboard** window:

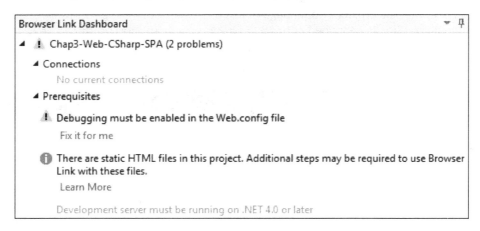

3. VS2015 can enable debugging for you automatically, but you can also do this yourself by ensuring that the `compilation` element is set to `true`, as shown in the following screenshot:

```
<system.web>
  <authentication mode="None" />
  <compilation debug="true" targetFramework="4.6.1" />
  <httpRuntime targetFramework="4.6.1" />
</system.web>
```

4. As soon as you save the changes, Browser Link will be available for use, so let's see what it can do. Open an HTML or **CSHTML** page in your editor. Then to browse with Browser Link, you will have to open the web browsers in the following manner. Select **Browse With...** as shown in the following screenshot:

5. Clicking on **Browse With...** will open the dialog box shown in the next image. Click on **Firefox** while holding down *Ctrl*. If **Internet Explorer** is not selected, *Ctrl* + click on its title as well. The following screenshot shows the desired selections:

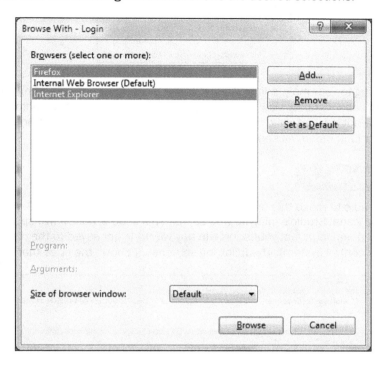

6. After making those selections, click on the **Browse** button. This will open up your web page in each browser selected.

7. You can verify this connection by leaving the browsers open and switching back to Visual Studio. Then open the **Browser Link Dashboard** window (if it is not already open) using the menu shown here:

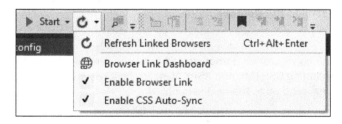

8. Once the dashboard is open, it will show that two connections are, in fact, present:

9. Returning to your main editor window, make a change, such as adding a few lines of text. You can instantly view the changes by reloading your website across all browsers with the hot key *Ctrl + Alt + Enter*, or by clicking on the **Browse** button under the Browser Link menu, as shown in *Step 5*.

How it works...

Visual Studio is able to make this feature work by injecting a snippet of JavaScript into the web pages served by Visual Studio's internal web server. This code is added transparently behind the scenes, and does not affect your source in any way (it is not saved to the disk or entered into your source control system). The following screenshot shows the code that is added:

```
114  <!-- Visual Studio Browser Link -->
115  <script type="application/json" id="__browserLink_initializationData">
116      {"appName":"Internet Explorer","requestId":"3e376790c15f4444a269eaffe04924c5"}
117  </script>
118  <script type="text/javascript"
     src="http://localhost:41536/8b5640adb8fa4911ab06925c0943fa8c/browserLink"
     async="async"></script>
119  <!-- End Browser Link -->
120
121  </body>
122  </html>
123
```

There's more...

Browser Link is tied to running your site through Visual Studio in the **Debug** mode; it turns itself off when switching to the **Release** mode.

The configuration demonstrated here works with dynamic files, including CSHTML and ASPX files. For best results with static HTML files, read on to the next section.

However, there may be situations where you want to absolutely guarantee that Browser Link is not running—perhaps you are tracking down a particularly nasty bug, and want to eliminate all outside factors. The following code fragments added to your project's `Web.Config` file under the `appSettings` tag can force Browser Link to always be ON (`true`) or always OFF (`false`), depending on your needs:

```
<system.web>
  <compilation debug="false" targetFramework="4.6.1" />
</system.web>
```

Separately, the following change to `appSettings` should be paired with the preceding change:

```
<appSettings>
  <add key="vs:enableBrowserLink" value="false"/>
</appSettings>
```

 VS2015 will notify you on the **Browser Link Dashboard** if either of these is set to `true`, but knowing the code behind the settings allows you to ensure it is set the way you want, especially if sharing files with coworkers or version control systems.

Supporting static HTML files

To ensure that Browser Link correctly displays the static HTML files, add the following to your `Web.config` file in the handlers section under `system.webServer`:

```
<add name="Browser Link for HTML" path="*.html" verb="*"
type="System.Web.StaticFileHandler, System.Web, Version=4.0.0.0,
Culture=neutral, PublicKeyToken=b03f5f7f11d50a3a"
resourceType="File" preCondition="integratedMode" />
```

Note that you should only include this while developing, as it should not be enabled for production use due to performance considerations.

Adding bundling and minification to JavaScript and CSS files

One of the most common techniques for improving website performance is to reduce the number of requests a browser needs to make in order to get the resources required for the page, and to reduce the size of the data requested.

When it comes to both JavaScript and CSS, this generally means combining all of the files of the same type into a single large file (bundling), removing unnecessary whitespace from them, and renaming variables to use the minimum amount of space possible while still leaving the functionality unchanged (minification).

Since version 4.5, ASP.NET supports automatic bundling and minification. By having these processes applied in an automatic way, you can work with the unmodified files to make development easier, while your users get the benefit of the optimized files.

In this recipe, you'll add bundling and minification to a site, and see how it impacts your development activities.

Getting ready

You can use Visual Studio Express 2015 for Web, Visual Studio 2015 Community Edition, or any of the premium editions for this recipe. We are going to use the project created in the *Getting started with a Bootstrap-based SPA* recipe, but feel free to substitute your own.

This recipe assumes that your browser of choice has developer tools that are able to capture network traffic. If you use Internet Explorer, you will need Internet Explorer 11 or higher, which is what this recipe assumes you are using.

How to do it...

Bundling and minification are important steps to remember when moving your code into production (even if just testing for production-like environments). Let's see how to do it:

1. Build the application, and run it without the debugger by pressing *Ctrl + F5* or navigating to **Debug** | **Start Without Debugging** from the menu.

2. Navigate to the `http://localhost:37271/Manage` page in your browser, and open the browser's developer tools. If you are using Internet Explorer 11, you can press *F12* to open them.

3. Go to the **Network** tab (*Ctrl + 4*), and click on the Start Capturing (*F5*) button. In the browser window, press *Ctrl + F5* to force a complete refresh of the page. The network trace should show that a lot of files are required to load the page. This can be seen in the following screenshot:

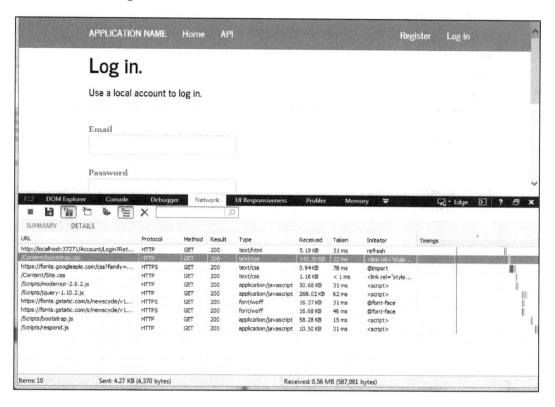

4. Look at all those requests! If you want a faster loading page, you need to reduce this. Leaving the browser open, switch back to Visual Studio, and in the **Solution Explorer** window, find and open the `BundleConfig.cs` file. (It is located in the project's `App_Start` folder.)

5. In this file, you will see the bundles defined for the project. Existing JavaScript files for this project are already configured. For example, look at how Bootstrap is bundled:

```
bundles.Add(new ScriptBundle("~/bundles/bootstrap").Include(
    "~/Scripts/bootstrap.js",
    "~/Scripts/respond.js"));
```

6. When you add custom JavaScript to your project (typically, in the project's `Scripts` folder), you will undoubtedly want the bundles file for your own custom JavaScript. To do that, you can define your own bundle by adding a new statement to the `RegisterBundles()` method as follows:

```
bundles.Add(new ScriptBundle("~/bundles/customjs").
Include("~/Scripts/myJavaScript.js"));
```

7. The preceding code assumes that you have added a JavaScript file to your project using the name shown in bold (`myJavaScript.js`).

8. Now is a good time for a checkpoint. Rebuild the solution, switch over to your browser, and perform a full page refresh (that is, press *Ctrl* + *F5* in Internet Explorer). Assuming that the **Network** tab is still open in the developer tools, you should see that everything is still operating as expected.

9. While you have defined the bundles, they still aren't actually being bundled or minified. Switch back to Visual Studio, and find and open the `Global.asax.cs` file in **Solution Explorer**. In the `Application_Start()` method, add the following highlighted line of code to enable optimizations, as shown in the following image:

```
protected void Application_Start()
{
    AreaRegistration.RegisterAllAreas();
    GlobalConfiguration.Configure(WebApiConfig.Register);
    FilterConfig.RegisterGlobalFilters(GlobalFilters.Filters);
    RouteConfig.RegisterRoutes(RouteTable.Routes);
    BundleConfig.RegisterBundles(BundleTable.Bundles);

    // When true, enable Bundles regardless of Debug mode
    BundleTable.EnableOptimizations = true;
}
```

The `EnableOptimizations` property forces bundling to occur. Without this call, bundling only occurs when running the site in the **Release** mode. In other words, when the debug = `true` attribute of the `system.web.compilation` tag of the `web.config` file is specified, bundling optimizations are disabled.

10. Rebuild the application, switch over to the browser, and perform a full page refresh again. The network trace will now show that JavaScript bundles are being downloaded instead of individual script files, and that the download size of the bundle files is less than the download size of the original JavaScript files, as shown in the following screenshot:

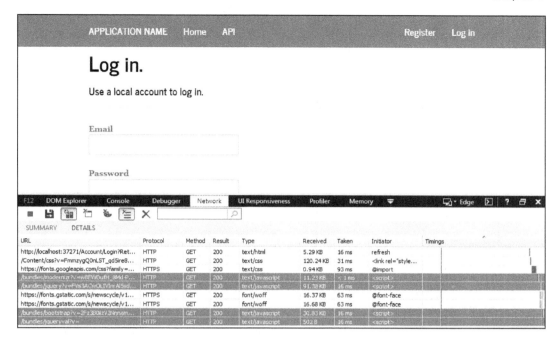

 The bundled files are now sourced from `/bundles/` rather than `/Scripts/`.

11. It's worth confirming that the scripts are not only bundled, but also minified. Navigate to the **Debugger** tab (*Ctrl + 3*) in the browser developer tools, and select the `bootstrap` file from the script's' drop-down list, as shown in the following screenshot:

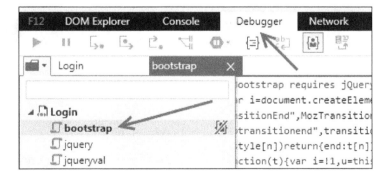

Once the file is open, as you can see in the following screenshot, not only has the whitespace been removed, but the variable names have also been shortened, and the code optimized. Exactly what you should expect minification to do:

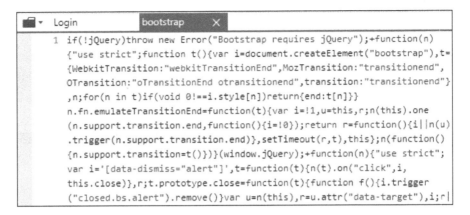

How it works...

Inside the ASP.NET runtime, when a browser requests a page with a bundle in it, ASP.NET will either render the names of the individual files in the bundle or the bundle name itself, depending on whether optimizations are turned on or not. When optimizations are on, browsers will request bundles by their name, and ASP.NET will group the individual bundled files into a single larger file before minifying them and sending the result back to the browser. The resulting minified file is cached by ASP.NET so that future requests do not impact site performance.

You can create your own custom bundle types by subclassing the Bundle class. This allows you to provide your own minification rules and bundling mechanisms, which is useful if you want to support web technologies such as LESS, Sass, or CoffeeScript.

Managing packages with NuGet

Watching the software releases that Microsoft has made in recent years, it is hard to miss the great strides that the firm has made in moving towards embracing open source software. Microsoft's approach to open source software and open source projects, in general, has softened over the years to the point where open source is now valued, embraced, and recognized as an integral part of the development ecosystem.

Microsoft is now so committed to open source that they are developing a number of projects, starting with .NET Core and ASP.NET Core, to providing contributions for a number of third-party open source projects such as jQuery, Node.js, and Git.

Developers using VS2015 need an easy way to locate and find open source packages that could be used in their own projects. To help facilitate this, Microsoft supports an open source project to create a package manager for Visual Studio called the **NuGet** package manager. NuGet (`https://www.nuget.org/`) allows developers to download packages of libraries that install themselves into a project, configure themselves, and then are ready for use by the developer. The package manager also does the work of looking for new updates, and applying those updates when they are available.

In this recipe, you'll see the ways to use the NuGet package manager in Visual Studio.

 This recipe uses a web application, but NuGet can be used across Visual Studio.

Getting ready

You can use Visual Studio Express 2015 for Web, Visual Studio 2015 Community Edition, or any of the premium editions for this recipe.

How to do it...

For this recipe, we will create a new ASP.NET web application, and then see how NuGet will let us easily add new packages to assist our application. Let's get started:

1. Start your copy of VS2015.
2. Create a new project by navigating to the template for **Visual C# | Web | ASP.NET Web Application**, and either accept the default project name, or enter one of your own.
3. In the next dialog box, choose the **MVC** template, as shown in the following screenshot:

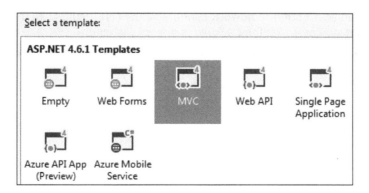

4. If prompted for a version control system, select your preference, or just click on **Cancel** to skip. For a quick check, make sure everything is in order, press *F5*, or navigate to **Debug | Start Debugging**. After a brief review, stop debugging and return to VS2015.

5. Let's add some packages. In **Solution Explorer**, right-click on the `References` node for the project, and select **Manage NuGet Packages**.

6. The **NuGet Package Manager** dialog box will appear. The default package source is `nuget.org`, which you can verify for your local environment, as shown in the following screenshot:

7. Enter `entityframework` into the search box on the bottom-left corner, and then review the results, as shown in the following screenshot:

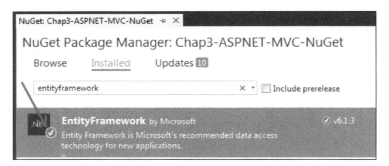

8. As you can see, **EntityFramework** appears as the first result. Note the green check mark that indicates that the package is already installed.

9. Now let's add a new package. Replace the `entityframework` search text with `json`.

10. The first result should be the **Newtonsoft.Json** .NET package. Click on the **Install** button. If it is already installed, you can instead **Update** your copy, as shown in the following screenshot:

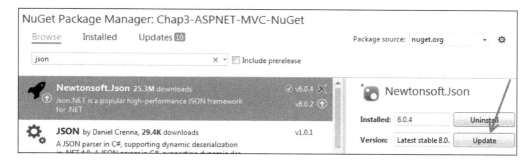

11. Once the package has been installed or updated, close the **NuGet Package Manager**.

12. Close the NuGet window, and then expand the `References` node for the project in **Solution Explorer**. You should see not only the **EntityFramework** and Json.NET assemblies, but also assemblies for other packages that the bundler relies on. A partial listing of the `References` are shown in the following screenshot:

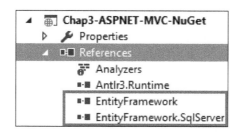

13. Now let's review how to update all of the installed NuGet packages that you may have. Open the **NuGet Package Manager** again by right-clicking on the `References` node, and selecting **Manage NuGet Packages**. Select the **Updates** tab, as shown in the following screenshot:

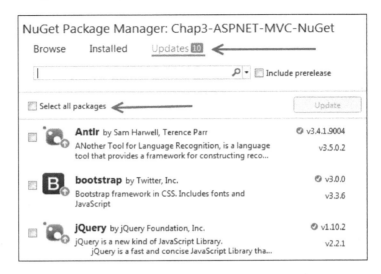

14. In the preceding screenshot, you can see that the **Updates** tab shows packages installed on your local system. It also provides an option to let you quickly update all of the installed packages from nuget.org, or individually choose the packages you would like to update.

15. The **NuGet Package Manager** is not the only way to use NuGet. So we will continue, and show you how to do a bulk update from the **Package Manager Console**.

16. From the main menu in Visual Studio, navigate to **Tools | NuGet Package Manager | Package Manager Console**.

17. The console will appear at the bottom of the screen. Click inside it, and enter the command `Get-Package -updates` before pressing *Enter*, as shown in the following screenshot:

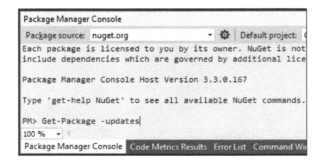

18. Since a particular package is not specified, NuGet will iterate over all installed packages to see if any updates exist. This will list all the packages that have updates available. To update all of them, execute the command `Update-Package`. NuGet will then locate and install updates for all packages automatically. Because package installation in web projects often affects the `Web.config` file, you may get prompted to reload it a number of times. Each time you do, just click on **Yes**.

19. Alternatively, you may enter a specific package to check for updates on that single package (for example, `Update-Package jquery`).

20. The results of the update will be shown in **Package Manager Console**, as shown in the following screenshot (note you may receive a notice to restart Visual Studio depending on the scope of the update):

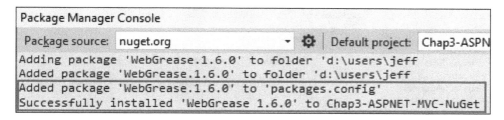

21. Compile and run the application to check that everything still works as expected.

How it works...

NuGet uses a central, well-known location for storing packages, located at `http://www.nuget.org`. Anyone can create and upload packages to this site, and the site features a gallery allowing you to search and browse all the available packages. For many people, the NuGet site is the first port of call when looking for a package to help them in their development efforts.

Apart from independent software packages being provided through NuGet, Microsoft itself is using NuGet to deliver their own packages. This provides Microsoft with an easier way to deliver updates, and provides you with an easier way to install them on your system, thereby keeping your software packages current.

There's more...

We just scratched the surface of what NuGet can do, but it offers a couple of more useful abilities. Let's take a look.

Automatically loading packages

If you are sharing solutions with different developers—perhaps you would like to try an open source project, or you may have recently changed your programming environments, for example—you will inevitably run into a situation where packages needed by your project are missing.

Visual Studio provides an option to automatically retrieve these packages for you, which can be especially helpful in situations when you want to focus on learning the code, and not be mired in troubleshooting build settings. To turn this feature ON or verify your current settings, navigate to **Tools | NuGet Package Manager | Package Manager Settings**, as shown in the following screenshot:

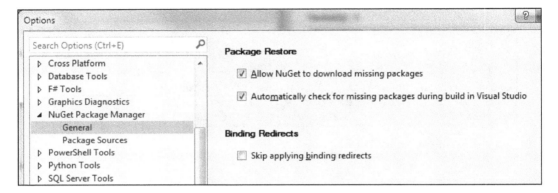

Selecting both the options (as shown in the preceding screenshot) will allow NuGet to download the missing packages automatically.

About binding redirects:

Binding redirects are used to help with versioning the packages provided by NuGet. For example, say you desire to install package A, which requires version 3.0.1 of package B. If the newest the version of package B is 3.2, that is what NuGet will install by default. Checking **Skip applying binding redirects** will enforce strict versioning, so a requirement to install version 3.0.1 means that is exactly what will be installed. For most purposes, you will want to leave this unchecked as shown.

Using custom package locations

A lot of organizations build their own utilities, frameworks, and libraries for use in their development, and wish to share them across various projects. Managing these dependencies can become difficult over time. Fortunately, NuGet can be configured to use custom locations for packages by either using a filesystem location, or your own network accessible NuGet server.

If you wish to host your own NuGet server, instructions can be found at `http://github.com/NuGet/NuGetGallery/wiki/Hosting-the-NuGet-Gallery-Locally-in-IIS`. If you wish to host just your own project-specific server via a custom feed, or take advantage of some advanced functionality, check out `http://docs.nuget.org/create/hosting-your-own-nuget-feeds`.

To configure Visual Studio to use a custom location for NuGet packages, go to **Tools | NuGet Package Manager | Package Manager Settings**, and add entries by filling in the **Name** and **Source** fields, and then clicking on the add button. The following screenshot shows two extra entries; one is configured to point to a local on-disk NuGet repository, and the other is pointing to a network share:

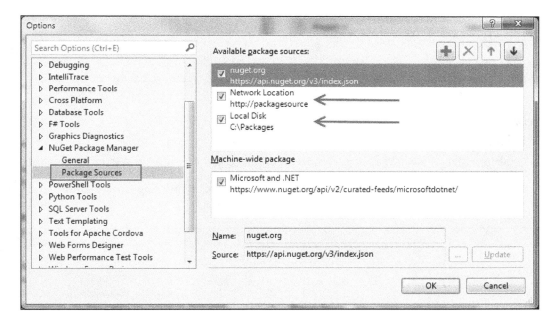

Fortifying JavaScript applications with TypeScript

JavaScript's role in web development has gone from being considered a starter language for hobbyist programmers to being regarded as a serious tool for building modern web applications on both the client and server. This change means that the size and scope of JavaScript applications has grown tremendously, and with that growth, the costs for managing the complexity have also increased. To address this, Microsoft has developed the open source project TypeScript, which is a superset of JavaScript that adds static type checking.

The result is that TypeScript can be used to build a new web application from the ground up just as well as it can be used on-demand to replace or refactor code in an existing JavaScript project. TypeScript can help depending on the needs of your project. Let's take a look at how TypeScript can benefit your web application.

Getting ready

You can use Visual Studio Express 2015 for Web, Visual Studio 2015 Community Edition, or any of the premium editions for this recipe. Please ensure Update 1 has been installed, regardless of the edition that you choose.

How to do it...

Let's perform the following steps to see how TypeScript can fortify your JavaScript applications:

1. Open Visual Studio 2015 and create a new project of **HTML Application with TypeScript** type, as shown in the following screenshot:

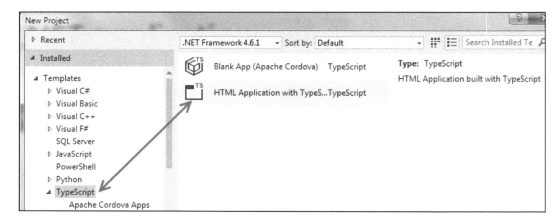

2. Accept the default project name, and create the project.

3. When executed, the default project will open with a small sample that will produce a web page that shows a simple clock. When you look at the source, it is pretty sparse, as shown in the following screenshot:

```
http://localhost:55812/ - Original Source
File  Edit  Format
 1  <!DOCTYPE html>
 2
 3  <html lang="en">
 4  <head>
 5      <meta charset="utf-8" />
 6      <title>TypeScript HTML App</title>
 7      <link rel="stylesheet" href="app.css" type="text/css" />
 8      <script src="app.js"></script>
 9  </head>
10  <body>
11      <h1>TypeScript HTML App</h1>
12
13      <div id="content"></div>
14  </body>
15  </html>
16
```

4. If you notice, beyond some HTML, there is not much except for a reference to a file called `app.js`. Returning to Visual Studio, it would seem that the only source code file is `app.ts`. So where did the `app.js` file come from? Going back to our original explanation of TypeScript, remember that it is a superset of the JavaScript language. This means that all valid JavaScript code is also valid TypeScript code. When TypeScript is compiled, JavaScript is generated. In this case, our file `app.ts` is compiled by Visual Studio to `app.js`. You can find the `app.js` file if you look inside your project folder; it is at the same location as your project's web config files.

5. Enable Show All Files in **Solution Explorer** to see the generated `app.js` file from within Visual Studio, as shown in the following screenshot:

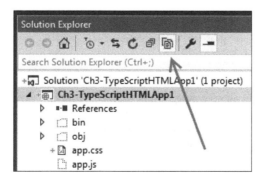

How it works...

Since TypeScript ultimately compiles down to JavaScript, you may be wondering about the advantages of using it. First, using TypeScript allows meaningful **IntelliSense** support. For example, examine the `app.ts` file that is part of our project. The following screenshot shows one of the available IntelliSense menus that can appear while editing:

```
window.onload = () => {
    var el = document.getElementById('content');
    var greeter = new Greeter(el);
    greeter.
};                  element        (property) Greeter.element: HTMLElement
                    span
                    start
                    stop
                    timerToken
```

Second, TypeScript (as its name implies) provides type checking. Consider the `greeter` class, and how Visual Studio is able to help by comparing the differences, as shown here:

```
window.onload = () => {
    var el = document.getElementById('content');
    var greeter = new Greeter(el);
    greeter.element = 42;
    greeter.star        (property) Greeter.element: HTMLElement
};
                        Type 'number' is not assignable to type 'HTMLElement'.
                        Property 'accessKey' is missing in type 'Number'.
```

Since TypeScript is being used, Visual Studio detects an error with the assignment, as shown in the preceding screenshot. Conversely, in the JavaScript code (which is shown in the following screenshot), Visual Studio did not detect the error:

```
var el = document.getElementById('content');
var greeter = new Greeter(el);
greeter = 10;
greeter.start();
```

The lack of type checking creates a bug that is easy to overlook. In smaller applications, the lack of type checking can usually be managed by the programmer. However, with larger applications or unfamiliar code bases, it becomes much more difficult. Catching the error immediately saves debugging time later.

Visual Studio works with the TypeScript compiler (`tsc.exe`) to produce valid JavaScript that works on any browser or platform that supports JavaScript. Since the nature of the TypeScript language is more specific than JavaScript, you can catch errors sooner and increase the power of IntelliSense. This allows you to keep the good parts of JavaScript (fast and powerful design capabilities) while increasing its safety and usability in large projects.

There's more...

You don't have to create a brand new project just to take advantage of TypeScript; it can be easily added to your existing web projects. From within an existing web project, add a new item (*Ctrl + Shift + A*), or right-click on your project name or directory within the **Solution Explorer** window and select **TypeScript File**, as shown in this screenshot:

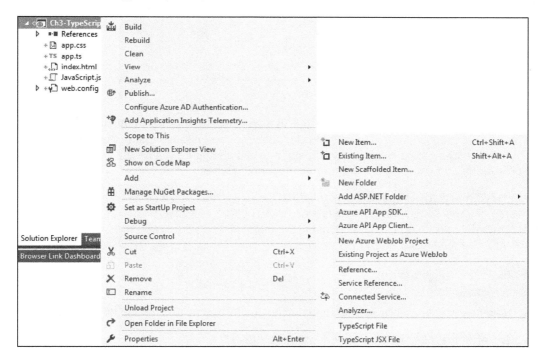

If you would like to try TypeScript but are wondering about all the existing JavaScript code that would have to be converted, don't worry. Library types for many popular JavaScript projects including Backbone.js, Node.js, and jQuery are available at DefinitelyTyped (http://definitelytyped.org/).

Using Visual Studio for Node.js development

The open source Node.js platform has become a popular way to deploy server-side applications written in JavaScript. Node.js can be hosted by numerous operating systems: Linux, Mac OS X, Unix variants, and Windows. If you are interested in developing for Node.js, you will be pleased to learn that you can use your existing Visual Studio knowledge with **Node.js Tools for Visual Studio** (**NTVS**).

This toolset provides a powerful new way to write Node.js applications while using Visual Studio to provide important features—including an IntelliSense-powered editor, debugging and profiling, and the Node.js package manager **npm**. In this recipe, we will see how VS2015 can be expanded to support Node.js development.

Getting ready

This recipe will require a bit more preparation than usual. The good news is that the NTVS supports VS2015 Community, premium editions, and VS2015 Express for Web—which means that a paid version of VS2015 is not required.

You can obtain NTVS from the project's GitHub page, or directly by using the link `http://aka.ms/getntvs`. Once that is installed, you will need to install Node.js. This is obtainable from `https://nodejs.org/`, and you should download the newest version to be sure that you have all the appropriate security patches.

Both NTVS and Node.js should be installed on the same machine where you have installed VS2015. For this recipe, we have installed v0.12.10 (LTS) using the 64-bit installer for Windows. (Be sure to download and install the installation package and not the binary runtime.) The default installation paths are acceptable to use for both NTVS and Node.js.

How to do it...

Let's see how NTVS can provide new capabilities to VS2015 by taking the following steps:

1. After installing NTVS and Node.js, start VS2015.

2. Upon startup, Visual Studio will automatically detect that NTVS has been installed. Create a new Node.js-based project by navigating to the template for **JavaScript | Node.js | Blank Node.js Web Application**, and either accept the default project name, or enter one of your own:

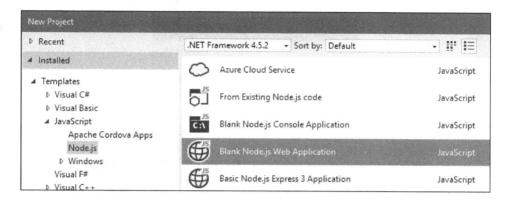

3. Once the project has been created, you can test it out to ensure that everything is in order. You may do so via the usual **Debug | Start Debugging** or *F5*. As the program starts, you may be prompted by the Windows Firewall. For proper operation, be sure to click on **Allow access**, as shown in the following screenshot:

4. After accepting the firewall changes, a debugging window starts, and your web browser displays the initial welcome page for the project, as shown in the following screenshot:

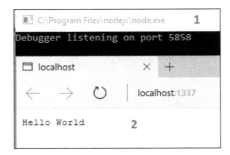

5. As you can see in the preceding screenshot, the debugging window is marked by the number **1**, while the web browser is marked with the number **2**. After confirming everything is in order, stop debugging and return to VS2015. (You can do this by closing your browser window and the debugger window.)

6. So far this makes sense, and we have a generic website. Let's see what else NTVS can do by using npm.

 npm is the Node.js package manager. Extensive documentation and a listing of the numerous packages available for installation can be found at https://www.npmjs.com/.

7. There are several ways to access npm. The easiest way to get a command prompt is to simply right-click on your project in **Solution Explorer**, and select **Open Command Prompt Here**. For this recipe, we will use an alternate method, which is found by right-clicking on the npm object in **Solution Explorer** and selecting **Install New npm Packages**. Note that the first time this is selected, the package catalog will be downloaded; while it is cached for subsequent requests, its download will introduce a brief delay.

8. After the catalog has downloaded, you will have a dialog box that will allow you to search for packages to install. It also provides an indication as to when it was last updated, so if it has been a while since it was downloaded, you can click **Refresh**. We will now install the finalhandler package, so enter that into the search box, as shown in the following screenshot:

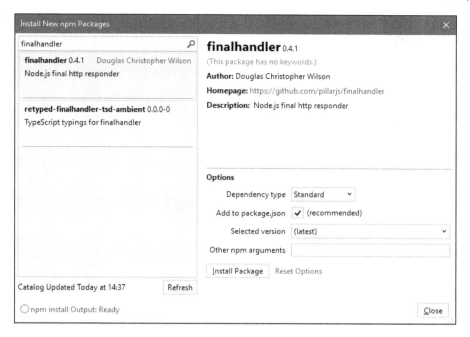

9. After installation has finished, you will note that the package catalog refreshes to reflect that `finalhandler` has been installed, as shown here:

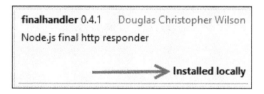

10. We will also need the package `serve-static` (also created by Douglas Christopher Wilson). The hyphen in the title is important, so make sure you get the right package. Install this using the process described in *Step 8*. Installation should also be verifiable, as shown in the following screenshot:

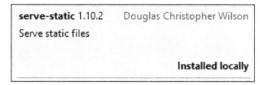

11. We are done with the package installer, so after verifying installation, click on **Close**.

12. Now that we have these packages installed and available for use with our Node.js project, it is able to serve static files. Let's add the finishing touches. First, replace the existing `server.js` code with this example based on the project's sample code:

```
var http = require('http')
var finalhandler = require('finalhandler')
var serveStatic = require('serve-static')

var port = process.env.port || 1337;
var serve = serveStatic('./')

// Create server
http.createServer(function (req, res) {
  var done = finalhandler(req, res)
  serve(req, res, done)
}).listen(port)
```

13. Next, add a new HTML file to your project by right-clicking on the project in the **Solution Explorer**, and selecting **Add | New Item** (or use *Ctrl + Shift + A*). Be sure to name the file `index.html`.

14. After you add the new HTML file, it will open in your editor. The default code is fine for what it is, but doesn't include any visible output. Add some text, as shown in the following code excerpt:

```
<!DOCTYPE html>
<html xmlns="http://www.w3.org/1999/xhtml">
  <head>
    <meta charset="utf-8" />
    <title>Hello from Node.js</title>
  </head>
  <body>
    Hello from Node.js
  </body>
</html>
```

15. Save your work, and now run the debugger (*F5*). If there are no errors, you will receive a welcome message, as shown in the following screenshot:

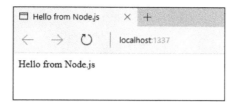

How it works...

NTVS provides a full-featured environment for developing Node.js applications, while enabling you to continue to use the familiar Visual Studio interface. The bundled Node.js templates allow you to start writing code quickly, and the inclusion of npm support means that you can take advantage of the same Node.js packages available to non-VS2015 users, so you don't have to reinvent the wheel.

There's more...

NTVS includes a remote debug proxy tool (`RemoteDebug.js`) that can be used to provide debugging capabilities in conjunction with a remote server. This means you can run your application in an environment more typical of a production-like setting (such as Linux server or virtual machine) while debugging it on your local workstation running VS2015.

NTVS also provides an interactive window for use with Node.js, which is accessible via **Tools | Node.js Tools | Node.js Interactive Window** (shortcut key *Ctrl + K, N*).

See also

▸ Full instructions on how to use remote debugging are available at `https://github.com/Microsoft/nodejstools/wiki/Remote-Debugging-Node.js-running-on-Linux`

4

.NET Framework Development

In this chapter, we will cover the following topics:

- ▶ Creating a task-based WCF service
- ▶ Unit testing .NET applications
- ▶ Sharing class libraries across different runtimes
- ▶ Detecting duplicate code
- ▶ Exploring C# through the Immediate window

Introduction

In *Chapter 3*, *Web Development*, we looked at web development, and how Visual Studio supports web developers. Of course, the .NET Framework is also useful for writing traditional desktop applications and server-side programming.

In this chapter, we turn the spotlight on Visual Studio 2015's support for the .NET platform for non-web applications. We will look specifically at functionality that has been added or enhanced. This chapter will start by discussing what was included with the .NET Framework 4.5, and then move on to discuss the new features found in 4.6.1.

You should be aware that like its previous version, .NET Framework 4.5, Framework 4.6.1 is an in-place upgrade of its 4.x predecessors. This means that while you may have only one version of the 4.x series installed, they will run side by side with the earlier versions of the framework (version 3.5 SP1 and its predecessors).

Be aware that, like the previous 4.5 release, .NET Framework 4.6.1 is not supported on Windows XP, Windows Vista, or Windows Server 2003. .NET Framework 4.6.1 ships with VS2015. The Framework is also available for use on Windows Vista SP2, Windows 7 SP1, and Windows Server 2008 R2 SP1. Your application's targeted audience should be a consideration when choosing which framework to use, but most new applications should use the latest version of the framework available.

Creating a task-based WCF service

Windows Communication Foundation (**WCF**) remains a mature technology, so there is little difference in developing these applications and services with VS2015. Since WCF is a technology focused on network communications, the visible changes in Visual Studio are quite small. However, with .NET Framework 4.6.2, there have been many bug fixes and stability enhancements to ensure that it performs as expected.

WCF is Microsoft's framework designed for use in creating applications based on service-oriented architecture. Some of the features provided by WCF include interoperability, service metadata, data contracts, and security. For in-depth information on using WCF, refer to Microsoft's introduction at https://msdn.microsoft.com/en-us/library/ms731082(v=vs.110).aspx, and the general reference guide at http://msdn.microsoft.com/en-us/library/dd456779(v=vs.110).aspx.

In this recipe, you'll create a task-based WCF service so that you can see what has changed. A sample WPF application will call this sample WCF service.

Getting ready

Simply start a premium version of VS2015 (or Visual Studio Community), and you will be ready to go.

How to do it...

As you create these WCF applications, you will see how Visual Studio simplifies the process. Let's get started:

1. Create a new project by navigating to **Visual C# | WCF | WCF Service Application**, and give it the default name.

2. Add another project to the solution by navigating to **Visual C# | Windows | WPF Application**, also giving it the default name. Be sure to select **Add to solution** in the **Solution** field.

3. Compile the solution and start the WCF service to make sure it starts correctly so that you have a working service for the next few steps. Stop the application once you are satisfied that it's working. Since you added the WCF project first, it should be the default project.

4. Back in Visual Studio, right-click on the WPF application, and select **Add Service Reference**.

5. Click on the **Discover** button. The **Service1** web service should be discovered, as shown in the following screenshot:

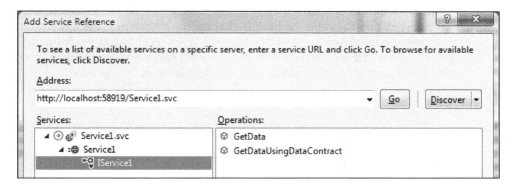

6. Click on the **Advanced** button in the bottom-left corner of the **Add Service Reference** dialog box. Ensure that in the options for service generation, **Generate task-based operations** is selected, and **Allow generation of asynchronous operations** is turned on, as shown in the following screenshot:

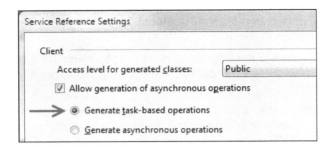

7. Click on **OK** in this option's dialog box (**Service Reference Settings**), and then again in the **Add Service Reference** dialog box to generate the service proxy. (In some cases, Visual Studio may erroneously throw an error here, such as **Unable to check out the current file**. If you get bitten by this bug, simply restart Visual Studio, and try again. Note that this is less likely in VS2015.)

8. Use **Solution Explorer** to open the app.config file for the WPF application, locate the <endpoint> configuration section, and hover the mouse over the name attribute. A tooltip will appear to explain what this attribute is for, as shown in the following screenshot. Given the issues people have historically had with understanding the details in WCF configuration, this IntelliSense information is very welcome.

9. Start adding a new endpoint configuration to the <client /> section by typing <endpoint binding=. IntelliSense will kick in to show you the values that can be placed inside the quotes. That makes editing WCF configurations much simpler than trying to remember what all the valid values are. Select the basicHttpBinding value, as shown in the following screenshot:

The recipe asks you to add it here so you can see the new IntelliSense support for WCF configurations. A complete WCF tutorial is outside the scope of this book, but once you finish the recipe, try manually adding support for https using the `basicHttpsBinding` class. For now, we will comment out the second endpoint that we just added.

10. Returning to the WPF project, open the `MainWindow.xaml` file, and change the `<Grid>` element to a `<StackPanel>` element. Add a button and a textbox to the `<StackPanel>` element, as listed in the following code:

```
<StackPanel>
  <Button x:Name="btnAsync" Click="btnAsync_Click_1">
  click!</Button>
  <TextBlock x:Name="txtText">Not yet populated
  </TextBlock>
</StackPanel>
```

11. Navigate to the code-behind file, `MainWindow.xaml.cs`, and add code for the button click event handler so that it calls out to the WCF service, as follows:

```
async private void btnAsync_Click_1(object sender,
RoutedEventArgs e){
  using (var client = new
  ServiceReference1.Service1Client())
  {
    var result = await client.GetDataAsync(3);
    txtText.Text = result;
  }
}
```

12. In **Solution Explorer**, right-click on the solution, and select the **Set as StartUp Project** option.

13. Choose **Multiple startup projects**, and set **Action** to **Start** for both projects. Click on **OK** to save the changes:

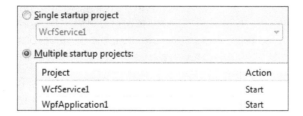

14. Press *F5* to start debugging, and when the WPF application appears, click on the **click!** button to make the `async` call to the WCF service. The text below the button should update to say **You entered: 3**, proving that the call to the service worked.

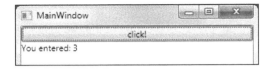

How it works...

As mentioned earlier, the **Add Service Reference** dialog box can generate task-based proxy classes that you can call from your code with an `await` keyword. This makes asynchronous calls to services much easier to write, though you can still call the blocking, synchronous methods if you need to. The generated code contains both the synchronous method call as well as the task-based call.

WCF's ServiceModel Metadata Utility Tool (`svcutil.exe`) can also be used to generate task-based proxies if you prefer to use the command-line tool instead of Visual Studio.

Unit testing .NET applications

Unit testing represents the practice of writing code to test other code. The term "unit" refers to identifying pieces of code (classes, methods, and so on) that represent useful functionality and can be tested by separate pieces of code. As a developer, establishing these tests allows you to easily verify that your code continues to work as changes and additions are made.

Visual Studio historically has been tightly tied to the **MSTest** framework when it comes to unit testing. The inclusion of a unit test framework inside Visual Studio has been excellent. It has encouraged developers to improve their quality by writing tests to prove code functions as expected. On the flip side, many developers regard MSTest as an inferior unit test framework when compared to NUnit, XUnit, and other frameworks.

The problem stems from the fact that MSTest does so much more than unit testing, and as a result, suffers from poor speed and bloat. Additionally, its assertion methods are fragmented across multiple classes, and it has a cumbersome approach to data-driven tests and expected exceptions. MSTest has also been tied to the release cycle of Visual Studio, so updates have been very slow, and it lags behind when compared to the other test frameworks.

Microsoft has ended the tight coupling between Visual Studio and MSTest by making the unit test framework pluggable. MSTest is still provided out of the box, but now developers can choose the framework that they like the most as long as their choice of framework implements a Visual Studio adapter.

Microsoft previously removed Test Impact Analysis from Visual Studio (it still exists in Microsoft Test Manager), and replaced it with a continuous testing style feature instead. **Continuous testing** is an approach that has been gaining popularity because of the incredibly rapid feedback cycle it gives developers. The idea is that each time a change is saved in the source files, the unit tests are run to see if anything has broken. This works well with dynamic languages such as Ruby; however, as .NET is a static language, this approach is not so simple. With Visual Studio 2015, instead of having all tests run whenever the source is saved, you can have them run automatically each time the code is compiled.

This overall testing functionality is viewed and controlled by **Test Explorer**. In this recipe, we will use the built-in test framework in a test-first manner to implement a very simple calculator, and you'll see how the continuous testing feature works. The important part of this recipe isn't so much the code you will write, but to see how Visual Studio can change your development practices when it comes to unit testing. Let's get to it!

Getting ready

You are going to need a premium version of Visual Studio (Professional or higher) for this recipe for best results. However, the basics of writing code and unit tests can be performed with Visual Studio Community.

How to do it...

1. Open Visual Studio and create a new **Unit Test Project** under **Visual C# | Test**; accept the default name, `UnitTestProject1`.

2. In the newly created solution, rename `UnitTest1.cs` as `CalculatorTests.cs`. You will be prompted to rename all references to `UnitTest1`. Click on **Yes** so that Visual Studio renames `UnitTest1` as `CalculatorTests` in the code itself.

3. In the `CalculatorTests` class file, add the following test method. Don't worry if the code doesn't compile yet—it will not. In a test-driven approach, the tests are written first to establish how your code should behave before you implement anything. Then, you write the following implementation code to make the test(s) succeed:

```
public class CalculatorTests
{
  [TestMethod]
  public void TestAdd()
  {
    Calculator calc = new Calculator();
    int result = calc.Add(3, 1);
    Assert.AreEqual(4, result);
  }
}
```

```
    [TestMethod]
    public void TestMultiply()
    {
      Calculator calc = new Calculator();
      int result = calc.Multiply(6, 6);
      Assert.AreEqual(36, result);
    }
}
```

4. Now let's write some code so our tests will pass. To do this, we need to add a `Calculator` class, but good practice dictates that you shouldn't place it in your test assembly project.

5. Add a new C# **Class Library** to the Unit Test solution by right-clicking on your solution, then select **Add | New Project**, and then select **Visual C# | Windows | Class Library**. Name this project `CalculationEngine`.

6. In your newly created project, rename the `Class1.cs` file as `Calculator.cs`, and when prompted, allow Visual Studio to rename `Class1` as `Calculator` across the project.

7. Return to the `UnitTestProject1` project, and add a project reference to the `Calculator` project. To do this, right-click on the **References** node for `UnitTestProject1`, and select **Add Reference...**. Make sure **Projects** is selected in the right-hand side column, and then click on the checkbox for `CalculationEngine`, as shown in the following screenshot:

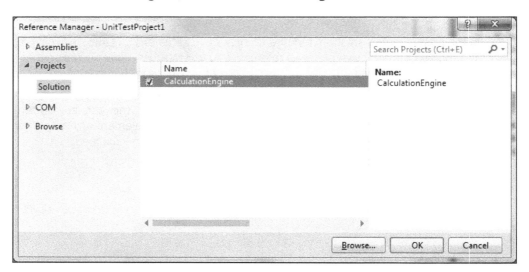

8. In the `CalculatorTests.cs` file, place the cursor on the `Calculator()` constructor call in the unit test. Then use the mouse to hover and click on the actions drop-down menu, or press *Ctrl + . (Ctrl* + Period) to show the available actions. Select the `using CalculationEngine;` option to add the required `using` statement to your test code, as shown in the following screenshot:

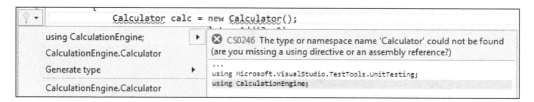

9. Now place the cursor on the `Add()` method in the next line, and bring up the available tasks. Again, do this either by hovering over the code with the mouse and then clicking on the options drop-down menu when it appears, or by pressing *Ctrl + . (Ctrl* + Period) and selecting the only available option to generate the method stub. Do the same for the `Multiply()` method.

10. Now let's see what happens when we haven't written any new tests. Open **Test Explorer** by navigating to **Test | Windows | Test Explorer**.

11. Select the **Run All** option in the **Test Explorer** window to compile the code, and run the tests in the project for the first time.

12. The unit tests should fail at this point, because the method stubs you generated for the `Add()` and `Multiply()` methods both simply throw the exception, `NotImplementedException`. The following screenshot shows the results for `Add()`:

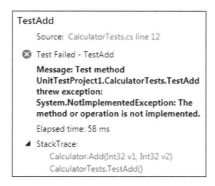

13. Let's fix our errors. Switch to the `Calculator.cs` file, and implement the `Add()` method by using the following code:

```
public int Add(int v1, int v2)
{
  return (v1 + v2);
}
```

14. Next, do the same for the `Multiply()` method, as shown in the following code:

```
public int Multiply(int v1, int v2)
{
  return (v1 * v2);
}
```

15. Now let's see what the passing tests look like. Update the **Test Explorer** screen by clicking on **Run All**. After rebuilding the solution, your unit tests will run, and this indicates that they passed successfully. This is shown in the following screenshot:

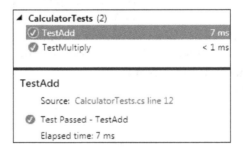

How it works...

When using projects and unit testing frameworks supported by test adapters, they will take care of the discoverability aspects for you. The adapter-driven approach has also allowed Microsoft to create a unit-test-optimized version of MSTest that is fast and light, and can be used in standard class libraries without a problem.

You can also mix and match your unit test frameworks. It is entirely valid to have MSTest, xUnit, and NUnit tests in one assembly. For example, you may have a suite of older tests in one framework, and may want to transit to a new framework without reworking all those old tests. Now you can, without any problem at all.

Out of the box, Visual Studio only supports the MSTest framework; however, adapters are available in the Visual Studio Gallery for the major test frameworks. The **Chutzpah** test adapter adds support for the QUnit and Jasmine unit test frameworks, which can be helpful when writing JavaScript or TypeScript. (Chutzpah is available at `http://chutzpah.codeplex.com/`.)

> As mentioned previously, MSTest no longer requires a TestSettings file for unit test projects. Test settings files can still be used with MSTest unit test projects; however, if they are included, MSTest reverts to the Visual Studio 2010 compatibility mode, and you will have a much slower execution of unit tests.

There's more...

The changes in the test runner are fairly dramatic, and with it come a number of other changes you should be aware of.

Can I restrict the unit tests that automatically execute?

In many projects, it is common to have unit tests in one test project and integration tests in a second project. Unit tests are considered to be those tests that execute entirely in memory, and have no interactions with external systems such as the network, filesystem, screen, or database. Integration tests are those tests that interact with external systems.

If you want to restrict the tests that run such that only unit tests run, and slower integration tests are excluded, you will need to use the **Test Explorer** filter to limit the tests to run. If you have your unit and integration tests in separate assemblies, then the **Fully Qualified Name** filter is likely to be the filter that will help you the most. Another option is to create playlists of different tests. This can be helpful if you are focusing on a specific area, and wish to temporarily avoid the default of **All Tests**.

Asynchronous tests

MSTest does support asynchronous tests that make use of the `await` keyword. You can see this in the following code where the method signature is no longer a `public void` method, but rather an `async` task:

```
[TestMethod]
async public Task Can_load_Bing_home_page()
{
  var client = new System.Net.WebClient();
  var page= await
  client.DownloadStringTaskAsync("http://www.bing.com");
  StringAssert.Contains(page, "bing");
}
```

The asynchronous test ensures that the test runner will wait for the test to end before starting the next test. It does not mean that multiple tests will be run in parallel; it is just that you can test methods that use the `async` and `await` keywords.

Automatically trigger test execution

With Visual Studio Enterprise, the **Test Explorer** window presents an additional feature: automatically executing tests every time a build is made. To select this, use the icon in the **Test Explorer** that is shown in the following screen:

See also

▶ For information on how to invoke MSTest from the command line (such as for automation purposes), consult `https://msdn.microsoft.com/en-us/library/ms182487.aspx`

▶ Beyond MSTest, there is NUnit `http://www.nunit.org/` and xUnit `https://github.com/xunit/xunit`

Sharing class libraries across different runtimes

There are a number of managed runtimes and profiles for .NET development including the .NET Framework, Silverlight, Windows Phone, Windows 8.X, and the **Universal Windows Platform** (**UWP**). When you have to write code that can be shared across more than one of these runtimes, various options are available. Frequently, it can involve either the use of copy-and-paste development, or multiple versions of the same project and the use of linked files. Neither approach is ideal as they introduce greater possibilities for errors and make updating difficult. It is all too easy to make changes to a piece code during an intensive debugging session, and then forget to copy them over to the other files.

The solution to all of these issues is to use **Portable Class Libraries** (**PCL**). The idea here is that you can build a class library that works across all desired runtimes by ensuring that all code that is general to all platforms is used. So whether you have business logic or math functions used for a game engine, this common code can be located in one or more PCLs. Then code that is platform-specific can be contained in its own projects and references these PCLs. Further, the compiler only builds the project once regardless of the number of runtimes supported, making the overall solution faster to build.

Let's look at a quick example of how a Silverlight application might talk to a .NET application using this approach. To keep the recipe focused, we're only going to look at the connection between the two runtimes, not at building a full application.

Getting ready

This recipe assumes you are using Visual Studio Community or one of the premium editions. Start the one that you have available, and you will be ready to go.

 Note some differences emerge depending on what version of Windows you are using, and so we will illustrate the differences.

How to do it...

1. Create a standard **WPF Application** project by navigating to **Visual Basic | Windows | Classic Desktop** and accepting the default name.

2. Right-click on the solution, and add a **Portable Class Library** project under **Visual Basic**; name it `PortableClassLibrary1`.

3. When you are prompted to choose **Targets**, change the selections so that only **.NET Framework 4.6** and **ASP.NET Core 5.0** are selected, and then click on the **OK** button, as shown in the following screenshot:

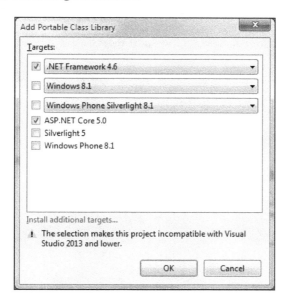

4. Navigate to the `Class1.vb` file in the `PortableClassLibrary1` project, and add a method to the `Class1` class, as shown:

```
Public Class Class1
    Public Function checkUser() As Boolean
    Return True
    End Function
End Class
```

5. Right-click on the `WpfApplication1` project in **Solution Explorer**, and select **Add Reference**. In the **Reference Manager** dialog box, navigate to **Solution | Projects**, and select the checkbox next to `PortableClassLibrary1`. Click on **OK** to add the reference to the project, as shown in the following screenshot:

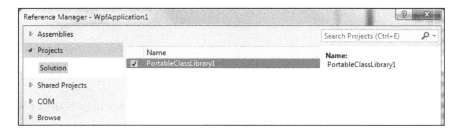

6. Build the solution, and ensure everything is in order.

7. Return to `WpfApplication1`. Double-click on `MainWindow.xaml` to open the XAML editor. We are going to add a default **Label** control and a default **Button** control. To do this, simply expand the **Toolbox**, and drag and drop the two controls. The following screenshot shows the open **Toolbox** and placement of the two controls:

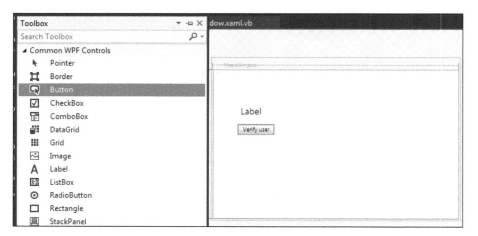

8. If you look carefully, the text for the button control has been changed. If you would like to do the same, simply right-click on the button in the editor, and select **Edit Text**. This is only the display name, so feel free to use whatever text you prefer.

9. Now we are going to put all of the pieces together. Double-click the button you have added to the editor so that a code stub is generated for it. Enter the following code into `MainWindow.xaml.vb`:

```
Class MainWindow
  Dim portable As New PortableClassLibrary1.Class1()
  Dim result = portable.checkUser()

  Private Sub button1_Click(sender As Object, e As
  RoutedEventArgs) Handles button1.Click
  label.Content = result
  End Sub
End Class
```

10. Compile the solution to confirm that there are no compiler errors, and confirm that the references are made successfully.

11. When you run the program, the label control will begin by showing its name, **Label**. Then, when the button control is clicked, the text will change, as shown in the following screenshot:

How it works...

The portable libraries themselves are just standard .NET class libraries with restrictions on the framework calls that can be made from within them. The set of calls that can be made is determined by the methods that are supported across all target runtimes selected in the project's properties.

A good practice to follow, when writing your portable libraries, is to avoid adding references to other libraries. Instead, try and design your PCLs as standalone libraries. Since most people tend to use portable library classes for WCF contracts, data transfer objects, or calculation libraries, this is unlikely to be too limiting. As you can see from our example, the business logic is separated from the presentation. Assuming this was a real application under development, a separate ASP.NET project could also use the same PCL. This code reuse simplifies development, and reduces errors.

At the time of writing, it was announced that Microsoft has purchased Xamarin. This arrangement should only increase the range of cross-platform targets that will be available to us as developers.

One example that demonstrates the advantages that PCLs provide is the `HttpClient` library (`https://www.nuget.org/packages/Microsoft.Net.Http`) published by Microsoft. This library allows an application to have a uniform way of making web calls without having to write specific code for each platform.

Viewing defined targets

If you would like to see which target(s) were selected for an existing project, or to change them, you can do so via **Solution Explorer**. For the Visual Basic-based project shown in this recipe, right-click on the my project file. This will provide the details as shown in the following screenshot:

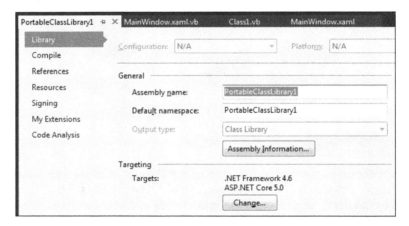

C#-based projects can find PCL details by right-clicking on the `Properties` file for their PCL project.

There's more...

Microsoft has loosened the license restrictions on the portable class library reference assemblies. From a licensing standpoint, this increases the utility of using PCLs across all of your target platforms for your client software. Take advantage of PCLs to make your development process more efficient—you can even add a **Windows 10** target (Windows Universal 10) so that you can prepare for the future while you write your current applications.

Xamarin offers products to add support to Visual Studio for the iOS and Android platforms. This includes support for writing PCLs. For more information on the integration, see `http://blog.xamarin.com/pcl-projects-and-vs2013/`, and for information on PCLs, check out `http://docs.xamarin.com/guides/cross-platform/application_fundamentals/pcl/`.

Detecting duplicate code

Copy and paste development is generally regarded as a bad practice, because bug fixes or enhancements in one area of code have to be repeated in all the other copies of the same code. Not only is this time consuming and tedious, but in large code bases, it's very easy to miss a change, leading to bugs and lower overall quality.

Frequently, code duplication can be unavoidable, especially on larger projects with multiple contributors. Not to mention that using an unfamiliar code base can make it easy to unintentionally write duplicate code. With Visual Studio, Microsoft has provided a way to detect these duplicates so that you can take remedial action to clean it up. Let's see how this is done.

Getting ready

You will need Visual Studio Enterprise 2015 for this recipe. Start it up, and you're ready to go.

Visual Studio 2013 Premium and Ultimate also support this feature.

How to do it...

1. Create a new **Class Library** project under **Visual C#**, and name the project `OriginalLibrary`.

2. Rename the `Class1.cs` file as `OriginalClass.cs`, and allow Visual Studio to rename the class itself when prompted.

3. In `OriginalClass.cs`, add the following method:

```
public string StringWithCheckDigit(int x, int y)
{
  if (x <= 0)
  throw new ArgumentOutOfRangeException("x", "must be
  positive");
  if (y <= 0)
  throw new ArgumentException("I don't like negatives", "y");

  var counter = "";
  for (int i = 0; i < x; i++)
  {
    counter += y;
  }

  var checkDigits = new List<char>() { 'a', 'b', 'c', 'd', 'e'
  };
  var checkDigit = checkDigits[y % 5];
  counter += checkDigit;
  return counter;
}
```

4. Add a second C# based **Class Library** project to the solution, giving it the name `DuplicateLibrary`.

5. Rename the `Class1.cs` file as `DuplicateClass.cs`, and, as in *Step 2*, allow Visual Studio to rename all references when prompted.

6. Copy and paste the code you just added into `DuplicateClass`, renaming the method as `DuplicatedCheckDigit`.

7. Rename the parameters in the `DuplicatedCheckDigit` method as `p1` and `p2`.

8. Rename `i` as `loop` and `counter` as `outString`. Your duplicated method should now look like the following code:

```
public string DuplicatedCheckDigit(int p1, int p2)
{
  if (p1 <= 0)
```

```
throw new ArgumentOutOfRangeException("p1", "must be
positive");
if (p2 <= 0)
throw new ArgumentException("I don't like negatives",
"p2");

var outString = "";
for (int loop = 0; loop < p1; loop++)
{
  outString += p2;
}
var checkDigits = new List<char>() { 'a', 'b', 'c', 'd',
'e' };
var checkDigit = checkDigits[p2 % 5];
outString += checkDigit;
return outString;
}
```

9. From the Visual Studio menu, navigate to **Analyze | Analyze Solution for Code Clones**. The **Code Clone Analysis Results** window will be displayed, and will show you where the duplication exists; this is shown in the following screenshot:

10. Right-click on the **Weak Match 1(2 Files)** result and select **Compare**, as shown in the following screenshot:

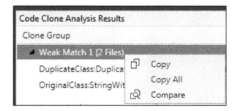

11. The two sections of duplicated code are shown in Visual Studio's new diff viewer, and you can decide what remedial action to take from there:

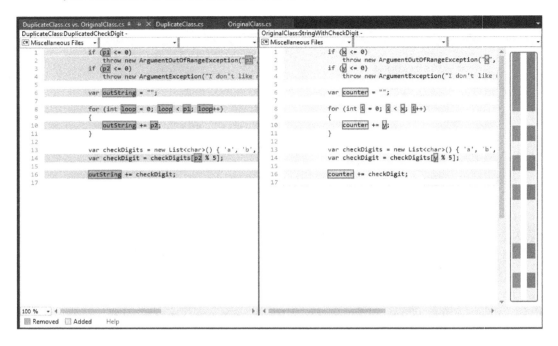

How it works...

This code would have been hard to find using just the **Find in Files**, and looking for variable names or a single line of code. The clone detection algorithm in Visual Studio ignores the differences in variable names, and instead, looks at the structure of the code itself. It also limits searches to duplicates that are a minimum of 10 statements long to prevent detection from taking a very long time.

If you do want to search for smaller or specific sections of code, you can highlight the code in the editor, right-click on it, and select **Find Matching Clones in Solution**, as shown in the following screenshot:

There's more...

There are a number of items that get ignored by the detection algorithm to help improve the speed of detection, and to exclude files that you are unlikely to be interested in. The following files can be ignored or excluded:

- ► Type declarations are ignored. Two classes with the same properties are not considered to be clones, nor are classes with the same method signatures. Only the code within the methods and properties is examined.

- ► The *.designer.cs and *.designer.vb files are automatically excluded, as is code within any InitializeComponent methods.

You can add a `.codeclonesettings` file to your project to exclude certain paths or file types from comparison. For example, if you are using T4 code generation, you may want to place all the generated code in a subfolder, and then exclude that folder from the clone detection engine by adding an entry for it in the settings file. Alternatively, you may be working on an external project or third-party code, for which you have no intention (or ability) to modify. Excluding those files would make sense to save time and avoid warnings that you will always ignore.

A sample exclusion could be like the following code snippet. This file was named `sample.codeclonesettings`, and placed at the top level of the project `DuplicateLibrary` used in the previous recipe. In this case, it blocks our `DuplicateClass` file from being examined.

```
<CodeCloneSettings>
  <Exclusions>
    <File>DuplicateClass.cs</File>
  </Exclusions>
</CodeCloneSettings>
```

It can be modified to use wildcards, and also ignore a whole directory, as shown in the following code snippet:

```
<CodeCloneSettings>
  <Exclusions>
    <File>ExcludeTheseFiles\*.cs</File>
```

Exploring C# through the Immediate window

Scripting languages enjoy great popularity, in part due to the immediate feedback they provide the developer. Rather than have to write code, compile it, and then execute it to see if the desired behavior occurs, many scripting languages offer a **read-eval-print-loop** (**REPL**). A REPL gives the developer the ability to watch their code execute about as fast as they can write it.

There are several advantages to this approach. First, you can explore a library or code fragment without having to first set up a new solution. Second, it allows one to experiment with different possible approaches when problem solving. By being able to quickly iterate, it can bring about a working solution more quickly.

Visual Studio had carried this feature in the past, but it disappeared in VS2013. Fortunately, it has returned in VS2015, and this is what we will explore in this recipe.

Getting ready

You can use any version of VS2015 that you like, although do make sure that you have applied Update 2. Without it, the Immediate Window will not be available in the manner described here. (A limited form of the Immediate Window functionality is provided by Update 1, but Update 2 is recommended.)

How to do it...

1.   Open up your copy of VS2015. Then start the REPL by navigating to **View | Other Windows | C# Interactive**.

2.   A new window, with a blank command prompt, will then appear, as shown in the following screenshot:

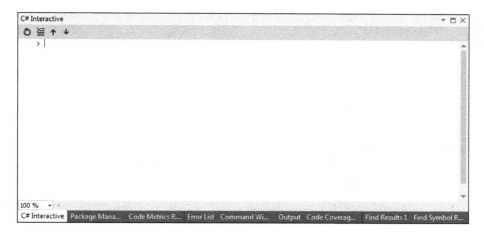

3.   This is ready to go immediately, and so, for our first test, try entering the following at the prompt 3 * Math.PI.

4.   As you type, notice that you have IntelliSense support, and that this REPL is able to easily process your C# snippet. The following screenshot shows the results:

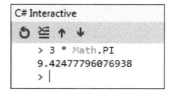

When you press *Enter* to execute a command, make sure you are at the end of the line. To easily navigate your command history, use *Alt* + Up Arrow or *Alt* + Down Arrow.

5. A C#-powered calculator is neat, but let's keep moving. Next, we will define a method from within the REPL. Let's add the following code:

```
public Boolean isEvenNumber(int x) { if (x % 2 == 0)
return true; return false; }
```

6. Once added, we can then use our new method, as shown in the following screenshot:

```
C# Interactive                                                    ▾ ☐
⟳ ≣ ↑ ↓
> public Boolean isEvenNumber(int x) { if (x % 2 == 0) return true; return false; }
> isEvenNumber(3)
false
> isEvenNumber(22)
true
> |
```

7. Once again, notice that after defining our method, we get IntelliSense support for it in the REPL, and can begin using it immediately.

8. Now let's expand our repertoire to take advantage of code outside the REPL. Create a new project on VS2015 via **Visual C# | Class Library**. The default project name is acceptable, but after the project has opened, rename `Class1.cs` in **Solution Explorer** as `InteractiveClass.cs`.

9. Once your class has been renamed, add the following method:

```
public int returnGreater(int x, int y)
{
  if (x > y)
  {
    return x;
  }
  else return y;
}
```

10. Build your solution to ensure there no errors, and so that a DLL will be available. Take note of the newly produced DLL—you will need the full path including filename. The easiest way to do this is to right-click on your project, and select **Open File** in **File Explorer**. Then, navigate to the `bin` folder, and from there to the `Debug` folder. For our example, the full path is `D:\Users\Jeff\Documents\Visual Studio 2015\Projects\SolutionName\ClassLibrary1\bin\Debug\ClassLibrary1.dll`.

11. Now return to your **C# Interactive** window. To ensure it is at a good starting point, click on the Reset icon, which is the far left icon shown in the following screenshot:

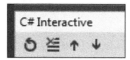

12. To make your newly compiled DLL available in the REPL, we will use the r command. Enter #r plus your local path.

13. Then you can introduce your DLL's name space, instantiate a new class, and then use its method, as shown in the following screenshot:

```
C# Interactive

> #r "D:\Users\Jeff \Documents\Visual Studio 2015\F
> using ClassLibrary1;
> InteractiveClass ic = new InteractiveClass();
> ic.returnGreater(45, 213012)
213012
>
```

14. As you can see, our code is available to us in the REPL, and we can interact with it with minimal effort.

How it works...

The **C# Interactive** window runs your code in a completely independent process from any open solutions or projects that you may have. This makes it easy to write C# without first creating a skeleton project. If you do have an open project, you can easily explore with different concepts without affecting your work.

There's more...

While the default, isolated nature of the **C# Interactive** window is very beneficial, what if you would like the window to have greater awareness of what is happening in a project that you have open? Thanks to VS2015 Update 2, there is a new context menu option called **Execute in Interactive**. As the name suggests, this will send the text you select in your editor window to the Interactive window for execution.

To see this in action, let's return to our previous example. Our `returnGreater()` method appears in the editor window, and is ready for us to manipulate. Simply highlight the method body and right-click on the selection (**1**), then select **Execute in Interactive** (**2**), as shown in the following screenshot:

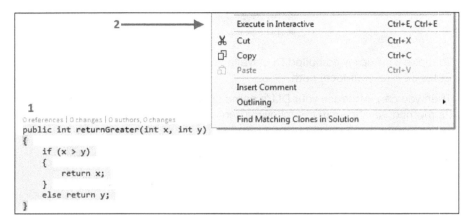

After doing this, the results of executing the selected method will appear in the Immediate Window, where the method can then be accessed the same as if you entered it by hand. Being able to select code and send it directly is much easier. The following screenshot shows the results:

```
C# Interactive

> public int returnGreater(int x, int y)
.            {
.                if (x > y)
.                {
.                    return x;
.                }
.                else return y;
.            }
> returnGreater(32, 64)
64
> |
```

5
Debugging Your .NET Application

In this chapter, we will cover the following recipes:

- ▶ Putting **Diagnostic Tools** to work
- ▶ Maximizing everyday debugging
- ▶ Debugging on remote machines and tablets
- ▶ Debugging code in production with IntelliTrace
- ▶ Debugging parallel code
- ▶ Visualizing concurrency

Introduction

It's an unfortunate reality, but modern software development still requires developers to identify and correct bugs in their code. The familiar edit-compile-test cycle is as familiar as a text editor, and now the rise of portable devices has added the need to measure for battery consumption and optimization for multiple architectures. Fortunately, our development tools continue to evolve to combat this rise in complexity, and Visual Studio continues to improve its arsenal.

Multithreaded code and asynchronous code are probably the two most difficult areas for most developers to work with, and also the hardest to debug when you have a problem such as a race condition. A race condition occurs when multiple threads perform an operation at the same time, and the order in which they execute makes a difference to how the software runs or the output is generated. Race conditions often result in deadlocks, incorrect data being used in other calculations, and random, unrepeatable crashes.

The other painful area to debug involves code running on other machines, whether it is running locally on your development machine or running in production. Hooking up a remote debugger in previous versions of Visual Studio has been less than simple, and the experience of debugging code in production was similarly frustrating. In this chapter, we will examine the improvements to the debugging experience in Visual Studio 2015, and how it can help you diagnose the root cause of a problem faster so that you can fix it properly, and not just patch over the symptoms.

Putting Diagnostic Tools to work

In Visual Studio 2013, Microsoft debuted a new set of tools called the **Performance and Diagnostics** hub. With VS2015, these tools have revised further, and in the case of **Diagnostic Tools**, promoted to a central presence on the main IDE window, and is displayed, by default, during debugging sessions. This is great for us as developers, because now it is easier than ever to troubleshoot and improve our code. In this recipe, we will explore how **Diagnostic Tools** can be used to explore our code, identify bottlenecks, and analyze memory usage.

Getting ready

The changes didn't stop when VS2015 was released, and succeeding updates to VS2015 have further refined the capabilities of these tools. So for this recipe, ensure that Update 2 has been installed on your copy of VS2015. We will be using Visual Studio Community 2015, but of course, you may use one of the premium editions too.

How to do it...

For this recipe, we will put together a short program that will generate some activity for us to analyze:

1. Create a new C# console application, and give it a name of your choice.

2. In your project's new `Program.cs` file, add the following method, which will generate a large quantity of strings:

```
static List<string> makeStrings()
{
  List<string> stringList = new List<string>();
  Random random = new Random();

  for (int i = 0; i < 1000000; i++)
  {
    string x = "String details: " + (random.Next(1000,
    100000));
    stringList.Add(x);
```

```
    }
    return stringList;
}
```

3. Next, we will add a second static method that produces an SHA256-calculated hash of each string that we generated. This method reads in each string that was previously generated, creates an SHA256 hash for it, and returns the list of computed hashes in hex format:

```
static List<string> hashStrings(List<string> srcStrings)
{
    List<string> hashedStrings = new List<string>();
    SHA256 mySHA256 = SHA256Managed.Create();

    StringBuilder hash = new StringBuilder();
    foreach (string str in srcStrings)
    {
        byte[] srcBytes =
        mySHA256.ComputeHash(Encoding.UTF8.GetBytes(str), 0,
        Encoding.UTF8.GetByteCount(str));
        foreach (byte theByte in srcBytes)
        {
            hash.Append(theByte.ToString("x2"));
        }
        hashedStrings.Add(hash.ToString());
        hash.Clear();
    }
    mySHA256.Clear();
    return hashedStrings;
}
```

4. After adding these methods, you may be prompted to add using statements for System.Text and System.Security.Cryptography. These are definitely needed, so go ahead and take Visual Studio's recommendation to have them added.

5. Now we need to update our Main method to bring this all together. Update your Main method to contain the following code:

```
static void Main(string[] args)
{
    Console.WriteLine("Ready to create strings");
    Console.ReadKey(true);
    List<string> results = makeStrings();
    Console.WriteLine("Ready to Hash " + results.Count() + "
    strings ");
    //Console.ReadKey(true);
    List<string> strings = hashStrings(results);
    Console.ReadKey(true);
}
```

6. Before proceeding, build your solution to ensure everything is in working order.

7. Now run the application in **Debug** mode (*F5*), and watch how our program operates.

 By default, the **Diagnostic Tools** window will only appear while debugging. Feel free to reposition your IDE windows to make their presence more visible or use *Ctrl + Alt + F2* to recall it as needed.

8. When you first launch the program, you will see the **Diagnostic Tools** window appear. Its initial display resembles the following screenshot. Thanks to the first `ReadKey` method, the program will wait for us to proceed, so we can easily see the initial state. Note that CPU usage is minimal, and memory usage holds constant.

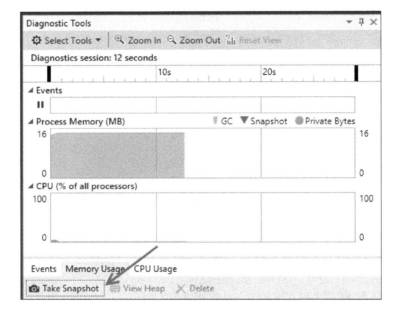

9. Before going any further, click on the **Memory Usage** tab, and then the **Take Snapshot** command as indicated in the preceding screenshot. This will record the current state of memory usage by our program, and will be a useful comparison point later on. Once a snapshot is taken, your **Memory Usage** tab should resemble the following screenshot:

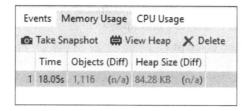

10. Having a forced pause through our `ReadKey()` method is nice, but when working with real-world programs, we will not always have this luxury. Breakpoints are typically used for situations where it is not always possible to wait for user input, so let's take advantage of the program's current state, and set two of them. We will put one to the second `WriteLine` method, and one to the last `ReadKey` method, as shown in the following screenshot:

```
static void Main(string[] args)
{
    Console.WriteLine("Ready to create strings");
    Console.ReadKey(true);
    List<string> results = makeStrings();
    Console.WriteLine("Ready to Hash " + results.Count() + " strings ");
    List<string> strings = hashStrings(results);
    Console.ReadKey(true);
}
```

11. Now return to the open application window, and press a key so that execution continues.

12. The program will stop at the first break point, which is right after it has generated a bunch of strings and added them to our `List` object. Let's take another snapshot of the memory usage using the same manner given in *Step 9*. You may also notice that the memory usage displayed in the **Process Memory** gauge has increased significantly, as shown in this screenshot:

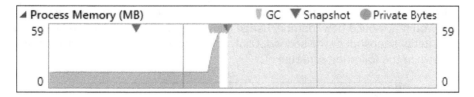

13. Now that we have completed our second snapshot, click on **Continue** in Visual Studio, and proceed to the next breakpoint.

14. The program will then calculate hashes for all of the generated strings, and when this has finished, it will stop at our last breakpoint. Take another snapshot of the memory usage. Also take notice of how the CPU usage spiked as the hashes were being calculated:

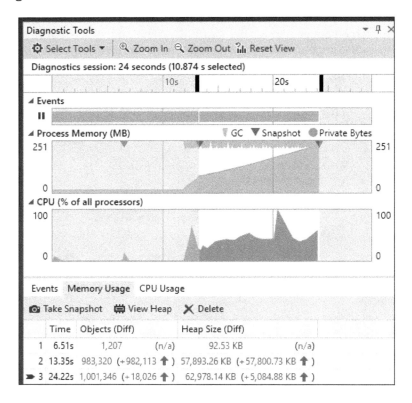

15. Now that we have these three memory snapshots, we will examine how they can help us. You may notice how memory usage increases during execution, especially from the initial snapshot to the second. Click on the second snapshot's object delta, as shown in the following screenshot:

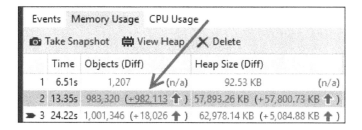

16. On clicking, this will open the snapshot details in a new editor window. Click on the **Size (Bytes)** column to sort by size, and as you may suspect, our **List<String>** object is indeed the largest object in our program. Of course, given the nature of our sample program, this is fairly obvious, but when dealing with more complex code bases, being able to utilize this type of investigation is very helpful. The following screenshot shows the results of our filter:

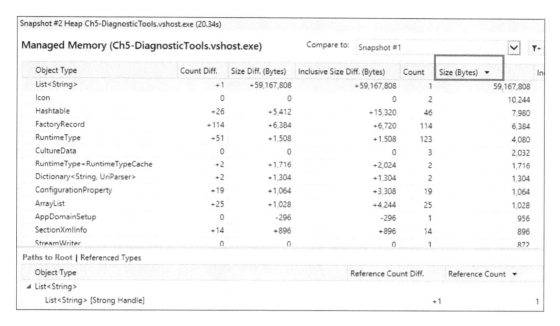

If you would like to know more about the object itself (perhaps there are multiple objects of the same type), you can use the **Referenced Types** option as indicated in the preceding screenshot. If you would like to try this out on the sample program, be sure to set a smaller number in the makeStrings() loop, otherwise you will run the risk of overloading your system.

17. Returning to the main **Diagnostic Tools** window, we will now examine CPU utilization. While the program is executing the hashes (feel free to restart the debugging session if necessary), you can observe where the program spends most of its time:

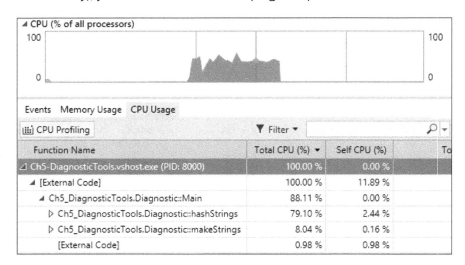

Again, it is probably no surprise that most of the hard work was done in the `hashStrings()` method. But when dealing with real-world code, it will not always be so obvious where the slowdowns are, and having this type of insight into your program's execution will make it easier to find areas requiring further improvement.

 When using the CPU profiler in our example, you may find it easier to remove the first breakpoint and simply trigger a profiling by clicking on **Break All** as shown in this screenshot:

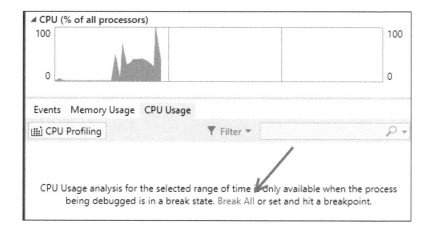

How it works...

Microsoft wanted more developers to be able to take advantage of their improved technology, so they have increased its availability beyond the Professional and Enterprise editions to also include Community. Running your program within VS2015 with the **Diagnostic Tools** window open lets you examine your program's performance in great detail.

By using memory snapshots and breakpoints, VS2015 provides you with the tools needed to analyze your program's operation, and determine where you should spend your time making optimizations.

There's more...

Our sample program does not perform a wide variety of tasks, but of course, more complex programs usually perform well. To further assist with analyzing those programs, there is a third option available to you beyond **CPU Usage** and **Memory Usage**: the **Events** tab. As shown in the following screenshot, the **Events** tab also provides the ability to search events for interesting (or long-running) activities.

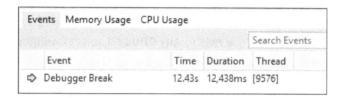

Different event types include file activity, gestures (for touch-based apps), and program modules being loaded or unloaded.

See also

▸   The *Debugging code in production with IntelliTrace* recipe

▸   The *Debugging parallel code* recipe

▸   The *Visualizing concurrency* recipe

Maximizing everyday debugging

Given the frequency of debugging, any refinement to these tools can pay immediate dividends. VS2015 brings the popular **Edit and Continue** feature into the 21st century by supporting a 64-bit code. Added to that is the new ability to see the return value of functions in your debugger. The addition of these features combine to make debugging code easier, allowing to solve problems faster.

Getting ready

For this recipe, you can use VS2015 Community or one of the premium editions. Be sure to run your choice on a machine using a 64-bit edition of Windows, as that is what we will be demonstrating in the recipe.

 Don't worry, you can still use **Edit and Continue** with 32-bit C# and Visual Basic code.

How to do it...

Both features are now supported by C#/VB, but we will be using C# for our examples. The features being demonstrated are compiler features, so feel free to use code from one of your own projects if you prefer. To see how **Edit and Continue** can benefit 64-bit development, perform the following steps:

1. Create a new C# console application using the default name.

2. To ensure the demonstration is running with 64-bit code, we need to change the default solution platform.

3. Click on the drop-down arrow next to **Any CPU** and select **Configuration Manager...**

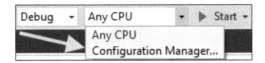

4. When the **Configuration Manager** dialog opens, we can create a new project platform targeting a 64-bit code. To do this, click on the drop-down menu for **Platform,** and select **<New...>**:

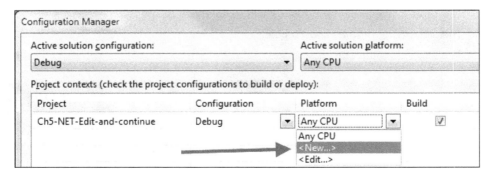

5. When **<New...>** is selected, it will present the **New Project Platform** dialog box. Select **x64** as the new platform type:

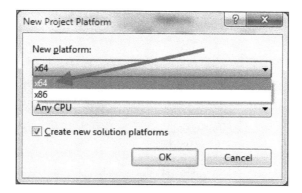

6. Once **x64** has been selected, you will return to **Configuration Manager**. Verify that **x64** remains active under **Platform**, and then click on **Close** to close this dialog. The main IDE window will now indicate that x64 is active:

7. With the project settings out of the way, let's add some code to demonstrate the new behavior. Replace the existing code in your blank class file so that it looks like the following listing:

```
class Program
{
  static void Main(string[] args)
  {
    int w = 16;
    int h = 8;
    int area = calcArea(w, h);
    Console.WriteLine("Area: " + area);
  }

  private static int calcArea(int width, int height)
  {
    return width / height;
  }
}
```

8. Let's set some breakpoints so that we are able to inspect during execution. First, add a breakpoint to the `Main` method's `Console` line. Add a second breakpoint to the `calcArea` method's `return` line. You can do this by either clicking on the left side of the editor window's border, or by right-clicking on the line, and selecting **Breakpoint | Insert Breakpoint**:

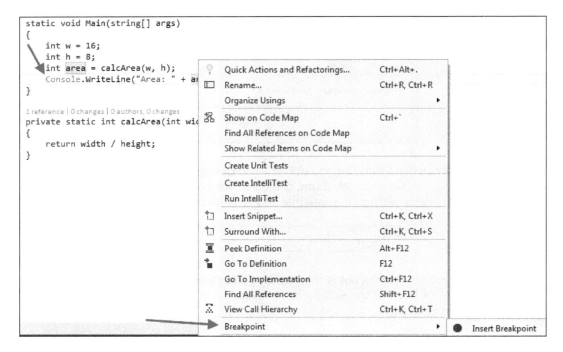

9. If you are not sure where to click, use the right-click method, and then practice toggling the breakpoint by left-clicking on the breakpoint marker. Feel free to use whatever method you find most convenient. Once the two breakpoints are added, Visual Studio will mark their location as shown in the following screenshot (the arrow indicates where you may click to toggle the breakpoint):

```
static void Main(string[] args)
{
    int w = 16;
    int h = 8;
    int area = calcArea(w, h);
    Console.WriteLine("Area: " + area);
}

1 reference | 0 changes | 0 authors, 0 changes
private static int calcArea(int width, int height)
{
    return width / height;
}
}
}
```

10. With the breakpoint marker now set, let's debug the program. Begin debugging by either pressing *F5* or by clicking on the **Start** button on the toolbar:

11. Once debugging starts, the program will quickly execute until stopped by the first breakpoint. Let's first take a look at **Edit and Continue**. Visual Studio will stop at the calcArea method's return line. Astute readers will notice an error (marked by **1** in the following screenshot) present in the calculation, as the area value returned should be width * height. Make the correction.

12. Before continuing, note the variables listed in the **Autos** window (marked by **2** in the following screenshot). (If you don't see **Autos**, it can be made visible by pressing *Ctrl + D, A,* or through **Debug | Windows | Autos** while debugging.)

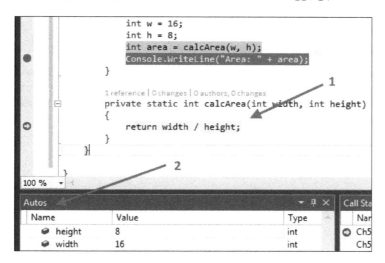

13. After correcting the area calculation, advance the debugging step by pressing *F10* twice. (Alternatively make the advancement by selecting the menu item **Debug | Step Over** twice). Visual Studio will advance to the declaration for the area. Note that you were able to edit your code and continue debugging without restarting.

14. The **Autos** window will update to display the function's `return` value, which is `128` (the value for `area` has not been assigned yet in the following screenshot—**Step Over** once more if you would like to see that assigned):

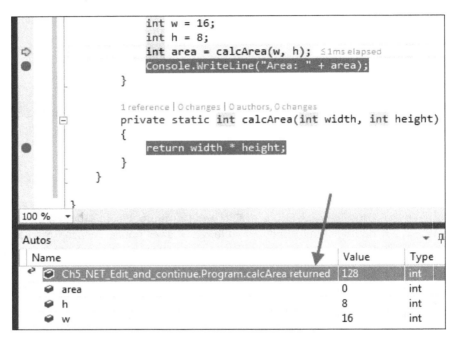

There's more...

Programmers who write C++ have already had the ability to see the return values of functions—this just brings .NET developers into the fold. The result is that your development experience won't have to suffer based on the language you have chosen to use for your project.

The **Edit and Continue** functionality is also available for ASP.NET projects. New projects created on VS2015 will have **Edit and Continue** enabled by default. Existing projects imported to VS2015 will usually need this to be enabled if it hasn't been done already. To do so, open the **Options** dialog via **Tools | Options**, and look for the **Debugging | General** section. The following screenshot shows where this option is located on the properties page:

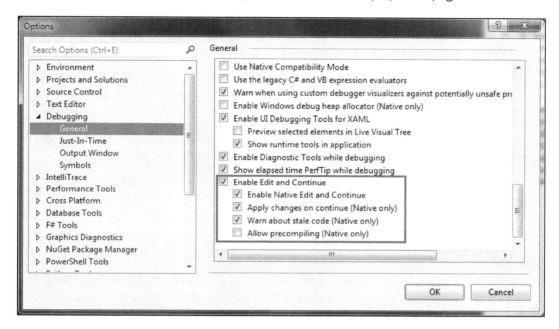

 Whether you are working with an ASP.NET project or a regular C#/VB .NET application, you can verify **Edit and Continue** is set via this location.

Debugging on remote machines and tablets

For most developers, debugging an application means setting a breakpoint with *F9* on a line of code, and then pressing *F5* (or **Debug | Start Debugging**), and stepping into and over statements with *F10* and *F11*.

This experience can work well when you are debugging code on your local machine, but what if you need to debug code running on a different machine that does not have Visual installed? This is where remote debugging tools come into play.

Even though many developers may not be aware of the functionality, debugging code on remote machines with Visual Studio isn't anything new. It's just that until now the debugging experience has been limited and unrefined. VS2015 builds on its predecessors, and the experience it provides is much improved as it combines improvement in speed with broader support for the wide range of devices that today's applications need to support.

Remote debugging is something every developer should know how to do, and this recipe shows you how to configure a machine for remote debugging, and then debug an application you have deployed to that machine.

Getting ready

For this recipe, you will need a second machine to act as your remote machine. It doesn't matter if it's a virtual or physical machine as long as your development machine and the remote machine can communicate over a network connection. This recipe assumes that you are running on VS2015.

The remote machine will need **Remote Tools for Visual Studio 2015** installed before we begin. If you don't have Remote Tools already installed, download them from the Microsoft website at `https://www.visualstudio.com/downloads/download-visual-studio-vs` (look under the section **Tools for Visual Studio 2015 | Remote Tools for Visual Studio 2015**), and then install them. Versions exist for each CPU architecture that Windows supports: X86, X64, and ARM. This recipe assumes that your local machine has a premium edition of VS2015, but note that Remote Tools does support Express for Windows Desktop and Express for Windows.

 Match the architecture of the Remote Tools to that of the remote machine's operating system. For best results, your development machine's OS should match that of the remote device.

There are several advantages to using Remote Tools. You will be able to debug on a remote machine that does not have Visual Studio installed, especially important for ARM-based devices such as the Surface RT where a native version of Visual Studio is not available. It also saves time and the hassle of maintaining a working development environment on each end-device you are targeting. Finally, remote debugging makes it easier to see how your application performs for end users by minimizing the influence of your development environment on your application's operation.

At the time of this writing, those seeking to use the ARM-version of Remote Tools should use Remote Tools for Visual Studio 2015 Update 1. You can use Remote Tools Update 1 with VS2015 Update 2.

How to do it...

Now that our tools are in order, let's see how to perform remote debugging in practice through the following steps:

1. Create a new C# console application using the default name.

2. Open the `Program.cs` file, and fill in the body of the `Main()` method as shown in the following code excerpt (there is an intentional bug in the code):

```
static void Main(string[] args)
{
  Console.Out.WriteLine("Press any key to begin");
  Console.ReadKey();  // Wait for keypress to start
  var charCode = 97;
  var outputBuilder = new StringBuilder();
  for (int i = 1; i < 26; i++)
  {
    outputBuilder.Append((char)(charCode + i));
  }
  var output = outputBuilder.ToString();
  Console.WriteLine(output); // should write "abcd...z"
  Console.ReadKey();
}
```

3. Run the program locally by pressing *F5*. When the console window appears, press any key and you should see a string of characters appear. Press any key again to close the program.

Debugging Your .NET Application

4. You should now check if it works on the remote machine. On your remote machine, start **Remote Debugger Configuration Wizard**, and ensure that the **Run the Visual Studio 2015 Remote Debugger service** checkbox is deselected.

Since our recipe uses a Console application, we do not need to run the remote debugger as a service. The Remote Debugger service is useful when working with web applications or in a known secure environment. More on this later.

5. Also ensure that the firewall configuration is set as appropriate for your network, and then complete the remaining steps of the wizard by taking the default values. The following screenshot illustrates the firewall settings we have selected:

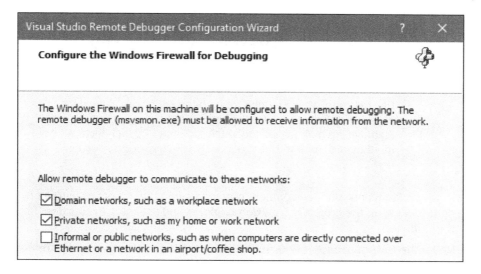

6. Now that you have finished configuring it, start the Remote Debugger on your remote machine.

7. When the debugger appears, you should see a message showing the machine name and port number that the debugger is listening on. Take a note of the machine name as you'll be using it later on. In the following screenshot, the machine is named **DESKTOP-SVJA20M**, and it is running on port **4020**:

8. For the smoothest development and debugging experience, the remote machine should be configured to run the code from your development machine via a network share. Either add a specific share to the `bin\debug` folder of your development machine, or access it via the inbuilt `C$` share, for example, `\\dev-machine\C$\Users\Jeff\Documents\Visual Studio 2013\Projects\ConsoleApplication1\bin\debug` (your location will vary).

Ensure that you can connect to your network share from the remote machine. Code Access Security is not applied to .NET 4.0 applications by default, but it is for .NET 2.0 applications. To debug a .NET 2.0 application on a remote machine via a file share, you need to make sure the share is a trusted location. Use the `caspol.exe` utility for both the x86 and x64 versions of the framework to modify the security settings of your machine (settings are maintained separately for each CPU architecture). For more details, refer to `https://msdn.microsoft.com/en-us/library/cb6t8dtz(v=vs.110).aspx`.

9. In Visual Studio on your development machine, open the project properties by right-clicking on the project in **Solution Explorer** and selecting **Properties**. Select the **Build** tab.

10. Under the **Output** section, set **Output path** to the network share on your remote machine, as shown in the following screenshot:

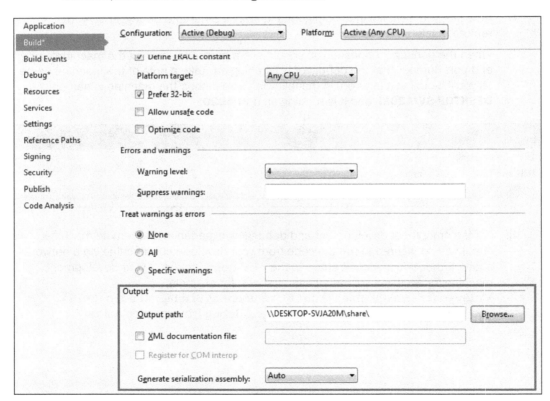

11. Build your solution so that the debug build of the application is deployed. Then return to the **Properties** dialog, and switch to the **Debug** tab.

12. Change **Start Action** to **Start external program**, and enter the path to the compiled application using the path that will be used by the remote machine to start the application, for example, `\\dev-machine\sharename\ConsoleApplication1.exe`.

13. In the **Start Options** section, check the **Use remote machine** checkbox and enter the name of the remote machine. This is the machine name you noted in *Step 6*. Your **Debug** tab should now look similar to the following screenshot:

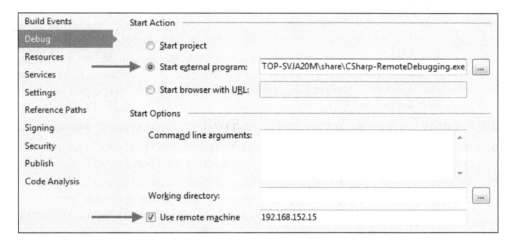

14. On your development machine, press *F5* to start debugging. Assuming there are no firewall issues and your permissions are okay, Visual Studio will communicate with the remote machine and launch the application for you automatically. Note that, depending on the accounts used on each machine, you may be prompted for login credentials. If that happens, enter the details of the user running the debugging monitor on the remote machine.

15. If you have a problem communicating with the remote machine, check that the firewall on the remote machine is allowing incoming connections. If it isn't, you can either rerun **Remote Debugger Configuration Wizard** to confirm the firewall settings, or manually add a rule to allow a connection on the port number the Remote Debugger is using (the port number is shown in *Step 6*).

16. If you switch to your remote machine, you should see that the application is running and displaying a console window with its output, and **Visual Studio 2015 Remote Debugger** reflects that a debugging connection has been made. The following screenshot shows the updated debugger:

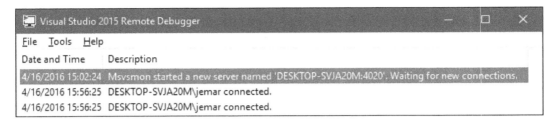

17. The application is now waiting for you to press a key. Before you do, set a breakpoint on your development machine in the `Main()` method of `Program.cs`, somewhere after the `ReadKey()` method. A good place would be where the `outputBuilder` variable is initialized.

18. Return to the remote machine, and press a key to continue program execution.

19. Switch back to the development machine. You should find that your breakpoint has been hit, and that the application is ready for you to continue debugging.

20. Step through the code in Visual Studio to get a feel of how quick the remote debugging experience is, and then continue execution down to the second `Console.ReadKey()` statement. The easiest way to do this, rather than looping through the `for` loop 26 times, is to right-click on that second `Console.ReadKey()` statement, and select **Run to Cursor**.

21. You may notice that the output has dropped the `a` at the start of the output string. Is that a display problem or a bug in the code? You can check the string length to be sure. Navigate to the **Immediate** window and type `?output.Length` to see how long the output string is.

22. If the **Immediate** window isn't visible, you can display it by pressing *Ctrl + Alt + I* or choosing **Debug | Windows | Immediate** from the menu.

23. You should see the value `25` displayed, as shown in the following screenshot:

```
Immediate Window
?output.Length
25
```

24. Note that this value is not from a process on the local machine, it is from the process running on your remote machine. To verify this, navigate to **Debug | Attach to Process** from the menu bar. In the **Qualifier** drop-down menu, select the remote machine. (If it does not appear, use the neighboring **Find...** button). It will be suffixed by the port number that the remote debugger is listening on. When the **Available Processes** list is populated, you should see that your application is the only process on the remote machine that the debugger is attached to (titled `Ch5-RemoteDebuggingWin10.exe` in the following screenshot):

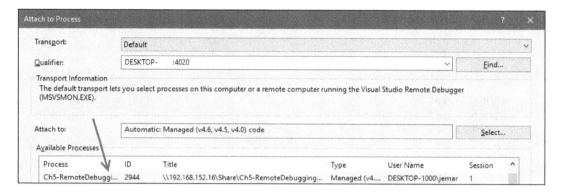

25. Stop debugging by either pressing *Shift + F5*, clicking on the stop button in the debugging toolbar, or choosing **Debug | Stop Debugging** from the menu. This will also terminate the process on the remote machine.

26. Since we have the project open already, fix the bug in the `for` loop by altering the loop variable to start from `0` instead of `1`. Your `for` loop should now look like the following code:

```
for (int i = 0; i < 26; i++)
{
    outputBuilder.Append((char)(charCode + i));
}
```

27. After making the changes and saving your work, press *F5* to start debugging again. Visual Studio will compile the application, and launch it on your remote machine for you.

28. Complete the execution of the application to verify that the output is now correct.

How it works...

The main thing to keep in mind when using the remote debugger is that you are looking at data from the remote machine. The debug experience can feel so smooth and transparent that it's easy at times to forget that a path name for a file, for example, is a path relative to the remote machine and not your local machine.

Normally, the debugger runs using **Windows Authentication**; however, it can be switched over to the **No Authentication** mode. The **No Authentication** mode enables debugging scenarios for managed and native debugging across versions of Windows that were previously not possible. The danger of this approach is that it opens up a security hole including allowing attackers to launch any application they choose. Be sure not to run the remote debugger on production machines in this way. The remote debugger is a developer tool, and should only be run when developers require it.

There's more...

If you don't want to install the remote debugger on the remote machine, you can run it directly from a file share. However, you won't be able to debug Universal Windows applications in the Windows Store or debug JavaScript this way.

Another thing to note is that when you are debugging a UWP app on Windows 10, you will not need to change the **Start Action** section of the project to start an external program. Leaving it set to **Start project**, and then ticking the checkbox and setting the value of the **Use remote machine** field will tell Visual Studio that the project should be packaged and deployed to the remote machine before debugging commences.

Debugging an ASP.NET process

To debug ASP.NET websites running under IIS, you do not need to make any changes to the project properties to configure the remote debugger. In fact, you can't. The options aren't available.

For remote debugging, you will either need to run the remote debugger as a service, or run the application as an administrator. On your development machine, you then use the **Attach to Process** dialog to connect to the ASP.NET worker process, and begin the debugging session.

To configure the remote debugger as a service, rerun **Remote Debugger Configuration Wizard**, and check the option to run it as a service.

Much like you did in this recipe, for the best debugging experience, you should configure the IIS application on the remote machine to run from a network share pointing to the web application's source folder on your development machine.

Once the web application is running in Visual Studio, select the **Debug | Attach to Process** menu option. The **Qualifier** drop-down menu is the name of the debugger instance you are connected to, and this should be the remote machine. If your target machine is not already listed, you can use the **Find...** button to locate the available debuggers.

Once you are connected to the correct machine, locate the ASP.NET worker process (w3wp) from the list, select **Attach**, and then close the window. You are now connected to the remote debugger for the web application, and can set breakpoints in your pages and step through code just as you would expect.

Deploying directly to a remote machine

The suggestion to run the programs on the remote machine via a file share is just a tip to make the development process simpler, and to eliminate the time it takes to redeploy the application you are trying to debug each time you make a change.

If you don't want to run the application from a file share, then you will need to deploy the application to the remote machine, and use the **Attach to Process** dialog to connect the debugging session each time.

Missing symbols

When debugging remote processes, you may find that after you attach to a process and set a breakpoint, it will look similar to the following screenshot:

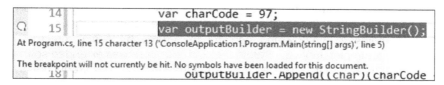

This message seen in the preceding screenshot appears because Visual Studio either can't load the symbol information (the PDB file) of the executable file, or the version that is running on the remote machine is not the same as the one on your development machine. For example, you may have recompiled the code on your development machine since you last deployed to the remote machine, causing the two environments to no longer match.

Fortunately, there is a way to fix this. Follow these steps:

1. Navigate to the **Debug | Windows | Modules** menu entry to display the **Modules** window. (You have to be actively running the debugger for this option to be available.)

2. The following screenshot shows a list of open modules, and whether or not a symbol file has been loaded for them. To load a symbol file, right-click on the entry from which you want to load them, and from the resulting menu, choose **Load Symbols From | Symbol Path**.

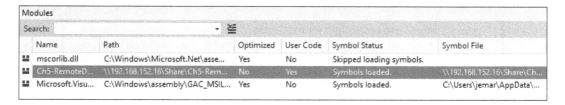

3. From the file selection dialog box, locate the correct symbol file (PDB file) to load. Once you do this, the debug breakpoints will change to show filled-in red dots, as expected, and the **Modules** window will indicate that symbols are loaded.

Debugging code in production with IntelliTrace

Frequently, applications seem to have the frustrating characteristic of performing very well during the development and test cycle, only to be followed up by randomly misbehaving in production environments for no apparent reason. This results in a frantic effort to try and figure out what's going wrong from bug reports that range from "it just stopped working" to "it works on my machine". Diagnosing these problems in a production environment can be rather tricky, especially if you are in an environment where you do not have production access. This is where **IntelliTrace** can help.

While a traditional dump file only provides a capture of the runtime environment as a moment in time, a more lengthy and detailed record is made with IntelliTrace. IntelliTrace was originally introduced in Visual Studio 2010 as a way for developers and testers to record what they'd just done leading up to a bug, and then step back through those actions to make a diagnosis of the bug simpler. In Visual Studio 2012, this feature was extended so that system administrators could capture IntelliTrace information from live, running production systems, and send the logs to developers for diagnosis.

IntelliTrace has continued to evolve over the years. It can be used directly to debug apps within VS2015, used to monitor a session in Test Manager, or it can be used in conjunction with Microsoft Monitoring Agent on production systems.

This recipe will show you how to gather information from a live application running in a production environment, and then diagnose and debug problems.

Getting ready

You will need a machine to use as your production machine. Of course, it doesn't have to be a genuine production machine—just a second machine without Visual Studio installed. A virtual machine is perfectly acceptable. For this recipe, a Windows Server 2012 R2 environment was used. The recipe does require VS2015 Enterprise to be installed on your development machine.

 If you are really tight for machines, and can't even run a virtual machine, then you can use your development machine as your production server for the purposes of this recipe.

Your nominated production machine will need to have .NET Framework 4.5, PowerShell, and—since you will be diagnosing a web application—Internet Information Server installed on it.

 If you would like to have a lighter footprint on your production machine, IntelliTrace Collector has been once again released as an individual software package. It can be downloaded from Microsoft via https://www.microsoft.com/en-us/download/details.aspx?id=44909.

How to do it...

1. On your development machine, create a new application with the default name by selecting **Visual Basic | ASP.NET Web Application**, and in the ensuing dialog, select **Web Forms** as the type of project.

2. Open the `Default.aspx` page, and add a button to the bottom of the page (just before closing the `asp:Content` tag). Give it an id of `ClickMe`, set the text attribute to `Click Me`, and ensure that a button click event is created as shown in the following code excerpt:

```
<div>
   <asp:Button ID="ClickMe" runat="server"
   OnClick="ClickMe_Click" Text="Click Me"
   CssClass="btn btn-default" />
</div>
</asp:Content>
```

3. In the code-behind file, add code for the button's click event handler, as shown in the following code excerpt:

```
Protected Sub ClickMe_Click(sender As Object, e As
EventArgs)
Dim second As Integer = DateTime.Now.Second
If (second Mod 2 = 0) Then
Throw New ApplicationException("Even second click triggered
exception")
Else
ClickMe.Text = "current second: " & second.ToString()
End If
End Sub
```

4. Now when you run the application and click on the button, an exception will be thrown whenever the current time has an even-numbered second. The following screenshot demonstrates a lucky click that occurred on an odd second, avoiding the exception (note some of the template's default code was removed for clarity):

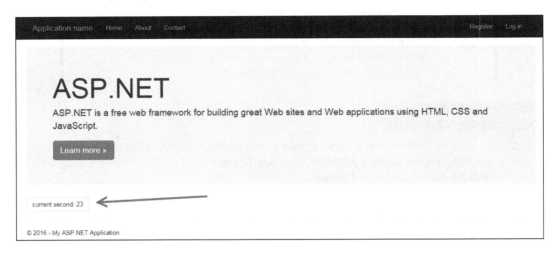

5. Deploy your web application to your production server. Confirm that it runs, and that it throws exceptions randomly when the button is clicked. You will want to note the **Site name** and the **Application Name** that you use here. In the following screenshot, the **Default Web Site** name was used, and the application was installed as VS2015:

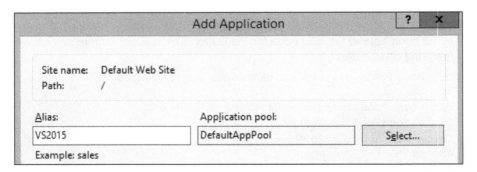

6. Create a directory on the production server to store the log files that we will be generating. For this example, we will use `C:\IntelliTraceLogs`. In an actual production environment, it is important to choose a secure location, since information in the IntelliTrace files can reveal potentially sensitive data from your application. Ideally, a physical disk, separate from your application's disk, should be used to record the IntelliTrace log files. This is to minimize I/O contention, as the server has to respond to application requests while simultaneously writing IntelliTrace logs.

7. Download the latest version of Microsoft Monitoring Agent 2013, available at `http://www.microsoft.com/en-us/download/details.aspx?id=40316`, and install it on your production environment.

8. Open a PowerShell prompt as an administrator, and enter the following command: `Start-WebApplication-Monitoring`.

9. You will be prompted for the name of the application to monitor, but you must also include the site it is located on. In our example, it is `Default Web Site\VS2015`. Next, you will be prompted for the mode of monitoring—enter `Trace`. Finally, you will be prompted for where the output should be logged. Enter `C:\IntelliTraceLogs`. The following screenshot shows the results of running the command:

```
Administrator: Windows PowerShell

PS C:\Users\Administrator> Start-WebApplicationMonitoring

cmdlet Start-WebApplicationMonitoring at command pipeline position 1
Supply values for the following parameters:
Name: Default Web Site\VS2015
Mode: Trace
OutputPath: C:\IntelliTraceLogs
Starting monitoring for 'Default Web Site/VS2015' ...
Monitoring started for 'Default Web Site/VS2015'

PS C:\Users\Administrator> _
```

10. If you want to now verify the status of your monitor, enter `Get-WebApplicationMonitoringStatus`, which will display the information we just entered. Verify that your monitor is operational, and then load your website and generate both, some successful and some unsuccessful clicks.

11. In true production environments, logging should minimize its interference with an application's performance as much as possible. To obtain a trace file while the monitor continues to run, you can enter `CheckPoint-WebApplicationMonitoring`. This will prompt for the name of the site whose performance you want to record, and once entered, the log file will be saved to the previously stated output directory. In this case, we will stop the monitor, and review our logs. Enter `Stop-WebApplicationMonitoring-all`, which will stop the monitoring service and a final log. The file will end in `.itrace`, and will be found in `C:\IntelliTraceLogs`. The following screenshot demonstrates the execution of both commands:

```
PS C:\Users\Administrator> Checkpoint-WebApplicationMonitoring

cmdlet Checkpoint-WebApplicationMonitoring at command pipeline position 1
Supply values for the following parameters:
Name: Default Web Site/VS2015
Creating checkpoint for 'Default Web Site/VS2015'.  This may take a few minutes ...
Monitoring checkpointed for 'Default Web Site/VS2015'

Monitoring results are available:
C:\IntelliTraceLogs\w3wp_000006b0_160417_121852_160417_123040.iTrace

PS C:\Users\Administrator> Stop-WebApplicationMonitoring -all
Stopping monitoring for all web applications.  This may take a few minutes ...
Monitoring stopped for all web applications

Monitoring results are available:
C:\IntelliTraceLogs\w3wp_000006b0_160417_121852.iTrace

PS C:\Users\Administrator>
```

12. Copy the log file back to your development machine. Double-click on the `.iTrace` file to open it in Visual Studio. Alternately, if Visual Studio is already open, you can either press *Ctrl + O*, or use the **File** | **Open** | **File menu** option to load it. Once the file loads, you should be able to see a **Web Requests** section that looks a little like the following screenshot:

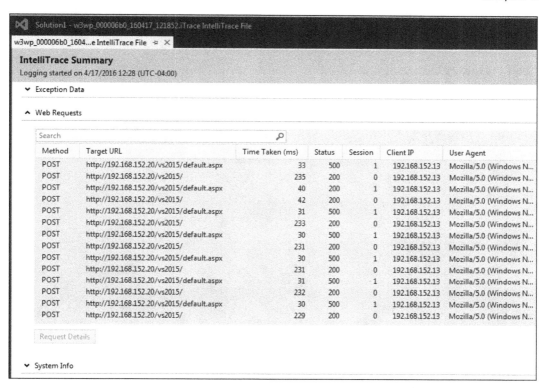

13. In the request list, find a request with a return code of **500**, select it, and then click on the **Request Details** button below the list:

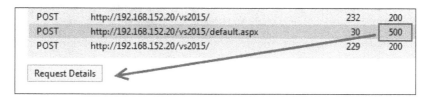

14. The details of the individual request are shown along with the actions that occurred and any exceptions that were thrown:

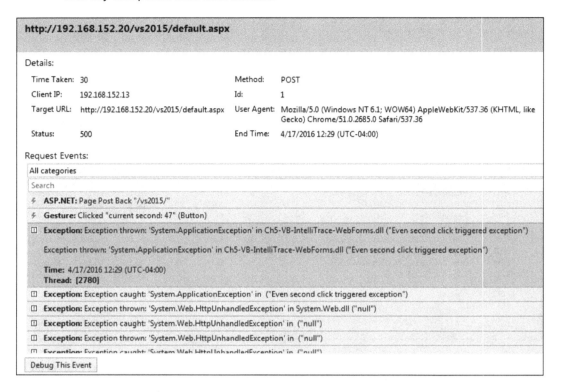

15. Select the entry in the list where the exception is first thrown, as in the previous screenshot in *Step 14,* and click on the **Debug This Event** button.

16. The code will be displayed, and the execution point will be positioned where the exception was thrown:

```
Protected Sub ClickMe_Click(sender As Object, e As EventArgs)
    Dim second As Integer = DateTime.Now.Second
    If (second Mod 2 = 0) Then
        Throw New ApplicationException("Even second click triggered exception")
    Else
        ClickMe.Text = "current second: " & second.ToString()
    End If
End Sub

End Class
```

17. You can then use the IntelliTrace debugging controls to move around the code, and diagnose what occurred by following the execution path and inspecting parameters.

How it works...

No recompilation of code was required for this to work. The application is untouched, and the website didn't need to be restarted. Collecting IntelliTrace data is something that your systems administrators can do on your behalf, safe in the knowledge that the application will be unchanged, and that existing web requests will complete normally. This makes debugging and diagnosing those tricky production problems a much more viable prospect, since checkpoints can be made periodically at intervals that minimize server disruption.

Is your application in break mode?

When using VS2015 and IntelliTrace, you may not see your code highlighted as shown in *Step 16*. Instead, you will see a dialog similar to the following screenshot:

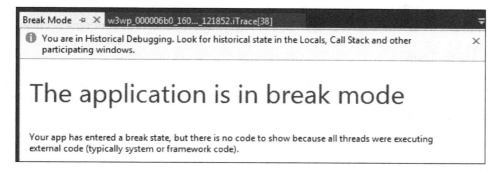

This occurs because the debugging feature **Just My Code** is enabled. To work around this situation, uncheck this feature in the **Options** dialog box, as shown in the following screenshot:

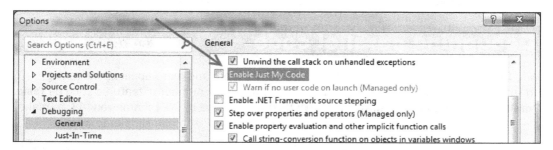

This can be useful if it's enabled under other circumstances, so feel free to re-enable it when you are finished with your IntelliTrace session.

There's more...

The IntelliTrace settings used in the recipe are the detailed trace settings (as configured in *Step 9*). They will record the execution flow as well as events, and will have some impact on production performance. The alternative option is to use the monitor setting, which has a minimal impact on performance as it focuses on exceptions and performance.

Don't forget that IntelliTrace files can get very big, very quickly. Make sure that the location you place them in has plenty of space if you want to capture data over a reasonable time period, and more so if you have a busy production server. Logging directly to the system drive like we did in the recipe is generally not recommended, since filling your system drive will bring your server to a grinding halt.

Finding the variable values

If you haven't used it before, you might expect IntelliTrace to be equivalent to the normal debugging experience. Unfortunately, the performance impact of recording all the data needed to simulate the full debugging experience makes this prohibitive.

By default, variable values are not recorded by IntelliTrace unless a breakpoint has been set or an event occurs. In the recipe, if during the debugging session you hovered your mouse over the second variable in the code window, you would see an indication that the data was not collected.

If you wanted to capture that information, you could configure IntelliTrace to record the tracing information and add trace statements for your code, or you could write custom IntelliTrace events (outside the scope of this book) and add them to the IntelliTrace configuration. In either case, it would require recompiling and redeploying code to production, so there is an assumption that you know the level of trace information you will need ahead of time.

Debugging parallel code

With the prevalence of multicore CPUs we are seeing more and more applications taking advantage of parallel processing to improve performance. A number of features such as **Task Parallel Library** (**TPL**) and **Parallel LINQ** (**PLINQ**) were added by .NET Framework 4.0 to make developing applications that take advantage of multicore CPUs much simpler to write.

The debugging experience for threaded applications in Visual Studio has gotten better with each release, and VS2013 is no exception. Let's take a look at what is available.

Getting ready

Start a premium edition of VS2015, and create a new C# console application with a name of your choice.

How to do it...

In order to debug a program with parallel code, perform the following steps:

1. Use the following code to populate the body of `Program.cs`. It's a pretty simple program that starts a parallel `for` loop, which, in turn, calls a method that performs meaningless calculations intended to keep the CPU busy:

```
class Program
{
  static void Main(string[] args)
  {
    Parallel.For(0, 100000, i => SlowMethod(i + 1));
  }

  private static void SlowMethod(int i)
  {
    var total = 0;
    for (int loop = 0; loop < 1000000; loop++)
    {
      total += loop;
      total /= i;
    }
  }
}
```

2. Press *F5* to run the program, and after a second or two, break into the debugger either by pressing the pause button in Visual Studio or by pressing *Ctrl* + *Alt* + Break.

3. You will most likely break inside `SlowMethod()`. When you do, you should be able to see the current value of the variable `i` by hovering over the variable name, as shown in the following screenshot:

```
1 reference | 0 changes | 0 authors, 0 changes
private static void SlowMethod(int i)
{
    var total = 0;
    for (int loop = 0; loop < 1000000; loop++)
    {
        total += loop;
        total /= i;
    }                    ● i   212   ⇦
}
```

4. So far, this is standard behavior when debugging. However, you can only see the value of i for a single thread (in our screenshot, that value is **212**). What about the value of i on all the other threads? From the menu, navigate to **Debug | Windows | Threads,** and you will see all the threads in the application including the threads that the parallel for loop has created. The following screenshot lists some of the threads present:

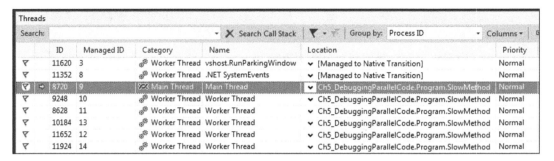

5. Right-click on a different thread from the one you are currently on, and select **Switch To Thread** from the context menu. Now look at the values of i, loop, and total, and you will see they are different.

6. This is useful for what it is, but still fairly cumbersome if you want to see the value of i across all threads. For a more useful holistic view, use the menu to navigate to **Debug | Windows | Parallel Watch | Parallel Watch 1** (or use the keyboard shortcut *Ctrl + Shift + D, 1*). This will bring up a new window with all of the current threads listed, and an area in the header of the last column for adding watch expressions. Any expression entered will be evaluated automatically across all threads for you.

7. Add watch expressions for i and **1000000-loop** as shown in the following screenshot, so you can see how this works (to enter a watch for each variable, click on the **<Add Watch>** column header):

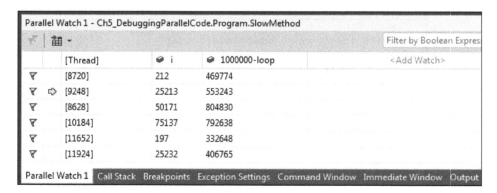

8. Stop debugging. Return to Visual Studio, and add a second console application named `Parallel2` to the current solution. In the new project's `Program.cs` file, use the following code for the body of the file:

```
class Program
{
  static void Main(string[] args)
  {
    Parallel.For(0, 100000, i => AnotherSlowMethod(i + 1));
  }

  private static void AnotherSlowMethod(int i)
  {
    var total = 0;
    var sb = new StringBuilder(1000 * i);
    for (int loop = 0; loop < 1000 * i; loop++)
    {
      sb.Append(loop);
    }
    total = sb.ToString().Length;
  }
}
```

9. Right-click on the solution in **Solution Explorer**, and select **Set Startup Projects** in the context menu. Select **Multiple startup projects**, and ensure that the **Action** value for both console applications is **Start**.

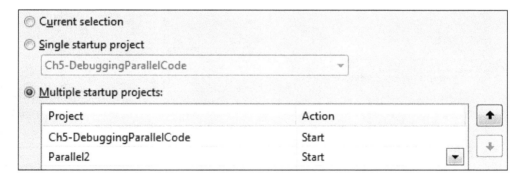

10. Click on **OK** to save the changes, and then press *F5* to start debugging.

11. Wait for a short period of time, and then again break into the debugger using the same process as explained in *Step 2*.

12. From the menu, navigate to **Debug | Windows | Tasks**. You will now see that you have multiple processes, each with multiple tasks. You can also see what thread each task is running on, as shown in the following screenshot:

	ID	Status	Location
⊽	7	▶ Active	System.Buffer._Memmove
⊽	61	▶ Active	Ch5_DebuggingParallelCode.Program.SlowMethod
⊽ ⇨	6	▶ Active	System.Threading.Thread.CurrentCulture.get
⊽	8	▶ Active	System.Text.StringBuilder.Append
⊽	9	▶ Active	System.Text.StringBuilder.Append
⊽	13	▶ Active	System.Text.StringBuilder.Append
⊽	14	▶ Active	Parallel2.Program.AnotherSlowMethod
⊽	15	▶ Active	System.Text.StringBuilder.Append

Tasks — Some scheduled tasks might be missing. Try restarting the debug session.

13. Now we will utilize a view that will let us visualize how the processes have been created. From the menu, navigate to **Debug | Windows | Parallel Stacks**. As can be seen in the following screenshot, you now have two processes being displayed, each with a main thread and the spawned threads created by the parallel `for` loops of each process:

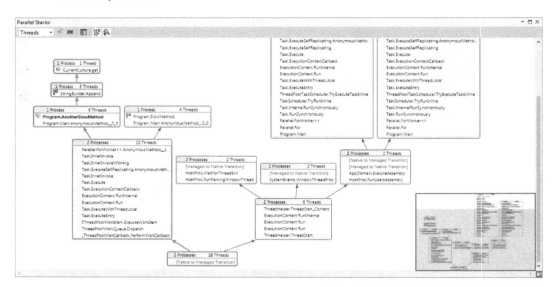

Note that the **Parallel Stacks** window has useful controls located in the top corner of the screen to assist in navigation (including zoom), and there is the minimap located on the bottom right. Both sets of controls are very helpful when dealing with larger diagrams.

How it works...

Apart from the debugging improvements themselves, Microsoft has worked hard on TPL, PLINQ, and other multithreading-related framework features, and gained some serious performance improvements for .NET 4.5. Since .NET 4.5+ is an in-place replacement of the .NET 4.0 runtime, it means that any of your .NET 4.0 code that uses these libraries will automatically benefit from the performance improvements without requiring you to make code changes or manage lengthy recompilations.

See also

▶ The *Visualizing concurrency* recipe

▶ For more information on TPL, refer to the *MSDN documentation* at `https://msdn.microsoft.com/en-us/library/dd460717(v=vs.110).aspx`

▶ Information on PLINQ is available at `https://msdn.microsoft.com/en-us/library/dd460688(v=vs.110).aspx`

Visualizing concurrency

The Concurrency Visualizer is another tool that was added in Visual Studio 2010 to assist with multithreaded code and, just like the other features of Visual Studio related to threading in Visual Studio 2012, it too has been the subject of a number of improvements. Starting with VS2013, it has been pulled out of the default installation, but is available on the Visual Studio Gallery.

In this recipe, we'll take a look at these improvements, and see how you can better understand what is happening inside your application when it runs.

Getting ready

You will need to use VS2015 or one of the premium editions for this recipe. Download and install the Concurrency Visualizer from the Visual Studio Gallery available at `https://visualstudiogallery.msdn.microsoft.com/a6c24ce9-beec-4545-9261-293061436ee9`. Once installed, reopen Visual Studio, and create a new C# console application named `Concurrency`.

This recipe is based on VS2015, but the VS2013 extension remains available at `https://visualstudiogallery.msdn.microsoft.com/24b56e51-fcc2-423f-b811-f16f3fa3af7a`.

How to do it...

1. Open the `Program.cs` file, and add the following statements to the `using` statements at the top of the file:

```
using System.Threading;
using System.Diagnostics.Tracing;
```

2. The following sample code is fairly straightforward. It will simply build up a list of tasks to run, and then execute them. Each task then calls `SpinWait` on the thread for a period of time. It's much the same as a `Thread.Sleep` method, but instead of the thread yielding back to the operating systems task scheduler, it keeps the CPU busy (to better assist with our demo). To proceed, add this code to the body of `Program.cs`:

```
static void Main(string[] args)
{
  var taskList = new List<Task>();
  for (int i = 0; i < 10; i++)
  {
    taskList.Add(Task.Run(() =>
    {
      MyEventSource.Log.RecordAnEvent(DateTime.Now.Second);
      Thread.SpinWait(10000000);
    }));
  }
  Task.WaitAll(taskList.ToArray());
}
```

3. Next, add a custom event source as shown in the following code excerpt. It will be called whenever a new task is created in the main program loop:

```
[EventSource(Guid = "EE8B671C-90FA-4D6F-A238-F779DBCA6128")]
class MyEventSource : EventSource
{
  internal static MyEventSource Log = new MyEventSource();

  [Event(1)]
  public void RecordAnEvent(int data)
  {
    WriteEvent(1, data);
  }
}
```

4. Launch the **Concurrency Visualizer**, either by pressing the keyboard shortcut of *Alt + Shift + F5*, or from the menu by navigating to **Analyze | Concurrency Visualizer | Start with Current Project**.

 For the purpose of this recipe, if you are prompted to configure a symbol cache or you see a warning about running without executive paging on an x64 machine, you can select **No** in each case.

If you are prompted for elevation, then select **Yes** since the collection analyzer requires administrative privileges.

5. When the process completes and the data collection ends, you will see a window like the following screenshot:

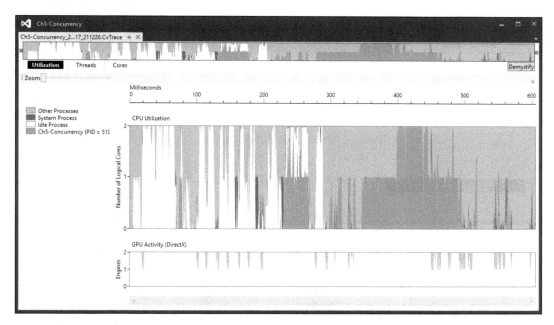

6. At the very top of the window is an overview area with drag handles that you can use to limit the amount of data displayed. Move the red drag handles toward each other so that the selected area contains the high activity area of the trace file.

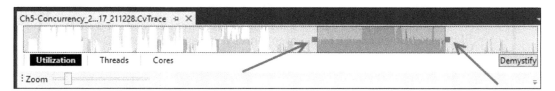

7. Navigate to the **Threads** view by clicking on the button just under the overview area. The following screenshot shows the **Threads** view:

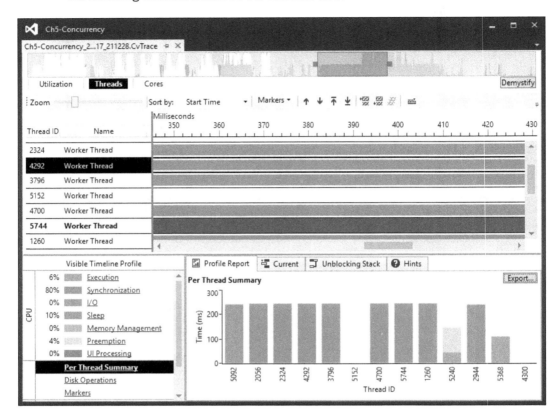

8. You will be shown what has been happening in each thread, and you can also see that your custom event isn't displaying yet. Let's figure out why.

9. Navigate to the **Analyze | Concurrency Visualizer | Advanced Settings** menu entry, and select the **Markers** tab.

10. Click on the green plus icon to add a new marker. Enter `RecordAnEvent` as the **Name** of the marker, and in the **Provider GUID** field, enter the GUID you used in the `MyEventSource Event` attribute (refer to *Step 3*). The following screenshot shows how this should look. Click on **OK** to close the dialog box.

 To make this step a little easier, copy the GUID from the code and paste it into the dialog. It'll help prevent errors when entering the GUID.

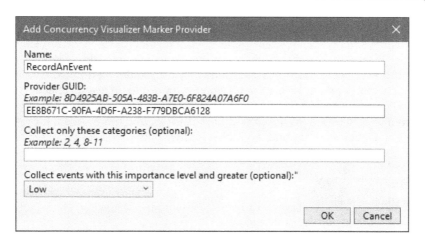

11. Repeat *Step 4* to reanalyze the application and collect updated results, including your newly-added event marker.

12. When **Concurrency Visualizer** opens, switch to the **Threads** view as before. You should be able to find the custom event information as shown in the following screenshot:

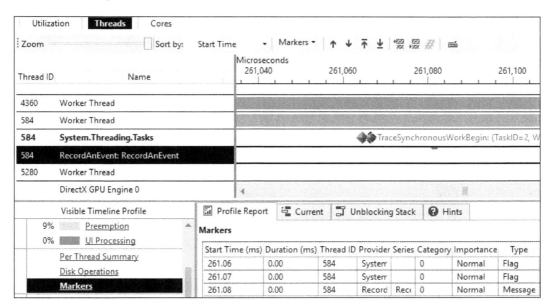

How it works...

The Concurrency Visualizer exists to help you understand what the CPU is doing when your application runs, and where performance issues may be originating from. The ability to add your own custom markers is very useful when you want to tie events specific to your application to the visualizer. Apart from custom event data, the visualizer also understands the events from TPL, PLINQ, synchronized data structures, and more. This information gives you great insight into your code, and will hopefully help you isolate the points where performance bottlenecks and bugs might be originating from.

See also

- ▶ The *Debugging parallel code* recipe
- ▶ Information on PLINQ is available at `http://msdn.microsoft.com/en-us/library/dd460688(v=vs.110).aspx`

6

Asynchrony in .NET

In this chapter, we will cover the following topics:

- ▶ Making your code asynchronous
- ▶ Understanding asynchrony and Universal Windows Platform apps
- ▶ Using asynchrony with web applications
- ▶ Working with actors and the TPL Dataflow library

Introduction

The use of asynchronous code has become more popular as programmers seek ways to deal with latency and blocking operations in their applications. For example, an application running with the benefit of significant local resources is still at the mercy of the response time of other systems that it has to communicate with. In many cases, applications wait for their users to respond, and they shouldn't consume all available system resources while they wait for the users to react.

To deal with these and similar challenges, multithreaded code has been used. With this approach, the work that needs to be done is handled by multiple threads, so while one thread is handling network communication, another may update the display. Sometimes, this approach has its own limitations, as additional threads increase complexity for the programmer, and there are practical limitations on how many threads can be effectively created and utilized.

Whether your code is currently multithreaded or not, the use of asynchronous techniques can be beneficial, as they eliminate blocking on an executing thread. This applies whether it is the sole main execution thread, or a particular thread devoted to the task at hand.

Microsoft realized that while most developers understand the benefits of asynchronous code and the improvements it can bring about in their applications, the programming models involved in asynchrony were fairly cumbersome, verbose, and in some cases, quite difficult to get right. As a result, most developers ignored asynchrony unless circumstances forced it upon them. The extra complexity, effort, time, higher chance of bugs, and difficulty of debugging meant that it simply wasn't worth it for most developers.

To ensure reading and writing asynchronous code is no longer restricted to domain experts, Visual Studio 2012 and .NET 4.5 introduced the `async` and `await` keywords for both the C# and Visual Basic languages. These keywords make asynchronous code as easy to read, write, and debug as normal synchronous code.

As you saw in *Chapter 5, Debugging Your .NET Application*, the debugging experience for .NET code has been greatly improved. When this is combined with the improved language features, the implementation cost of asynchronous code is made much easier, and so, should be considered for use to see if it is appropriate for your projects.

In this chapter, you'll be looking specifically at the `async` and `await` keywords, and see how VS2015 supports them.

Making your code asynchronous

Let's begin by examining a scenario where you have an application that might be lacking in the performance department. While users feel it is very unresponsive, yet when the performance counters on the host machine are examined, it doesn't seem to be doing all that much. The odds are high that your existing code is performing a slow operation and blocking the execution thread while it waits for this operation to complete, which prevents other code from executing.

It gets even worse in web applications that come under heavy load. Soon, every request thread that gets blocked becomes a point where other requests can get queued, and before long, your application server starts throwing **503 Service Unavailable** errors.

Time to take that synchronous code, stick an **a** at the front, and take advantage of your production system's hardware more efficiently. Keep in mind that before you make all of your code asynchronous, you should understand where it blocks, and where it doesn't (refer to *Chapter 5, Debugging Your .NET Application*, for some tips on getting started with this).

The overhead of using asynchronous code everywhere can actually make your application run slower if you aren't careful (this is similar to the fact that you cannot improve application performance solely through adding dozens of execution threads). While techniques such as multithreading and asynchronous programming can help in many situations, they do not represent a magical cure-all that is appropriate in every situation.

The sample application we are about to build will read RSS feeds from a number of sites and display them on the console. At the end of the display, the total time required for the feeds to be fetched and displayed will be shown.

Getting ready

You will need an Internet connection for this recipe to work, since you will be loading data from various RSS feeds and displaying the results.

So ensure you have a working connection, then simply start one of the Premium editions of VS2015 or VS2015 Community, and you will be ready to begin.

How to do it...

Perform the following steps:

1. Create a C# console application named `FeedReader`.

2. In the program, classes from a number of different namespaces will be used. To save some time, add the following code to the `using` statements at the top of `Program.cs`:

    ```
    using System.Diagnostics;
    using System.Net;
    using System.Net.Cache;
    using System.Xml.Linq;
    ```

3. Before you implement the main method, you need to create some supporting methods. Add a `ReadFeed()` private method, as shown after the `Main()` method. It creates a web client to read an RSS feed with the cache setting turned off. This will ensure that we always pull data from the Internet and not a local cached copy.

    ```
    private static string ReadFeed(string url)
    {
      var client = new WebClient()
      {
        CachePolicy = new
        RequestCachePolicy(RequestCacheLevel.NoCacheNoStore)
      };
      var contents = client.DownloadString(url);
      return contents;
    }
    ```

4. Add a `PublishedDate()` method below the `ReadFeed()` method. It will convert dates in the feed that `System.DateTime` doesn't handle into dates that can be parsed:

```
public static DateTime PublishedDate(XElement item)
{
    var s = (string)item.Element("pubDate");
    if (s != null)
    {
        s = s.Replace("EST", "-0500");
        s = s.Replace("EDT", "-0400");
        s = s.Replace("CST", "-0600");
        s = s.Replace("CDT", "-0500");
        s = s.Replace("MST", "-0700");
        s = s.Replace("MDT", "-0600");
        s = s.Replace("PST", "-0800");
        s = s.Replace("PDT", "-0700");
    }
    DateTime d;
    if (DateTime.TryParse(s, out d)) return d;
    return DateTime.MinValue;
}
```

5. Now return to the `Main()` method and create a variable for the list of feeds to read from (feel free to customize to suit your personal tastes):

```
static void Main(string[] args)
{
    var feedUrls = new List<string>() {
        "http://www.engadget.com/rss.xml",
        "http://www.wired.com/feed/",
        "http://apod.nasa.gov/apod.rss",
        "http://arstechnica.com/feed/",
    };
}
```

6. Continuing in `Main()`, create a `Stopwatch` so that you can start timing how long the execution takes, and then add the code to load the data from the feeds:

```
var stopwatch = Stopwatch.StartNew();
var feeds = (from url in feedUrls select
ReadFeed(url)).ToArray();
```

7. You need to parse the feed so you can extract something to show on screen. Add the following code to the `Main()` method to do so:

```
var items = from feed in feeds
from channel in XElement.Parse(feed).Elements("channel")
```

```
from item in channel.Elements("item").Take(2)
let date = PublishedDate(item)
orderby date descending
select new
{
  Title = (string)channel.Element("title"),
  Link = (string)channel.Element("link"),
  PostTitle = (string)item.Element("title"),
  PostLink = (string)item.Element("link"),
  Date = date
};
```

8. Complete the `Main()` method by adding the following code to display an item from each feed on the console, and to show the total time it took to process all feeds:

```
foreach (var item in items)
{
  Console.WriteLine("Title: {0} [{1}]", item.Title,
  item.Link);
  Console.WriteLine("  Post: {0}[{1}]", item.PostTitle,
  item.PostLink);
  Console.WriteLine("  Date: " + item.Date);
  Console.WriteLine("---------");
}
Console.WriteLine("Total Time: " + stopwatch.Elapsed);
Console.ReadKey(); // this line will be removed in Step 17
```

9. Compile the program, and check that it runs. Don't panic if the console takes a little while to show some text—you've got some slow code running here. When it does eventually complete, you should see output similar to the following screenshot:

```
Title: Ars Technica [http://arstechnica.com]
  Post: When the next Twitterbot loses it, remember that its tweets are protected[http://arstechnica.com/
16/04/when-the-next-twitterbot-loses-it-remember-that-its-tweets-are-protected/]
  Date: 4/23/2016 10:30:14
---------
Title: Engadget RSS Feed [http://www.engadget.com/rss.xml]
  Post: Recommended Reading: Is Instagram ruining our vacations?[http://www.engadget.com/2016/04/23/recom
-4-23-16/]
  Date: 4/23/2016 10:00:00
---------
Title: WIRED [http://www.wired.com]
  Post: Ratchet and Clank Remakes Itself, Yet Refines Nothing[http://www.wired.com/2016/04/ratchet-clank-
kes/]
  Date: 4/23/2016 07:00:57
---------
Title: APOD [http://antwrp.gsfc.nasa.gov/]
  Post: Milky Way in Moonlight[http://antwrp.gsfc.nasa.gov/apod/astropix.html]
  Date: 1/1/0001 00:00:00
---------
Title: APOD [http://antwrp.gsfc.nasa.gov/]
  Post: NGC 7635: The Bubble Nebula[http://antwrp.gsfc.nasa.gov/apod/ap160422.html]
  Date: 1/1/0001 00:00:00
---------
Total Time: 00:00:01.0305328
```

10. As you can see, since each request is being made in a synchronous manner, this does not execute very quickly. This program contacts each site sequentially, waits for a response, and then contacts the next site in the list. Even though they are independent servers, each delayed response increases the overall execution time. This isn't very efficient, so let's introduce the `await` and `async` keywords in an effort to speed this thing up. First, locate the `ReadFeed()` method, and change the return type from `string` to `Task<string>`.

11. You will then need to return a `Task<string>` object from the method, but you can't just cast the contents variable to that type. Fortunately, the `WebClient` class includes a task-based version of `DownloadString` called `DownloadStringTaskAsync` that returns a `Task<string>` object. Perfect for our needs. Change the code to use `client.DownloadStringTaskAsync(url)`:

```
private static Task<string> ReadFeed(string url)
{
  var client = new WebClient()
  {
    CachePolicy = new
    RequestCachePolicy(RequestCacheLevel.NoCacheNoStore)
  };
  var contents = client.DownloadStringTaskAsync(url);
  return contents;
}
```

12. Navigate back up to the `Main()` method, and you will see a problem with the `Parse()` method in the LINQ statement. The root cause is that the feeds variable is now an array of the `Task<string>` objects, and not `string` objects.

13. Change the code where `feeds` is assigned to wrap the LINQ statement in a `Task.WhenAll()` call instead of using `.ToArray()`. The `Task.WhenAll` method creates a task that waits until all of the inner tasks returned by the enclosed LINQ statement are complete. The `await` keyword tells the compiler that the task should be executed asynchronously and the result assigned to the `feeds` variable. The variable `feeds` is now defined as follows:

```
var feeds = await Task.WhenAll(from url in feedUrls select
ReadFeed(url));
```

14. There is still a problem. The compiler now complains about the `await` keyword not being valid, as shown in the following screenshot:

```
var feeds = await Task.WhenAll(from url in feedUrls select ReadFe
|
// parse feeds        The 'await' operator can only be used within an async method.
var items = fror
            fror  Show potential fixes (Ctrl+.)
```

15. Any method where the `await` keyword is used must have the `async` keyword in its declaration. Go to the declaration of the `Main()` method and add the `async` keyword, as shown in the following code:

```
static async void Main(string[] args)
```

 You can also accept the change recommended by VS2015 in the preceding screenshot.

16. Attempt to compile the application. You will get an error indicating that the `Main` method can't be made asynchronous, as it is the program entry point.

17. This is easy enough to work around. Retitle the `Main()` method `static async Task ProcessFeedsAsync()`, and insert a new `Main()` method above it, using the following code. Also, remove the `ReadKey()` method from the end of the `ProcessFeedsAsync()` method so that you are not prompted for user input twice. The result should be like the following code:

```
static void Main(string[] args)
{
    Console.WriteLine("starting...");
    ProcessFeedsAsync().Wait();
    Console.WriteLine("finished...");
    Console.ReadKey();
}
static async Task ProcessFeedsAsync()
```

18. Compile and run the program. You should see an output somewhat similar to the following screenshot, and the elapsed time should be shorter than before:

```
Title: Ars Technica [http://arstechnica.com]
   Post: When the next Twitterbot loses it, remember that its tweets are protected[http://ars
16/04/when-the-next-twitterbot-loses-it-remember-that-its-tweets-are-protected/]
   Date: 4/23/2016 10:30:14
---------
Title: Engadget RSS Feed [http://www.engadget.com/rss.xml]
   Post: Recommended Reading: Is Instagram ruining our vacations?[http://www.engadget.com/201
-4-23-16/]
   Date: 4/23/2016 10:00:00
---------
Title: WIRED [http://www.wired.com]
   Post: Ratchet and Clank Remakes Itself, Yet Refines Nothing[http://www.wired.com/2016/04/r
kes/]
   Date: 4/23/2016 07:00:57
---------
Title: APOD [http://antwrp.gsfc.nasa.gov/]
   Post: Milky Way in Moonlight[http://antwrp.gsfc.nasa.gov/apod/astropix.html]
   Date: 1/1/0001 00:00:00
---------
Title: APOD [http://antwrp.gsfc.nasa.gov/]
   Post: NGC 7635: The Bubble Nebula[http://antwrp.gsfc.nasa.gov/apod/ap160422.html]
   Date: 1/1/0001 00:00:00
---------
Total Time: 00:00:00.7234464
```

How it works...

The final version of the program written using asynchronous techniques provides better results based on the nature of the work we are trying to accomplish (I/O dependent processing). The primary impediment to timely execution is the wait imposed by each server's response time. In the original program, even one slow server can impede the results, as the delay cascades through each request. The asynchronous version avoids this by making each request in a non-blocking manner, so each request can be started without waiting for the preceding request to complete.

The `DownloadStringTaskAsync()` method shows off an important convention to be aware of in the .NET 4.5 Framework design. There is a naming convention to help you locate the asynchronous versions of methods, where methods that are asynchronous all have an `async` suffix to their names. In situations where an asynchronous method exists from previous framework versions, the newer, task-based, asynchronous methods are named with the `TaskAsync` suffix instead.

The line `ProcessFeedsAsync().Wait();` calls the `Wait()` method so that the program does not terminate before receiving a response from all the asynchronous tasks that were started. This use of `Wait()` is what allows the overall program flow to run as we would expect: the phrase **starting...** is displayed, the RSS feeds are retrieved and displayed, and then upon completion the program displays the total execution time.

As you've seen, Visual Studio offers enough warnings and errors through IntelliSense to make the conversion of synchronous code to asynchronous reasonably straightforward, as long as you make changes in small, incremental steps. Large scale changes of code, regardless of what those changes may be, are always difficult and error prone, especially if you lack unit tests or other mechanisms to verify that your changes haven't broken any functionality.

There's more...

It's possible to overdo it. Every piece of asynchronous code comes with a certain amount of overhead. There is a CPU cost to context switching, and a higher memory footprint used for maintaining the memory state of each asynchronous task/method, and it is possible to reduce the performance of your application when they are used inappropriately.

The original design guideline for the **Windows Runtime (WinRT)** libraries in Windows 8 was that any method that was likely to take more than 50 ms to complete was changed to be asynchronous. This is a good rule of thumb to continue following as you work on your applications whether they are **Universal Windows Platform (UWP)**-based or traditional .NET applications. Before attempting to improve all the methods in your application at once, start by determining which of your current methods are the slowest. Also take into consideration what a function is trying to do.

An initial guideline would be to start by only improving methods that take more than 500 ms to complete, and resolving those before targeting faster methods. Using asynchronous code for this example was ideal, since each feed is located on a separate server, and obtaining results from one server isn't dependent on another.

Whenever determining the appropriate balance between synchronous and asynchronous code, you should be doing performance and load testing on your application to determine what the current performance profile is, and what effect your changes will have on it. Because each and every application is different, finding the right mix can be an art. As a tip, identify the slowest areas of your application, and target them first. I/O-based methods are good candidates for consideration. As you improve performance, keep an eye on how much time it costs you to make your code asynchronous versus the improvement you are seeing in the overall application performance.

See also

▶   Stephen Cleary has written an informative article for *MSDN Magazine*, *Best Practices in Asynchronous Programming*, available at `http://msdn.microsoft.com/en-us/magazine/jj991977.aspx`

Understanding asynchrony and Universal Windows Platform apps

When developing the original Windows Runtime for Windows 8.x, Microsoft followed a design guideline in which any synchronous method that might take longer than 50 ms to complete was to be removed and replaced with an asynchronous version. The goal behind this design decision is to dramatically improve the chances of developers building applications that feel smooth and fluid by not blocking threads on framework calls.

In this recipe, you're going to revisit the RSS feed reader concept, just as you did in the *Making your code asynchronous* recipe, though this time you're going to be creating a UWP application.

There are a few differences between a UWP application and a console one, including differences in the classes available. For example, the `WebClient` class doesn't exist in WinRT, so you'll be using the `HttpClient` class instead.

For additional variety, we will be writing this app using Visual Basic, but of course, the concepts are applicable to any UWP application.

Getting ready

Ensure you are running Windows 10, and then launch VS2015. You will need either one of the Premium editions or Visual Studio Community 2015.

How to do it...

Perform the following steps to create the UWP version of our `FeedReader` program:

1. Create a new project by navigating to **Visual Basic | Windows | Universal | Blank App (Universal Windows)** and name it `FeedReaderApp`.

2. Depending on your particular installation of Windows 10 and VS2015, you may be prompted to define platform versions. For this recipe, we will use a **Target Version** of **Build 10586** and a **Minimum Version** of **Build 10240**, as shown in the following screenshot:

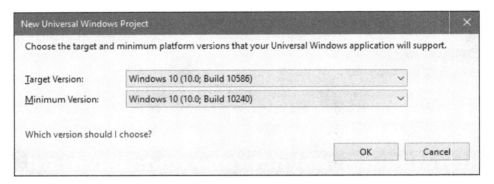

3. Add a class named `Post` by right-clicking on your project and then selecting **Add | New Item | Class**.

4. After `Post.vb` is created, insert the following code. This class will be used to hold the details of each post from the RSS feed that we will show on screen:

```
Public Class Post
    Public Property Title As String
    Public Property Link As String
    Public Property PostTitle As String
    Public Property PostLink As String
    Public Property PostDate As DateTime
End Class
```

5. Open `MainPage.xaml` and add the following XAML to the existing `<Grid/>` element to define the markup of how the results should appear. The layout consists of a button to start the feed loading and a `ListBox` element in which the results are displayed. You also have a `TextBlock` element in which you'll post the time it takes to read the feeds:

```
<Grid Background="{ThemeResource
ApplicationPageBackgroundThemeBrush}">
    <Button Name="LoadFeeds" Margin="116,60,0,0"
    VerticalAlignment="Top">
```

```
    Load Feeds
</Button>
<TextBlock Name="TimeTaken" HorizontalAlignment="Left"
Height="36" Margin="257,60,0,0" TextWrapping="Wrap"
VerticalAlignment="Top" Width="360" FontSize="32">
    Waiting for click
</TextBlock>
<ListBox Height="450" HorizontalAlignment="Left"
Margin="116,140,0,0" Name="PostsListBox"
VerticalAlignment="Top" Width="500" >
    <ListBox.ItemTemplate>
      <DataTemplate>
        <StackPanel Orientation="Vertical" Height="110">
          <TextBlock Text="{Binding Title}" />
          <TextBlock Text="{Binding Link}" />
          <TextBlock Text="{Binding PostTitle}" />
          <TextBlock Text="{Binding PostLink}" />
          <TextBlock Text="{Binding PostDate}" />
        </StackPanel>
      </DataTemplate>
    </ListBox.ItemTemplate>
  </ListBox>
</Grid>
```

 Feel free change to the selected device in the XAML designer so that there is enough room for our layout. This setting is located in the top-left corner of the designer window. For our recipe, we will target an **8" Tablet**, as shown in the following screenshot:

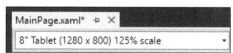

6. Next, navigate to the code behind the file `MainPage.xaml.vb`, and add a couple of `Imports` statements that you will need later:

```
Imports System.Net.Http
Imports System.Net.Http.Headers
```

7. Now add some initial code to define the RSS feeds to use and a collection to hold the `Post` objects:

```
Public NotInheritable Class MainPage
  Inherits Page

  Public Property Posts As List(Of Post)
```

```
        Dim feedUrls As New List(Of String)

        Public Sub New()
          InitializeComponent()
          feedUrls = New List(Of String) From {
            "http://www.engadget.com/rss.xml",
            "http://apod.nasa.gov/apod.rss",
            "http://arstechnica.com/feed/"
          }
          Posts = New List(Of Post)
        End Sub
      End Class
```

8. Add the `PublishedDate()` helper method to the class after the `New()` method:

```
Public Function PublishedDate(item As XElement) As DateTime
  Dim s As String = ""

  If item.Element("pubDate") IsNot Nothing Then
    s = CType(item.Element("pubDate"), String)
    s = s.Replace("EST", "-0500")
    s = s.Replace("EDT", "-0400")
    s = s.Replace("CST", "-0600")
    s = s.Replace("CDT", "-0500")
    s = s.Replace("MST", "-0700")
    s = s.Replace("MDT", "-0600")
    s = s.Replace("PST", "-0800")
    s = s.Replace("PDT", "-0700")
  End If
  Dim d As DateTime
  If DateTime.TryParse(s, d) Then
    Return d
  End If
  Return DateTime.MinValue
End Function
```

9. Add the `ReadFeed()` helper method below the `PublishedDate()` method using the following code:

```
Private Async Function ReadFeed(url As String) As Task(Of
String)
  Dim client As New HttpClient
  Dim cacheControl As New CacheControlHeaderValue With {
    .NoCache = True,
    .NoStore = True
  }
```

```
client.DefaultRequestHeaders.CacheControl = cacheControl
client.MaxResponseContentBufferSize = Integer.MaxValue
Dim response As HttpResponseMessage = Await
client.GetAsync(url)
Dim content As String = Await
response.Content.ReadAsStringAsync()

Dim _posts = From channel In
XElement.Parse(content).Elements("channel")
From item In channel.Elements("item").Take(1)
Let _date = PublishedDate(item)
Order By _date Descending
Select New Post With {
    .Title = CType(channel.Element("title"), String),
    .Link = CType(channel.Element("link"), String),
    .PostTitle = CType(item.Element("title"), String),
    .PostLink = CType(item.Element("link"), String),
    .PostDate = _date
}
Dim post = _posts.First
Posts.Add(post)
Return content
End Function
```

10. It's now time to add some functionality to the button that loads the feeds. Write a handler for the `LoadFeeds` button's click event using the following code:

```
Private Async Sub LoadFeeds_Click(sender As Object, e As
RoutedEventArgs) Handles LoadFeeds.Click
    Dim _stopwatch = Stopwatch.StartNew
    Await Task.WhenAll(From url In feedUrls Select
    ReadFeed(url))
    Dim _timespan As TimeSpan = _stopwatch.Elapsed
    TimeTaken.Text = _timespan.ToString
    PostsListBox.ItemsSource = Posts
End Sub 'End of method
```

11. Compile and run the program. When the UI appears, click on (or press if your machine is touch-enabled) the **Load Feeds** button, wait a few seconds, and you should see the results of your work appear, as in the following screenshot:

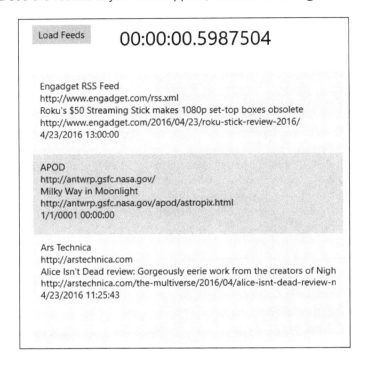

How it works...

In *Step 10*, you added a `LoadFeeds.Click` event handler. The important thing to note about this method is that it is an `async` method, and that `await` is used with the `Task.WhenAll` method. When the application runs and you click on the button, the click event fires the event handler, which in turn starts the background processing that reads the feeds. While the application is waiting for that background process to complete, control is returned to the main application for any other work that needs to be done, ensuring you do not block the application while waiting for the feeds to be retrieved. When the feed retrieval completes, execution returns back to the click event handler, which then updates the UI with the results.

In *Step 9*, the `ReadFeed()` method looks similar to what you used in the console application in the *Making your code asynchronous* recipe; however, you will now see that you are using the `HttpClient` class instead of the `WebClient` class for asynchronous support. The `HttpClient` class also requires different code to set up the cache control values, and you have to specify the response buffer size, otherwise you can get runtime exceptions on long feeds.

Since you are targeting the UWP, it is a good idea to use asynchronous code whenever possible. This makes using the `await` and `async` keywords critical for UWP apps. Without these keywords, developing asynchronous applications that meet UWP design guidelines would be so much harder to do, and probably, more fragile and difficult to debug. These two little keywords will make asynchronous programming much easier.

Using asynchrony with web applications

Internet Information Server (**IIS**) has limits on the number of requests and I/O threads it can use. Blocking any of these threads means IIS is forced to wait until the thread is released before another request can be processed. When there are no threads available to process requests (because of blocking or high-server load), requests start to queue up, and over time, that queue can grow until it reaches its maximum size, at which point the dreaded **503 Service Unavailable** message will be displayed to your site's visitors. This is not a good thing.

Historically, developers may have overlooked the benefits of using an asynchronous design when it came to web application design. This oversight may have been due to mindset, or have been limited by available technology. In any case, the rise of Node.js and similar asynchronous-based technologies demonstrates that this mentality is quickly changing. Most developers want a responsive, scalable web application that can support hundreds, if not thousands, of users, and are willing to consider new approaches if it means better results.

High server load due to a large volume of visitors is not something you can control. What is in your control, however, is your ability to write code that doesn't block threads, and allows IIS to scale and process more requests than would have been possible otherwise. If you want a responsive, scalable web application that supports hundreds or thousands of users per server, you need to make the best use of the hardware you are on, and you must consider the problems that are caused by blocking threads.

Once again, you'll use the feed reader scenario, but for simplicity, you'll just make the network calls to retrieve the RSS feeds and then display the time it took to do so.

Getting ready

Simply start a Premium edition of Visual Studio or Visual Studio Community 2015, and you're ready to go.

How to do it...

We will create an asynchronous web application by taking the following steps:

1. Start a new C# **ASP.NET Web Application**, and then choose the **Web Form** project type. Keep the default project name, or pick one of your own.

2. Right click on the project, select **Add | New Item** (*Ctrl + Shift + A*), and add a new **Web Form** item to the project using the default name of WebForm1.

3. In the newly created WebForm1.aspx file, add Async="true" to the end of the page directive. This tells ASP.NET to allow the page life cycle events prior to the PreRender event to execute asynchronous tasks. This insertion is shown in the following screenshot:

```
WebForm1.aspx  ⊕ ✕
    <%@ Page Language="C#"
        AutoEventWireup="true"
        CodeBehind="WebForm1.aspx.cs"
        Inherits="Ch5_CSharp_ASP_Asynch.WebForm1"
        Async="true"  %>

    <!DOCTYPE html>
```

4. Further down in the page body, add an id attribute to the <div> element and a runat="server" attribute so that you can place the timing results in it when the page executes:

```
<body>
  <form id="form1" runat="server">
    <div id="timeTaken" runat="server" />
    <div>
    </div>
  </form>
</body>
```

5. Now navigate to the WebForm1.aspx.cs code-behind file, and add the following using statements to what is already listed:

```
using System.Diagnostics;
using System.Threading.Tasks;
using System.Net;
using System.Net.Cache;
```

6. In the same file, that is, WebForm1.aspx.cs, add the supporting ReadFeed() method to read a single RSS feed:

```
private async static Task<string> ReadFeed(string url)
{
  var client = new WebClient()
  {
    CachePolicy = new
    RequestCachePolicy(RequestCacheLevel.NoCacheNoStore)
  };
  return await client.DownloadStringTaskAsync(url);
}
```

7. Now that you have the `ReadFeed()` method implemented, you should override the `Page_Init()` method in `WebForm1.aspx.cs` so that it will read all of the feed information during page startup. Because you want the page to load asynchronously, you will need to register a `PageAsyncTask` object. This lets ASP.NET know that you are performing an asynchronous operation, which is important since page life cycle events themselves are not asynchronous, and without them the page would render before your tasks were complete:

```
private TimeSpan duration;

protected void Page_Init(object sender, EventArgs e)
{
  var feedUrls = new List<string>() {
    "http://www.engadget.com/rss.xml",
    "http://apod.nasa.gov/apod.rss",
    "http://arstechnica.com/feed/"
  };

  RegisterAsyncTask(new PageAsyncTask(async (ct) =>
  {
    var stopwatch = Stopwatch.StartNew();
    var feeds = await Task.WhenAll(
      from url in feedUrls select ReadFeed(url));
    foreach (var feed in feeds)
    {
       Debug.WriteLine(feed.Length);
    }
    duration = stopwatch.Elapsed;
    timeTaken.InnerText = duration.ToString();
  }));
}
```

8. Finally, add the `Page_PreRender()` method so that the duration of the entire page life cycle, inclusive of the RSS reading, can be seen in the debug console in Visual Studio:

```
protected void Page_PreRender(object sender, EventArgs e)
{
  Debug.WriteLine("Duration: {0}", duration);
}
```

9. Press *F5* to start debugging the application. After a few seconds, the page load should complete and render a screen similar to the following screenshot:

10. Leaving the web page open, switch back to Visual Studio, which should still be in debug mode. Look at the contents of the **Output** window and the **Debug** messages in particular. As shown in the following screenshot, you should see that the debug message from the `PreRender` event is displayed before the three numbers, which indicate the size of data pulled from the RSS feeds.

   The duration shows as zero, because the `Page_Init` method has been completed, but `PageAsyncTask` that you registered has not yet been executed by the time the `PreRender` method is called.

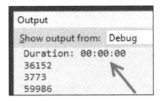

How it works...

It's important to keep in mind that with ASP.NET Web Forms, the page methods are executed synchronously even if you put the `async` keyword on the method declarations. You must use `RegisterAsyncTask`, just as you needed to in the previous versions of .NET.

Because of the `async` keyword, the registering of tasks is now simply a matter of including a lambda in the code. You don't need to follow the old style of asynchronous programming anymore, and you don't have to write any begin and end methods for the framework to call.

You will also notice that the page itself still takes a while to load. The asynchronous approach you used allows the web server as a whole to scale and process more requests concurrently. But this approach doesn't have the ability to make those slow network calls to the RSS feeds any faster, so other methods will have to be used to indicate to your users that something is happening, and that they are waiting for a reason.

There's more...

When it comes to ASP.NET MVC-based applications, things are even easier. Your controller still inherits from the `AsyncController` class, however, instead of having to write method pairs for the beginning and ending of an asynchronous operation, you simply have to create a controller method that returns `Task<T>`.

For example:

```
public async Task<ActionResult> Index()
{
  await LongRunningMethod();
  return View();
}
```

As you can see, this is much better than the way asynchronous controllers worked in previous versions of ASP.NET MVC.

See also

 ▸ The *Making your code asynchronous* recipe at the beginning of this chapter

Working with actors and the TPL Dataflow library

With Visual Studio 2010 and .NET 4.0, we were given the **Task Parallel Library** (**TPL**), which allowed us to process a known set of data or operations over multiple threads using constructs such as the `Parallel.For` loop.

Coinciding with the release of Visual Studio 2012, Microsoft provided the ability to take data that you may have and process it in chunks through a series of steps, where each step can be processed independently of the others. This library is called the **TPL Dataflow Library**.

An interesting thing to note about this library is that it was originally included as part of .NET Framework in the pre-release versions, but the team moved it to a NuGet distribution model so that changes and updates to the package could be made outside of the normal .NET life cycle. A similar approach has been taken with the **Managed Extensibility Framework** (**MEF**) for web and Windows 8.x apps. This change to the distribution model shows a willingness from Microsoft to change their practices so that they can be more responsive to developer needs.

From a terminology perspective, the processing steps are called actors, because they "act" on the data they are presented with, and the series of steps performed are typically referred to as a pipeline.

A fairly common example of this is in image processing where a set of images needs to be converted in some way, such as adding sepia tones, ensuring all images are in portrait mode, or doing facial recognition. Another scenario might be taking streaming data, such as sensor feeds, and processing that to determine the actions to take.

This recipe will show you how the library works. To do this, we will take some keyboard input, and display it back on the screen after having converted it to upper case and Base64 encoding it. If you would like to explore further after completing this recipe, you will find some references to more information listed later in this recipe.

In order to do this, we will use an `ActionBlock` object and a `TransformBlock` object. An `ActionBlock` object is a target block that calls a user-provided delegate when it receives data, while a `TransformBlock` object can be both a source and a target. In this recipe, you will use a `TransformBlock` object to convert characters to upper case, and encode them before passing them to an `ActionBlock` object to display them on screen.

Getting ready

Simply start a Premium of edition VS2015 or use Visual Studio Community 2015, and you're ready to go.

How to do it...

Create a Dataflow-powered application using the following steps:

1. Create a new application targeting .NET Framework 4.5 by navigating to **Visual C# | Console Application** and name it `DataFlow`.

2. Using NuGet, add the TPL Dataflow Library to the project. The package name to use for installation when using the **Package Manager Console** is `Microsoft.Tpl. Dataflow`; otherwise, search for TPL on the **Manage NuGet Packages for Solution** dialog. (Refer to the *Managing packages with NuGet* recipe in *Chapter 3, Web Development*, if you need a refresher on how to do this.)

3. Open `Program.cs`, and at the top of the file, add the following `using` statements:

```
using System.Threading;
using System.Threading.Tasks;
using System.Threading.Tasks.Dataflow;
```

4. In the `Main()` method of `Program.cs`, add the following code to define `ActionBlock`. The method in the `ActionBlock` object displays a string on the console and has a `Sleep` method call in it to simulate long-running work. This gives you a way to slow down processing, and force data to be queued between steps in the pipeline:

```
var slowDisplay = new ActionBlock<string>(async s =>
```

```
  {
    await Task.Run(() => Thread.Sleep(1000));
    Console.WriteLine(s);
  }
  new ExecutionDataflowBlockOptions {
  MaxDegreeOfParallelism = 4 }
);
```

5. In the `Main()` method again, continue by adding the code for `TransformBlock`. The `TransformBlock` object will take a `char` as input, and return an upper case Base64-encoded string. The `TransformBlock` object is also linked to the `ActionBlock` object to create a two-step pipeline.

```
var transformer = new TransformBlock<char, string>(c =>
{
  var upper = c.ToString().ToUpperInvariant();
  var bytes = ASCIIEncoding.ASCII.GetBytes(upper);
  var output = Convert.ToBase64String(bytes);
  return output;
});
transformer.LinkTo(slowDisplay);
```

6. Now add code to take input from the console, and pass it to the first step of the pipeline (the `TransformBlock` object in this case). You also need to close and flush the pipeline when you hit *Enter* so that you can exit the program:

```
while (true)
{
  var key = Console.ReadKey();
  if (key.Key == ConsoleKey.Enter)
  {
    transformer.Complete();
    Console.WriteLine("waiting for the queue to flush");
    transformer.Completion.Wait();
    slowDisplay.Complete();
    slowDisplay.Completion.Wait();
    Console.WriteLine("press any key");
    Console.ReadKey();
    break;
  }
  transformer.Post(key.KeyChar);
}
```

7. Run the program. When the console window appears, just randomly press characters, and hit *Enter* when you are done. You should see an output similar to the following screenshot. How the encoded strings appear (typically batches of 1-4) will depend on the number of CPU cores in your machine:

```
zikoshzhj893498shfvWg==
Tw==
waiting for the queue to flush
Uw==
Sw==
SA==
SQ==
SA==
Sg==
OA==
Wg==
Mw==
OQ==
OQ==
NA==
OA==
Uw==
SA==
Rg==
Vg==
press any key
```

How it works...

Let's look at what just happened. First, you defined two actors, the first being the `ActionBlock` object that takes a string and displays it on screen, and the second, the `TransformBlock` object, which takes a character as input and returns an encoded string as output. You then linked the `TransformBlock` object to the `ActionBlock` object to create the pipeline for the data to flow through.

Next, you took data that was streaming to you (the console key presses), and passed each key press to the pipeline as soon as it arrived. This continued until the user hit *Enter*, at which point the `Complete()` method is used to tell the actors that they should expect no more data. Once the queues have been flushed, the user is prompted to hit a key to close the program. (If you don't flush the queues, you will lose the data that is still in them when the program completes—never a good thing.)

 You can watch the queue flushing process by entering a bunch of characters, and then immediately pressing *Enter*. Depending on the speed of your machine, you will see the **waiting for the queue to flush** message scroll past followed by the remaining characters.

Now when you ran the program, the `TransformBlock` object did its work very quickly and passed its output to the `ActionBlock`. The interesting thing to note is that even though the data was queuing up to be processed by the `ActionBlock` object, the amount of code you had to write to do that was zero. The TPL Dataflow Library takes care of all the difficult plumbing code, thread management, and the communication of data between actors as well as determining how many actors it can run at once.

There's more...

You may also be wondering what happens in less straightforward scenarios, such as when you want to conditionally pass data or messages to the next actor. Fortunately, the TPL Dataflow Library is quite powerful, and this recipe is just an introduction to what it offers. For example, the `LinkTo()` method has a predicate parameter that you can use to filter the messages and decide which actors should do what.

You could also batch data for processing in the later steps by adding data to a buffer using the `BufferBlock` object and only passing buffered data to subsequent pipeline steps when the buffer is full. There are lots of possibilities, so feel free to go and explore what the library has to offer.

The eagle-eyed among you may also have noticed that the lambda function used by the `ActionBlock` object featured the `async` keyword. This was done so that the action block doesn't itself block execution of the program when performing the long-running task and prevent any more input from being processed.

See also

▶ For more information about TPL, visit `http://msdn.microsoft.com/en-us/library/dd460717(v=vs.110).aspx`

▶ For more information on Dataflow, visit `http://msdn.microsoft.com/en-us/library/hh228603(v=vs.110).aspx`

▶ The *Making your code asynchronous* recipe

▶ The *Debugging parallel coded with IntelliTrace* recipe in *Chapter 5, Debugging Your .NET Applications*

7

Unwrapping C++ Development

In this chapter, we will cover the following topics:

- ▶ Using XAML with C++
- ▶ Unit testing C++ applications
- ▶ Analyzing your C++ code
- ▶ Using a custom ruleset
- ▶ Edit and Continue C++ style
- ▶ Working with DirectX in Visual Studio 2015
- ▶ Creating a shader using DGSL
- ▶ Creating and displaying a 3D model
- ▶ Using the Visual Studio Graphics Diagnostics

Introduction

Before the rise of .NET, Java, and newer languages, C++ occupied a dominant position as the go-to choice for development of Windows applications. As the 21st century progressed, the use and popularity of these other languages grew, while C++ seemed to suffer somewhat without a vocal champion. This led to C++ becoming more of a specialist language to the point where it is now commonly seen as the language for writing operating systems, device drivers, game engines, and similar applications where speed is of the essence.

In recent years, this decline has somewhat moderated due to a renewed push in C++ support by Microsoft as well as renewed interest by developers who find that so called **bare metal** programming may provide better performance for applications running on portable devices. Microsoft has contributed to this resurgence by increasing Visual Studio's C++ standards compliance and improving the C++ toolset. VS2013 began this trend by including several components of the C++11 language standard and some long-requested pieces of the C99 standard.

Now with the arrival of VS2015, Microsoft is continuing these advances with the introduction of C++ concepts from the C++14 and C++17 language standards. The result is that C++ development is now easier and more efficient than with the previous editions of Visual Studio.

This chapter will cover a variety of areas to show how VS2015 can make your C++ development more productive. We will start by looking at XAML, spend some time on some useful diagnostic tools, and then conclude with a look at some DirectX-based features.

 As you may be aware, Microsoft has increased the pace of the updates it makes to Visual Studio. The most obvious of these are the usual quarterly "Update X for Visual Studio". But there can also be smaller specific updates such as **KB3151378** available at https://msdn. microsoft.com/en-us/library/mt695655.aspx. So stay informed, and keep your system patched.

Using XAML with C++

User interface development with C++ for Windows applications can be a challenging experience. When Visual Basic first appeared all those years ago, developers flocked to it, in part, because building a user interface in it was so much more productive than building the equivalent UI using C++ at that time, and C++ has never really caught up since.

Over recent years, with Microsoft moving away from WinForms, and the rise of declarative interface design with XAML, building a flexible yet powerful user interface has never been easier. The functionality offered by XAML based UI technologies is impressive, with data binding, in particular, being a genuine productivity enhancement.

Meanwhile, C++ developers have been left further and further behind, with the mainstream interface development typically found in the work being done by game studios and some in-house Microsoft product teams. Starting with VS2012, the power and flexibility of the XAML based user interface design is now available for C++ developers, making C++ a legitimate choice for business applications.

C++ can use XAML only when creating **Universal Windows Platform (UWP)** applications. You cannot use this combination together to create traditional Windows desktop applications.

It's not just business applications that benefit though. Developers of DirectX applications can use XAML to render interface elements, compositing them with their application's DirectX output. For game developers, this might be things such as application menus, score displays, and so on. Alternatively, you can have XAML-based applications interspersed with portions of DirectX code in them, allowing developers of applications with a need for 3D imaging, such as medical or geospatial systems, to mix and match DirectX and XAML as required.

The choice and flexibility is up to you. For this recipe, you'll create a simple XAML-based interface with data binding to see how it all fits together.

Getting ready

Ensure that you are on a Windows 10 machine. UWP app development is not supported on prior versions of Windows.

Start a premium version of VS2015 or use VS2015 Community, and you will be ready to go.

 As noted elsewhere, keep your copy of Visual Studio current, and be sure the latest updates are applied. For this recipe, ensure you have applied Update 2 or newer.

How to do it...

Create the app by following these steps:

1. Create a new **Blank App (Universal Windows)** project by navigating to **Visual C++ | Windows | Universal**, and name it `CppDataBinding`.

 For this recipe, the project name is important, as it is referenced below in the sample code. If you pick a different name, be sure to update the code accordingly!

2. Open the `MainPage.xaml` file, and add the following code inside the `<Grid>` element:

```
<Border BorderBrush="LightBlue" BorderThickness="4"
CornerRadius="20" Margin="5">
  <StackPanel Margin="5">
    <TextBlock Text="Red level" Margin="5" />
```

```
      <Slider x:Name="redLevelSlider" Minimum="0"
        Maximum="255" Value="{Binding Path=RedValue,
        Mode=TwoWay}"
        Margin="5" Width="255" HorizontalAlignment="Left" />
      <TextBlock Text="Numeric value:" Margin="5"/>
      <TextBox x:Name="tbValueConverterDataBound"
        Text="{Binding Path=RedValue, Mode=TwoWay}"
        Margin="5" Width="150" HorizontalAlignment="Left"/>
    </StackPanel>
  </Border>
```

3. For the data binding to work, you will need an object to bind to. Add a new header file to your project, and call it `MyColor.h`. The header can be added by right-clicking on your project name, selecting **Add | New Item** from the context menu, and then choosing **Header File**. Be sure to hold off compiling the code until you get to *Step 9*, as compiling before that will result in compiler errors.

4. Enter the following code as the content of the `MyColor.h` source file:

```cpp
#pragma once
#include "pch.h"
using namespace Platform;
using namespace Windows::UI::Xaml::Data;
namespace CppDataBinding
{
  [Bindable]
  public ref class MyColor sealed : INotifyPropertyChanged
  {
    public:
    MyColor(void);
    virtual ~MyColor(void);
    virtual event PropertyChangedEventHandler^
    PropertyChanged;
    property String^ RedValue
    {
      String^ get() { return _redValue; }
      void set(String^ value)
      {
        _redValue = value;
        RaisePropertyChanged("RedValue");
      }
    }
    protected:
    void RaisePropertyChanged(String^ name);
    private:
    String^ _redValue;
  };
}
```

5. Next, we will need to add a new C++ file named `MyColor.cpp`. Similar to the header file, right-click on the project, and select **Add | New Item**—only this time, choose **C++ File**. Once it has been created, enter the following code as its content:

```
#include "pch.h"
#include "MyColor.h"
using namespace CppDataBinding;
using namespace Windows::UI::Xaml::Data;
MyColor::MyColor(void) {}
MyColor::~MyColor(void) {}
void MyColor::RaisePropertyChanged(String^ name)
{
    PropertyChanged(this, ref new
    PropertyChangedEventArgs(name));
}
```

6. Now go to the `MainPage.xaml.h` file, and add the `MyColor.h` file to the `#include` list.

7. While in the `MainPage.xaml.h` file, go to the public members of the `MainPage` class, and add the following line of code that is highlighted:

```
public:
    MainPage();
    property MyColor^ _myColor;
```

8. Next, navigate to the code-behind file for the `MainPage` class (`MainPage.xaml.cpp`), and add the following highlighted lines of code to the constructor:

```
MainPage::MainPage()
{
    InitializeComponent();
    _myColor = ref new MyColor();
    this->DataContext = _myColor;
}
```

9. Compile and run the application. You should see a screen similar to the following screenshot. As you enter values in the text field or move the slider, the two fields should remain in sync, as shown in the following screenshot:

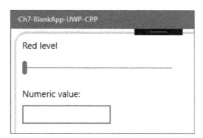

How it works...

The C++ code you have been writing is C++/CX, an extension of normal C++. You can still use normal C++ (without extensions) if you prefer, but it will mean dealing with the `IInspectable` interface and writing more COM code than would otherwise be the case.

The `ref` keyword you used for creating an instance of the `MyColor` class tells the compiler that you are using a Windows runtime object. The carat (^) symbol on variable declarations is a reference counting smart pointer to a Windows runtime object. It is similar to a normal pointer, but performs reference counting and automatic cleanup of resources when the last reference is cleared.

Data binding in C++ kicks into action when you insert the `[Bindable]` attribute into a class. When the compiler sees this, it automatically generates code in a file called `xamltypeinfo.g.cpp`, which implements the appropriate binding behaviors for interacting with the XAML markup.

In your code, you implemented the `INotifyPropertyChanged` interface. This was done so that you could use the two-way binding between the data class and the UI elements on the screen. The implementation of the interface should look familiar to anyone who has worked with the `INotifyPropertyChanged` interface in either WPF or Silverlight.

If you were compiling the code after each step of the recipe, you may have seen a few compiler errors, some of which might have not made much sense.

If you compiled the application after *Step 5*, you may have seen a number of errors in the `XamlTypeInfo.g.cpp` file.

This occurs because of the way the compiler handles the `[Bindable]` attribute and the generation of the code. The generated code not only includes the `.h` files from the XAML pages in the application, but also includes generated code for any types that are bindable. This means that if you have a bindable type, but no references to it in any of the `.xaml.h` files, you will have undeclared identifier errors. Adding the `#include` statement for the bindable class' header file as you did in *Step 6* fixes this compiler error.

There's more...

Microsoft continues to add functionality to the XAML toolset, and with Update 2, there are some additional tools available to us when the project is compiled in **Debug** mode beyond the frame rate counters.

The following screenshot shows the expanded XAML toolbar:

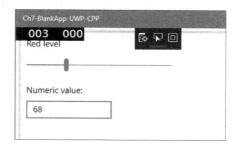

The toolbar provides three different functions (from left to right): **Go to Live Visual Tree**, **Enable selection**, and **Display layout adorners**. The first opens a new dialog in Visual Studio that lists the hierarchical relationship of the XAML controls present in your app, and provides a two-way connection between this dialog window and the control(s) on your application. From the application side, you can click on a particular control and locate it within the hierarchy, or you can pick an element from the hierarchy and see it highlighted in your application.

Enable selection is a toggle that lets you highlight and select various XAML elements for inspection. Finally, **Display layout adorners** is a toggle that will show the various borders of the XAML elements, as shown in the following screenshot:

These tools provide another way to examine your application's appearance, and to troubleshoot any layout issues you may be experiencing.

Unit testing C++ applications

Previously, we saw the .NET-based _Unit testing .NET applications_ recipe in _Chapter 4, .NET Framework Development_, but C++ developers have not been forgotten, and VS2015 includes built-in support for unit testing with **CppUnit**.

C++ developers can choose from several types of unit test projects, including the **Native Unit Test Project**, the **Managed Unit Test Project**, and the **Unit Test App (Universal Windows)** project. The first applies exclusively to desktop C++ development, the second applies exclusively to managed (C++/CX) code, and the third is for UWP-based apps.

In this recipe, we'll create a simple piece of code, and add some unit tests to it, which take advantage of the **Native Unit Test Project**.

Getting ready

Simply start VS2015 (Community or a Premium version), and you're ready to go. You can do this in any version of modern Windows, since you're going to be creating a **Native Unit Test Project**.

How to do it...

To unit test your code, perform the following steps:

1. Create a new **Native Unit Test Project** by navigating to **Visual C++ | Test** and accepting the default project name.

2. In the **Solution Explorer** window, right-click on the project, and select **Class Wizard...** from the menu to create a new class.

3. Click on the **Add Class...** button in the dialog box to add a new class to the project. Use the class name `BankVault`, and click on the **Finish** button as shown in the following screenshot:

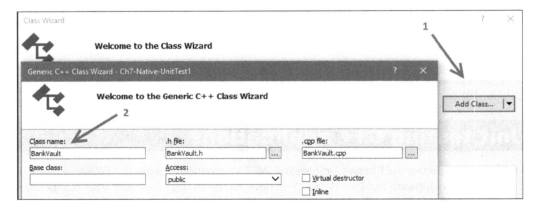

4. The **Class Wizard** will update its context to the newly-added `BankVault` class. Click on the **Methods** tab, and then click on the **Add Method...** button within that tab.

5. In the **Add Member Function Wizard**, set **Function name** to `AddFunds`, and add a **Parameter name** as `amount` of type `int` (yes, this bank vault only accepts whole units of currency). Be sure to click on the **Add** button to add the parameter, which is shown in the following screenshot:

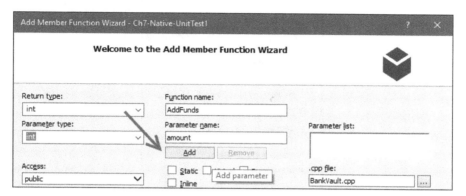

6. Click on **Finish** in the **Add Member Function Wizard**, and then click on **OK** in the **Class Wizard** window.

7. Open the `unittest1.cpp` file under the `Source Files` folder from **Solution Explorer**, and at the top of the file, add a #include statement for the `BankVault.h` file:

```
#include "BankVault.h"
```

8. Update the body of the `TestMethod1` method as follows:

```
TEST_METHOD(TestMethod1)
{
  // TODO: Your test code here
  auto vault = new BankVault();
  auto totalFunds = vault->AddFunds(100);
  Assert::AreEqual(100, totalFunds);
}
```

9. From the Visual Studio menu, select **Test | Run | All Tests** (or press *Ctrl + R, A*).

10. The code will compile. The **Test Explorer** screen will then appear and show the results of running the test, as shown in the following screenshot:

If you are using Visual Studio Enterprise, **Test Explorer** can be configured to automatically run after each build. To do this, select **Test | Test Settings | Run Tests After Build** so that the unit tests runs automatically each time the solution is built.

11. Switch back to the `BankVault.cpp` file, and navigate to the line after the `BankVault` destructor. Add the following code, as shown:

```cpp
int total = 0;
int BankVault::AddFunds(int amount)
{
  total += amount;
  return total;
}
```

12. Once again, select **Test | Run | All Tests** (or press *Ctrl + R, A*). As soon as the build completes, the test results will be executed, and the **Test Explorer** window should refresh to show the results of the unit test. Assuming you made the correct changes, the code should now look like the following screenshot:

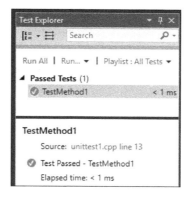

13. Let's continue to examine what **Test Explorer** can do by adding a few more methods. In the `BankVault.h` file, add the following lines of code that are highlighted:

```
class BankVault
{
  public:
  BankVault();
  ~BankVault();
  int AddFunds(int amount);
  void StageHeist();
  int CurrentFunds();
};
```

14. In the `BankVault.cpp` file, add the implementation for the two methods as follows:

```
void BankVault::StageHeist()
{
  total = 0;
}
int BankVault::CurrentFunds()
{
  return total;
}
```

15. Now, add another test to the `unittest1.cpp` file just after the `TestMethod1` parameter for these new methods by adding the following code:

```
TEST_METHOD(RobTheBank)
{
  auto vault = new BankVault();
  auto totalFunds = vault->AddFunds(200);
  Assert::AreEqual(200, totalFunds);
  vault->StageHeist();
  totalFunds = vault->CurrentFunds();
  Assert::AreEqual(0, totalFunds);
}
```

16. Compile the solution, and wait for **Test Explorer** to rerun the tests. You should now see one failing test result and one passing result, as shown in the following screenshot:

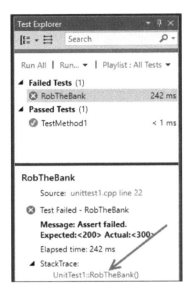

17. There's a small mistake in your code (originally inserted for illustrative purposes), and clicking on the first line of the stack trace in the error detail (indicated by the arrow in the preceding screenshot) should help you isolate the problem (the initial funds aren't as expected). Let's begin to fix the problem by first navigating to the `BankVault.h` file and adding a private `int` variable named `total`:

```cpp
class BankVault
{
  public:
  BankVault();
  ~BankVault();
  int AddFunds(int amount);
  void StageHeist();
  int CurrentFunds();
  private:
  int total;
};
```

18. In the `BankVault.cpp` file, remove the `int total = 0;` declaration, and change the class constructor to initialize `total` to zero.

19. Compile the code one last time, and rerun the unit tests. **Test Explorer** will show all tests working as expected.

How it works...

The test project you created already includes a reference to the CppUnit test framework as well as the necessary header files to define the various Assert methods available and the macros for creating the test methods.

You could build all of this by hand, but there's really no need to do so when the project template has defined it for you up front.

> When writing UWP apps, do make use of the specific **Unit Test App** project type to ensure that the proper references are available and have been configured correctly.

There's more...

For those using Visual Studio Enterprise, there is an option to run unit tests with code coverage within **Test Explorer**; however, for unit test library projects of a UWP app, you will not get any results as the diagnostic data adapters are not supported for unit tests of UWP app libraries.

Coverage information is only supported for native unit test projects, and the results of the analysis will be displayed in the **Code Coverage Results** window.

Debugging unit tests

In the .NET languages, you can right-click inside a test method in the code window and select the option to run and debug a unit test. This isn't available for C++ unit tests.

To debug C++ unit tests, you must select them from **Test Explorer**, and either right-click on them and choose the **Debug Selected Tests** context menu option, or select **Test | Debug | Selected Tests** from the Visual Studio menu.

See also

▶ The *Unit testing .NET applications* recipe in *Chapter 4, .NET Framework Development*

Analyzing your C++ code

Static analysis of C++ code is a feature offered in VS2015 Community and the Premium editions of Visual Studio. Static analysis is a useful way to locate potential problems in your code, and provides a way to catch a wide range of problems early in the development cycle.

In this recipe, we will show you how to use Visual Studio's built-in static analysis tools.

Getting ready

Start Visual Studio, and create a new project using the **Empty Project** template under **Visual C++**, giving it a name of your choice.

How to do it...

For this project, perform the following steps:

1. Right-click on the project, and select **Properties**.

2. Navigate to **Configuration Properties | General**, change **Configuration Type** to **Static Library (.lib)**, and click on **OK**.

3. Add a new **Header File** to the project, and name it `AnalyzeThis.h`.

4. Enter the following code in the body of the header file:

```
class AnalyzeThis {
  public:
  int LookHere(int param);
};
```

5. Add a new **C++ File** to the project, and name it `AnalyzeThis.cpp`.

6. Enter the following code to the body of the file:

```
# include "AnalyzeThis.h"
int AnalyzeThis::LookHere(int param)
{
  int x;
  int y;
  if (param > 0) x = param;
  if (param < 0) y = param;
  return x + y;
}
```

7. Compile the project. There should be no errors or warnings.

8. Right-click on the project and select **Properties** again. Select the **Code Analysis** group and ensure that **Enable Code Analysis on Build** is checked. Click on **OK** to close the window.

9. Right-click on the solution in the **Solution Explorer** window and select **Analysis | Run Code Analysis on Solution** (*Alt + F11*). This option is also available in the menu by navigating to **Build | Run Code Analysis on Solution**.

10. The **Code Analysis** results will be displayed, and it will show a single warning about the use of uninitialized memory, as shown in the following screenshot:

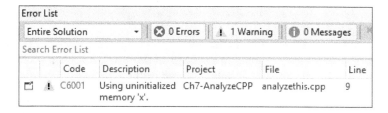

11. Double-click on the entry to receive more details. The reasons for the analysis warning will be shown, and the code where the warning occurs will be highlighted, as shown in the following screenshot:

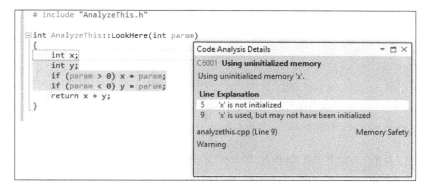

12. To address these details, change the code in the `LookHere` method so that both `x` and `y` are initialized correctly with zero values.

13. Rerun the analysis. No messages should be displayed.

How it works...

Visual Studio ships with a set of predefined rules to examine your project for common mistakes and poorly written code. In our example, the code may have compiled cleanly, but it could cause problems in operation, as the `x` and `y` variables are not initialized. Static code analysis seeks to find these types of mistakes earlier in the development cycle rather than waiting and hoping for them to be caught later by unit tests or the QA department.

There's more...

Selecting Active ruleset

The ruleset used by the analyzer can be modified to suit your preferences. The **Rule Set** setting, which can be accessed by going to **Settings** in the **Code Analysis** window, offers several choices based on the level of details required or the type of application being developed, as shown in the following screenshot:

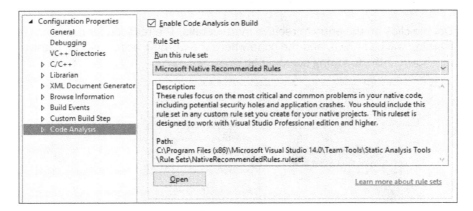

Improving C++ source navigation speed

Update 2 has added a new SQLite-based system that is designed to speed up source code navigation tools including **Go To Definition** and **Find All References**. To make sure it is enabled for your project, open the **Options** menu, then navigate to **Text Editor | C/C++ | Advanced**, and ensure the **Enable New Database Engine** option is set to **True**, as shown in the following screenshot:

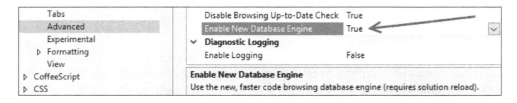

See also

▶ The *Using a custom ruleset* recipe

Using a custom ruleset

The built-in rulesets that come with Visual Studio cover a variety of usage scenarios, and provide a way to use the **Code Analysis** tool in your projects immediately. They are also of great value when exploring an unfamiliar code base, as you can take advantage of the static analysis tools to identify areas where code should be rewritten to meet your in-house standards. All this means that the existing default rules may need to be customized depending on the needs and complexity of your project as this recipe will demonstrate.

Getting ready

We are going to continue with the project we created in the *Analyzing your C++ code* recipe. You will need VS2015 Community or higher in order to modify rulesets.

How to do it...

To use a custom ruleset, perform the following steps:

1. Open the project created in the previous recipe.

2. Open the `AnalyzeThis.cpp` file, and add the following highlighted code:

   ```
   # include "AnalyzeThis.h"
   int x = 0;
   ```

3. Right-click on the project (not solution) in **Solution Explorer** and select **Properties**. Then navigate to the **Code Analysis** section.

4. As shown in the following screenshot, the **Microsoft Native Recommended Rules** are highlighted by default. You may use this or select another. There is also the option to select multiple rulesets. For our purposes, take the default, and click on **Open**.

By convention, rulesets have the `.ruleset` extension, and are stored at the following location:

`C:\Program Files (x86)\Microsoft Visual Studio 14.0\`
`Team Tools\Static Analysis Tools\Rule Sets.`

5. The ruleset editor will open. Go to `Microsoft.VC.AmbiguousIntent` or enter `C6244` in the search box. The rule we will enable is **C6244: Local declaration hides global**, which is shown in the following screenshot:

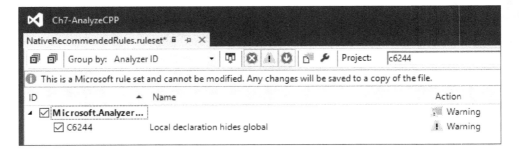

6. After enabling the rule, save it by pressing *Ctrl* + *S*. Since the base Microsoft rulesets are read-only, the changes will be saved in a new file based on your project name and made a part of the project. If desired, you can rename this by right-clicking on it in the **Solution Explorer**, and selecting **Rename**.

7. Verify that your new rules are being used by right-clicking on the project, choosing **Properties**, and selecting your newly created ruleset under **Configuration Properties | Code Analysis | General** (the same process as in *Step 3*).

8. Rebuild the solution (*Ctrl* + *Shift* + *B*), and then rerun the code analyzer (*Alt* + *F11*). With our new rule activated, our second variable's declaration was detected, as shown in the following screenshot:

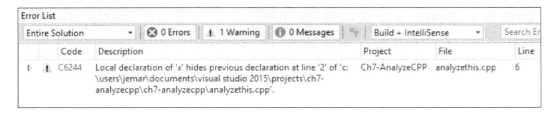

How it works...

This preceding recipe shows how existing rulesets can be combined and/or modified to suit the needs of your project. If you are inheriting a legacy code base, this analysis can provide a great starting point for where improvements can be made. The customization allows you to focus on items of a particular importance or, just as easily, minimize the clutter from rules that don't concern you. If you are starting a new project, you may opt for a rigorous approach so that best practices are followed from the start. Finally, having the ability to save these changes into an external file allows them to be stored with a project so that all developers can follow the same practices.

 You may have noticed that in the screenshot for *Step 4*, the dialog box indicates that VS2015 Professional or higher is required—but don't worry, they work just fine on VS2015 Community.

There's more...

There are two rulesets provided for native code in VS2015:

- The **Microsoft Native Minimum Rules** ruleset contains rules for basic correctness, such as potential security holes and application crashes (invalid memory access, buffer overruns, and so on)
- The **Microsoft Native Recommended Rules** ruleset is a superset of the minimum rules, and provides a more in-depth set of rules to evaluate, and also includes rule checks for lock problems, race conditions, and other concurrency-related issues

To get an understanding of the rules that each ruleset uses, go to the project's properties, and select the **Code Analysis** settings. Clicking on the **Open** button will display the rules that are enabled for the ruleset. In order to see all available rules, click on the red down arrow in the toolbar. For Microsoft's official definitions of all available rulesets, consult *Code analysis rule set reference* at `http://msdn.microsoft.com/en-us/library/dd264925.aspx`.

Edit and Continue C++ style

As demonstrated in *Chapter 5, Debugging Your .NET Application*, C# and Visual Basic support the **Edit and Continue** (**EnC**) functionality under Visual Studio. While users of those languages have had a pleasant experience, the situation has been a little bit different for C++ users. VS2013 had EnC for C++, although it had some restrictions that limited its usefulness. Fortunately, the EnC support for C++ code is much improved in VS2015. Microsoft has updated the component that provides debugging services, which combined with some other modernization ensures that EnC is supported for both 32-bit and 64-bit C++ code. The end result is that now C++ programmers can use this ability to save time while debugging their programs.

For best results, be sure that your copy of VS2015 has applied Update 2 or newer.

Getting ready

Simply start VS2015 Community or one of the premium editions, and you're ready to go.

How to do it...

To observe **Edit and Continue** in action, take the following steps:

1. Create a new **Win32 Console Application** under **Visual C++ | Win32 Console Application** with the default name.

2. If the **Win32 Application Wizard** appears, accept the default settings by clicking on **Finish**.

3. Next, ensure that **Edit and Continue** has been enabled for your project. Under the **Debug** menu, select **Options**.

4. Select **Debugging | General,** and make sure that **Enable Native Edit and Continue** is checked, as shown in the following screenshot:

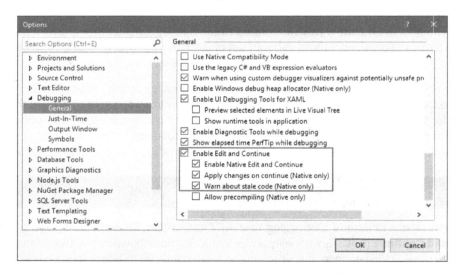

5. After clicking on **OK** to close the **Options** dialog box, return to your open C++ file.

Microsoft ultimately plans to make Enable/Disable Native Edit and Continue support as a single option, so the multiple options shown here could be removed in a future update.

6. Change the target to **x64**, as shown in the following screenshot:

7. Start with the following code:

```cpp
#include <iostream>
using namespace std;
int main()
{
    int x = 2;
    int y = 16;
    cout << "Computed answer: " << (x*y) << endl;
    cout << "Processing... " << endl;
    cout << "Computed answer 2: " << (x*y) << endl;
    return 0;
}
```

8. Add a breakpoint to the `Processing...` and `return 0` lines, as shown in the following screenshot:

```cpp
    cout << "Computed answer: " << (x*y) << endl;
    cout << "Processing... " << endl;

    cout << "Computed answer 2: " << (x*y) << endl;

    return 0;
}
```

9. Start debugging. The program will be compiled, and will stop at the first breakpoint; the output will display **Computed answer: 32**.

10. While the debugger remains stopped at the first breakpoint, add a new line `y=8;`, before the last `cout` statement, as shown in the following screenshot:

```cpp
    cout << "Computed answer: " << (x*y) << endl;
    cout << "Processing... " << endl;
    y = 8;
    cout << "Computed answer 2: " << (x*y) << endl;

    return 0;
}
```

11. Click on **Continue** (or press *F5*) to move to the next breakpoint. As soon as you do this, you may notice (depending on the speed of your computer) the **Edit and Continue** informational dialog appear as your new statement is included in the executable. This is shown in the following screenshot:

12. After the recompile, the second output of the program will display **16** rather than **32**.

How it works...

VS2015 uses additional compiler options and an improved debugger to provide us with the ability to modify C++ code while debugging it. This saves debugging time, because a complete project recompilation is not required, as is the case when EnC is not enabled. EnC is available on UWP apps and those using DirectX, removing some restrictions that previously limited its usefulness.

Ultimately, the usefulness of this feature depends on the size of your codebase. In the sample shown here, the presence of EnC is negligible, because the file is only a few lines long. In a more realistically sized code base, EnC will be much more useful, as it will reduce the amount of time spent waiting for dozens or hundreds of files to recompile.

Working with DirectX in Visual Studio 2015

C++ and DirectX are being promoted by Microsoft as the primary way to build high-performance games in Windows 10.

 Developers looking for the spiritual (if not outright) successor to the popular XNA Framework are encouraged to check out *MonoGame*, an open source implementation of XNA at http://www.monogame.net/.

As a DirectX developer, you will be pleased to know that there is no longer a separate DirectX download required for Windows 10. The DirectX SDK is now incorporated into the Windows SDK, and the DirectX runtime is built into the Windows 10 operating system. For older versions of Windows, the current requirement to download a separate SDK and runtime remains in place.

Windows 10 includes two major versions of DirectX—DirectX 11.x representing the latest evolution of a higher-level API, and the new DirectX 12, which is a lower-level API providing much greater control in an effort to provide greater performance. When designing a project, you will have to choose the one that best fits the goals of your project. A project based around reusing an existing DirectX code could probably stick to the DirectX 11 series, while one being created from scratch may take advantage of DirectX 12's focus on greater performance.

If you have used previous versions of DirectX and C++, then you will find VS2015 somewhat different, as you will be using C++/CX. Many of the DirectX calls have differences in them, not only due to the use of `ref` pointers but also in the way displays are referenced, and restrictions are enforced by the UWP app sandbox. It will most likely require some tweaking to the approaches you may have used in the past.

For this recipe, we'll use the default application template to display a rotating cube on the screen, and then alter the code to stop and start the rotation when we touch the screen, click the mouse, or press a key.

Getting ready

Start VS2015 with update on Windows 10, and you're ready to go. You will need to use VS2015 Community or one of the premium editions, as we are creating a UWP app.

How to do it...

Create the app by performing the following steps:

1. Create a new **DirectX App** project by navigating to **Visual C++ | Windows | DirectX 11 App (Universal Windows)**, and name it `RotatingCube`.

2. The default project template includes all the code to display a cube, apply shaders to it, and then rotate it. Before you go any further, ensure that the application works by compiling and running it. You should see a screen similar to the following screenshot:

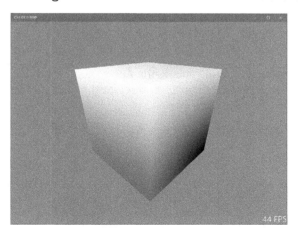

3. Stop the application by pressing *Alt + F4*, and then switch back to Visual Studio. In the `App.h` file, add the following code block to the protected event handler declarations:

```
void OnPointerReleased(Windows::UI::Core::CoreWindow^
sender, Windows::UI::Core::PointerEventArgs^ args);
void OnKeyDown(Windows::UI::Core::CoreWindow^ sender,
Windows::UI::Core::KeyEventArgs^ args);
```

4. To the private variables in that same header file, add the `bool m_isRotating;` statement.

5. In the `RotatingCubeMain.cpp` file, locate the `RotatingCubeMain` method. Add the following highlighted code to register the event handlers for the user input events and to set the `m_isRotating` flag:

```
// Start receiving touch/mouse events and keyboard events
window->PointerReleased +=
ref new TypedEventHandler<CoreWindow^,
PointerEventArgs^>(this, &App::OnPointerReleased);
window->KeyDown +=
ref new TypedEventHandler<CoreWindow^,
KeyEventArgs^>(this, &App::OnKeyDown);
m_isRotating = true;
```

6. Now add the following code for the event handlers at the end of the `App.cpp` file. The handlers simply toggle the `m_isRotating` flag to indicate whether to rotate the cube or not:

```
void App::OnPointerReleased(Windows::UI::Core::CoreWindow^
sender, Windows::UI::Core::PointerEventArgs^ args)
{
  m_isRotating = !m_isRotating;
}
void App::OnKeyDown(Windows::UI::Core::CoreWindow^ sender,
Windows::UI::Core::KeyEventArgs^ args)
{
  m_isRotating = !m_isRotating;
}
```

7. While still in the `App.cpp` file, locate the `App::Run()` method, and wrap the `m_main->Update();` call in an `if` statement that checks the `m_isRotating` flag, as shown in the following code snippet:

```
if (m_isRotating) {
  m_main->Update();
}
```

8. Run the application, and notice that you can start and stop the rotation by pressing any key, clicking with the mouse, or tapping on the screen.

9. Stop the application when you have finished testing.

10. The colors on the cube are determined by a combination of a vertex shader and a pixel shader. The vertex shader uses the color assigned to each vertex in the cube's definition, in the `Sample3DSceneRenderer::CreateDeviceDependentReso urces()` method. Each pixel shader is shaded based on blending the colors of the vertices nearest to it. Open the `SamplePixelShader.hlsl` file in the project's `Content` folder to look at the pixel shader.

11. At the moment, the shader simply takes the color passed to it, and sets the alpha channel to `1.0f`, making it opaque. Alter the shader to remove all traces of red from the cube by changing the body of the `main()` method to the following code snippet:

```
float4 main(PixelShaderInput input) : SV_TARGET
{
  float3 removedRed;
  removedRed = float3(0.0f, input.color.g, input.color.b);
  return float4(removedRed, 1.0f);
}
```

12. Rebuild and run the application. The cube should now look similar to the following screenshot, with no red color visible:

How it works...

The key areas to focus on in this application involve creating the drawing surface and the handling of the user input. You saw how the user input can be handled via the event listeners, and that the `PointerEventArgs` class is used for both touch- and mouse-based input.

Most of the work done while creating the rendering surface is encapsulated in the `Direct3DBase` class (`DeviceResources`). It is in here that the call to the `D3D11CreateDevice` method is made as is the call to the `CreateSwapChainForCore Window` method, which is needed in order to get DirectX up and running correctly.

It is also useful to note that an application manifest is included in the project, and that the linker has prepopulated references to the required DirectX libraries so that you don't have to remember to add them yourself.

There's more...

The pixel and vertex shaders used in the application are written using **High-Level Shading Language** (**HLSL**), a C++ style **Domain Specific Language** (**DSL**) for describing how the color should be calculated for each rendered pixel in an object.

When the compiler sees an HLSL file, it compiles it into a `.cso` file that you can then use in your application. You can see this in the `Sample3DSceneRenderer::CreateDeviceDepe ndentResources()` method where the `.cso` files of the two shaders are read into memory, and then passed to the DirectX calls to create shader instances. The shaders are then used later in the `Sample3DSceneRenderer::Render()` method, with the vertex shader being called before the pixel shader to ensure that the cube renders correctly.

Is managed DirectX supported?

Microsoft's suggested approach is to use C++ with DirectX 11 or 12 on Windows 10, and this recipe shows one way to do that. But this isn't the only way, and third-party libraries exist that enable using DirectX with a managed language such as C#. If you are interested in accessing DirectX in this fashion, you may want to keep an eye on open source projects such as **SharpDX** (`http://sharpdx.org/`).

Just keep in mind that this approach is not supported by Microsoft, and that DirectX applications written in .NET will run a little slower than native C++ applications; but in many cases, the benefits of using C# outweigh these concerns. In any event, applications built using third-party libraries should still be able to pass the verification process, and be listed in the store.

See also

- ▸ The *Creating a UWP app* recipe in *Chapter 2, Getting Started with Universal Windows Platform Apps*
- ▸ The *Creating a shader using DGSL* recipe
- ▸ The *Using the Visual Studio Graphics Diagnostics* recipe

Creating a shader using DGSL

Starting with Visual Studio 2012, Microsoft has added a new mechanism for building shaders using a language called **Directed Graph Shader Language** (**DGSL**). This language can be used to create very complex shaders that are still easily understandable at a high level, and are thus more maintainable than shaders written in pure HLSL.

In this recipe, we'll create a shader that applies a texture to an object and colors it.

Getting ready

Ensure that you are running Windows 10, and start either VS2015 Community or one of the premium versions.

How to do it...

Create a shader by performing the following steps:

1. Create a new **DirectX 12 App (Universal Windows)** project by navigating to **Visual C++ | Windows**, and give it a name of your choice.
2. Right-click on the project, select **Add | New Item**, and then choose **Graphics | Visual Shader Graph (.dgsl)**. Leave the name as the default one, Shader.dgsl, and click on **Add**.

3. The shader will be added to the project, and the design surface will be displayed. Open the toolbox (located on the left-hand side of the screen, or use *Ctrl + Alt + X*) to see all the nodes that can be used in your shader. Click on the black background of the design surface to see the properties of the shader. In the following screenshot, the **Toolbox** is marked on the left (first (**1**) arrow), and the **Properties** window is marked on the right (second (**2**) arrow):

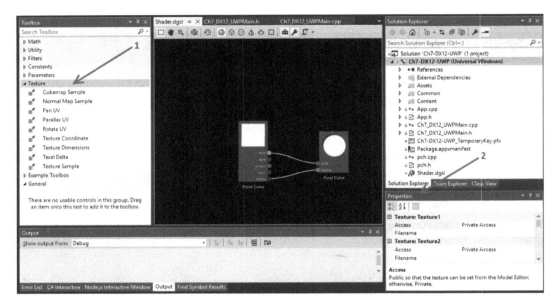

4. From the **Toolbox** window, drag a **Texture Sample** node onto the design surface.

 If you have trouble finding the **Texture Sample** node in the **Toolbox**, use the search box at the top of the **Toolbox** to filter the items displayed.

5. In the properties for the **Texture Sample** node you just added, set the **Filename** property to the full path (not relative path) of the `StoreLogo.png` file in the `Assets` folder. You can do this fairly easily by selecting the image file in **Solution Explorer**, copying the full path from the **Properties** window for the file, and then pasting that value into the **Filename** property of the **Texture Sample** node.

6. Drag a **Texture Coordinate** node from the **Toolbox** window onto the design surface.

7. On the side of each of the shader nodes are connectors, the small circles that represent the input and output variables for each node. Drag the **Output** connector of the **Texture Coordinate** node to the **UV** input connector of the **Texture Sample** node to link the two nodes together, as shown in the following screenshot:

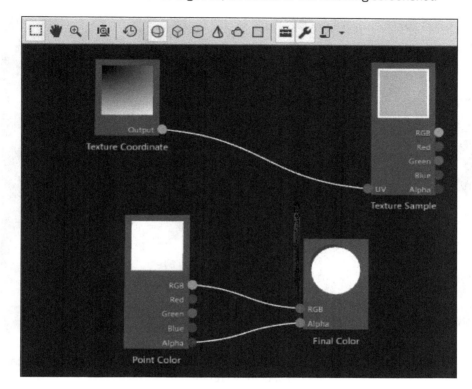

8. Next, you should color the texture based on the color of the point at which it will be applied. To do this, drag a **Multiply** node (found under **Math**) onto the designer, and connect the **RGB** output of both the **Point Color** and **Texture Sample** nodes to the **X** and **Y** inputs of the **Multiply** node.

9. Then, drag the output of the **Multiply** node to the **RGB** input of the **Final Color** node. In doing so, the **RGB** link from the **Point Color** node to the **Final Color** node will be removed, as inputs can only have one source; this is shown in the following screenshot:

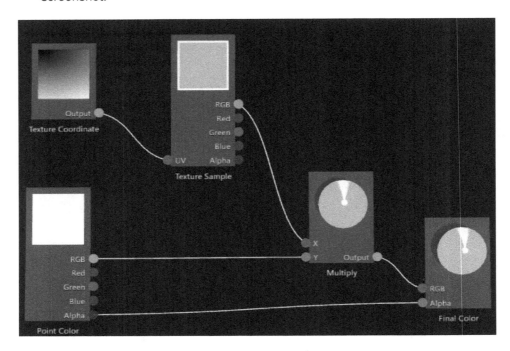

10. In the document toolbar, click on the **Preview with teapot.** button so that we can see the results using the classic object in 3D rendering demos:

11. In the shader designer, select the **Final Color** node, and then hold down the *Ctrl* key while you move the mouse scroll wheel forward to zoom in on the element until you can zoom no further. You will now see a better 3D representation of what the shader will do to a model, as shown in the following screenshot:

12. If you want to rotate the object itself, press and hold *Alt* and then click and drag on the teapot to rotate it.

 We used `StoreLogo.png` only because it is guaranteed to be available on all systems. Feel free to use a graphic file of your own choice for a more interesting display.

13. Save the `Shader.dgml` file by pressing *Ctrl + S*.

14. On the left side of the designer toolbar, click on the Advanced icon. It will display a menu where you can choose to export the shader as **HLSL**, a **compiled pixel shader (.cso)**, or a **C++ header file (.h)**. Select the **HLSL** file option, and save the shader into your `Documents` folder. The following screenshot shows where the **Export As...** command is located:

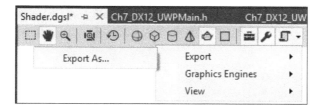

15. From the Visual Studio menu, select **File | Open | File** or press *Ctrl + O,* and then open the file you just saved. You can now see the HLSL version of the shader you created.

How it works...

Shaders are, effectively, a pipeline of instructions that affect the rendering of an object on the screen. They can be applied to vertices, pixels, and geometries to produce varying effects. The key to all shaders is to try and do as few operations as possible, since the higher the number of nodes in a shader, the more computationally expensive they will be, and the slower your overall frame rate in the application.

In this particular recipe, the shader we built was fairly rudimentary, since the intent was to show how a shader can be built in Visual Studio. For complex shaders such as flame or smoke, there are parameter nodes for **Time** and **Normalized Time** that you may want to use. For geometry shaders, you can consider using nodes such as **World Position** and **Mask Vector**.

See also

> ▸   The *Creating and displaying a 3D model* recipe

> ▸   The *Working with DirectX in Visual Studio 2015* recipe

Creating and displaying a 3D model

In the previous *Creating a shader using DGSL* recipe, you created a shader that applies a texture to a predefined model. However, most applications will need more variety than the default models offered. Fortunately, Visual Studio provides a mechanism for creating your own 3D models.

Visual Studio offers a fairly basic 3D modeling tool, and while it's nowhere near as fully featured as **Maya** or other specialist modeling tools, it does come in the box, and it meets the needs of the homebrew developer, or those simply wanting to rough in some models or tweak some properties of a model supplied by a designer.

Getting ready

This recipe uses the shader from the previous *Creating a shader using DGSL* recipe. So, if you haven't already completed that, go ahead and do so now. If you have already completed it, then open up the solution you created, as you're ready to get started.

How to do it...

Create a 3D model using the following steps:

1.   Right-click on the project, and select **Add | New Item**.

2.   In the dialog box, choose **Graphics | 3D Scene (.fbx)**, and leave the name as `Scene.fbx` before clicking on **Add**.

3. Visual Studio will open the scene editor where you can create your model. Ensure that the **Toolbox** and **Properties** panes are visible, and then add a cylinder to the scene by double-clicking on the **Cylinder** node in the **Toolbox** window.

4. Select the cylinder in the designer by clicking on it. In the scene editor toolbar on the left-side of the design surface, click on the Scale icon. The cylinder will be overlaid with **x**, **y**, and **z** drag handles (the red, green, and blue boxes) that you can use to resize the object in any single direction, and a central drag handle (a white box) for scaling the object evenly in all directions. Resize the cylinder to make it larger by clicking on the central white handle and dragging it to the right, as shown in the following screenshot:

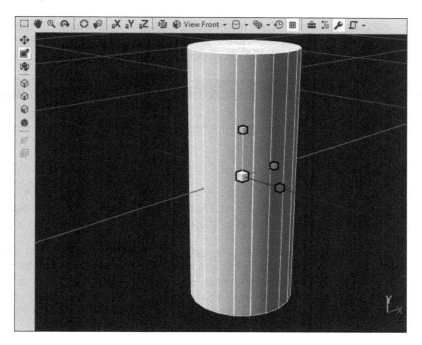

5. In the **Properties** window, locate the **Effect** property:

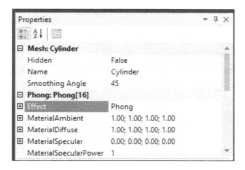

6. Click on the plus next to the **Effect** property to expand its details, as shown in the preceding screenshot. Now click on the ellipsis (**...**) on the **Filename** property to open the file selection dialog box.

7. Browse to the `Shader.dgsl` file you created in the previous recipe, and click on **OK**.

8. Change the value of the **Name** property in the shader's property group to `MyShader`.

9. In some cases, the change will not take place immediately, but it will refresh the next time the **Properties** window is asked to display properties for the cylinder. You can force this by clicking on a file in **Solution Explorer**, and then clicking on the cylinder again. You should also see that the scene has been updated to show the effects of the shader on the cylinder.

10. A common way of looking at 3D models is to look at the wireframe. To view the scene in wireframe mode, click on the wireframe icon on the main toolbar (not the embedded toolbar). It's the last icon in the list, as shown in the following screenshot:

How it works...

At this point, you now have a model that is ready to be used. As mentioned in the introduction, the modeling tool is not meant to compete with full-featured 3D modeling tools, and is, instead, offered only as an entry-level modeling toolkit.

Given that the packaging of models is typically application-specific, Visual Studio provides neither an inbuilt method for packing models into a data file nor a method to load them. The choice of how you package models depends on your application, its performance characteristics, and any of the restrictions you have to work within. Because of that diversity, Visual Studio provides a single, simple method for editing a model, and for everything else, it's up to you.

There's more...

There are many more features available in the model viewer than were covered in this recipe. Most of these features are self-explanatory, and deal with the basics of moving and rotating objects within the scene, changing selection modes, and changing view modes. Advanced functionality such as merging objects is contained under the **Advanced** menu on the left side of the designer's toolbar.

See also

▸ The *Creating a shader using DGSL* recipe

Using the Visual Studio Graphics Diagnostics

One of the hard things to do in DirectX applications is to determine the cause of a visual glitch or bug on the screen. Despite the best efforts of developers to avoid bugs, there are many websites featuring screenshots taken by gamers of weird things happening in a game.

Visual Studio addresses some of the debugging issues for DirectX applications by including a new **Graphics Diagnostics** toolset that lets you look at pixel history to determine just how a specific pixel came to be rendered on the screen. Let's see how it works.

Getting ready

Simply start VS2015 Community or one of the premium editions on Windows 10, and you're ready to go.

[Unlike VS2013, a paid version is no longer required to use the Graphics Diagnostics toolset.]

How to do it...

For this recipe, perform the following steps:

1. Create a new **DirectX 12 App (Universal Windows)** project by navigating to **Visual C++ | Windows**, and leave the default name as it is.

2. The project template includes code to display a spinning cube, so build the application to ensure it compiles.

3. Start the diagnostics by pressing *Alt + F5* or by choosing **Debug | Graphics | Start Diagnostics** from the Visual Studio menu.

4. When the application starts, you should see the debugger's HUD displayed in the top-left corner of the application.

5. While the application is running, press Print Screen (*PrtSc*) a few times to capture some frames from the application. The debugger HUD should update to display the captured frame indicating the capture was successful.

6. Stop debugging when you are ready (by closing the app or using the stop button in Visual Studio), and you should see something similar to the following screenshot:

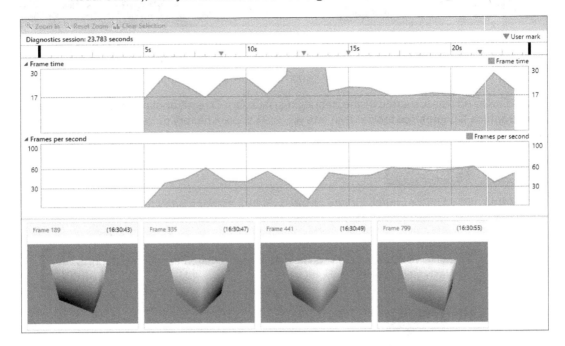

7. Select one of the frames you captured from the Frame List window, and in the frame view, click on one of the pixels in the cube. If you can't see the entire frame, you can hold *Ctrl* and drag with the left mouse button to pan around the frame. (In our previous screenshot, this would be **Frame 189**, **Frame 335**, and so on.)

8. After selecting a frame, the **Visual Studio Graphics Analyzer** window should appear. Your screen will then resemble the following screenshot:

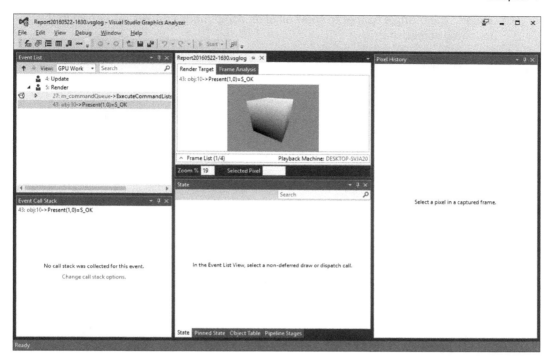

9. In the center **Render Target** window, click on a pixel for your cube. The history for that pixel will then be displayed, as shown in the following screenshot:

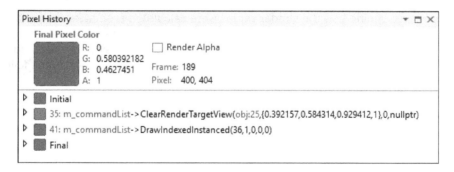

10. In the preceding screenshot, this selected pixel was initially green, then blue, and then returned to green. Your color will most likely be different. Click on the expansion arrow for the event when the color changes to expand it.

11. Expand the triangle further to show all of its component's details, as shown in the following screenshot:

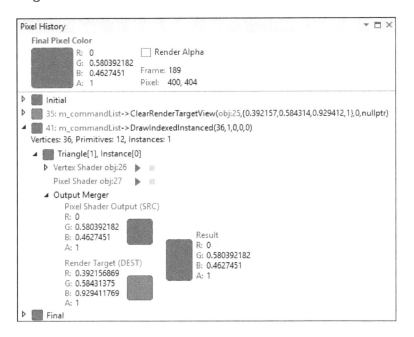

12. Clicking either on the **Vertex Shader** or **Pixel Shader** links will take you to the HLSL source for the shader so that you can see the shader calculation.

13. You can examine how the shader values were calculated even after normal debugging has concluded. Click on the debug icon (the play button) for one of the vertices in the **Vertex Shader** link or for the **Pixel Shader** link to debug it using the captured values. Step through the shader code until the debugger finishes, as shown in the following screenshot:

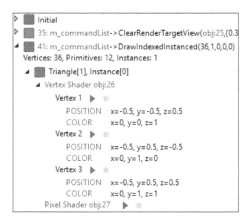

14. You can click on one of the triangles (shown in the previous screenshot) to jump directly to the code responsible for that shader. One window shows the HLSL source, while the second pane shows the output from the HLSL compiler, as shown in the following screenshot:

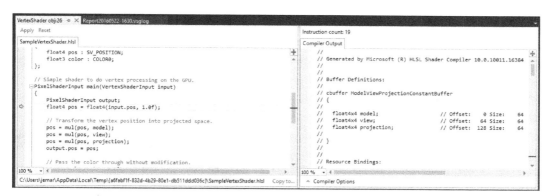

How it works...

The Graphics Diagnostics toolset featured in VS2015 has seen several improvements over the previous versions. Moving the tools from a minor overlay to a separate mini application window allows you to see more information at once, and really focus on examining how graphics are being rendered in your application. The level of detail presented by these tools is extensive, and should help you track down the root cause of many of your rendering problems.

There's more...

One thing that wasn't touched on in the recipe was the rendering pipeline. If you want to look at the way a frame was built up, then understanding how the object meshes were used can be very useful.

If you select a DirectX Draw event from the **Events List** window and then select **Pipeline Stages** from the menu, you will see how the frame was put together. Clicking on one of the stages in the Graphics **Pipeline Stages** window will show you the details of that stage in a document preview tab, as shown in the following screenshot:

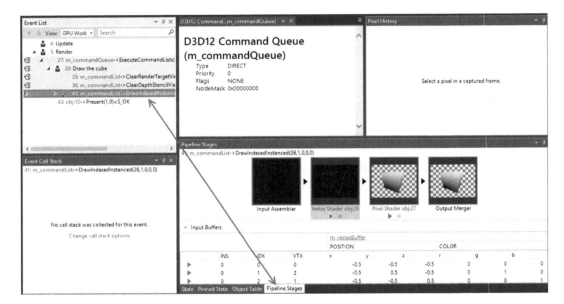

8

Working with Team
Foundation Server 2015

In this chapter, we will cover the following topics:

- ▶ Creating a new TFS project
- ▶ Managing your work
- ▶ Using local workspaces for source control
- ▶ Performing code reviews
- ▶ Getting feedback from your users
- ▶ Using Git for source control
- ▶ Taking Advantage of Git's command line

Introduction

Team Foundation Server (**TFS**) is a popular companion for users of Visual Studio, which provides Microsoft's approach to source control and project management. Developers working in traditional corporate software development will frequently use TFS as a way to coordinate their activity with that of product owners, quality assurance, and release engineers.

TFS is a separate product from VS2015, and exists in both paid and free (TFS Express) versions. The primary difference between the two is that TFS Express is designed for smaller developer teams and thus supports five users, while the full version has no such restrictions. Day to day usage will typically involve connecting to TFS from within Visual Studio or through the TFS web browser interface.

A couple of years ago when VS2013 launched, Microsoft created **Visual Studio Online (VSO)**. This has since been renamed as **Visual Studio Team Services (VSTS)**. VSTS can best be thought of as the cloud-based, hosted version of TFS. It provides developers with an area to create and store their projects without having to also take on the task of administrating a server. VSTS is also free for up to five users just like TFS Express.

 Those who have a subscription to Visual Studio Professional or Enterprise can join any number of VSTS projects as a benefit of their subscription.

When deciding on what type of TFS to use, you should first consider the benefits (if any) provided by your copy of Visual Studio as well as the type of environment you will be a part of. For example, larger corporations typically have an existing source code repository and build system that you will utilize. Smaller teams or individual developers will be able to set up something new.

Beyond TFS, there is also the option to use a Git based repository from within Visual Studio. Providers such as GitHub make it easy to have a cloud-based Git instance, and using Git with TFS is also an option. Finally, as Git is an open source, freely available tool, it is also possible to run a private Git server.

The key takeaway is that using a source code repository system is an important part of modern software development, and should be used regardless of the size of your development team. Since the focus of this book is on Visual Studio, this chapter will look at how to utilize these various systems from within Visual Studio to promote good practices and improve your workflow. The recipes in this chapter will walk you through using these new improvements and features, so let's get started.

 Just what is source control anyway? For those readers who are unfamiliar with source control, read on. Source control is a way to manage the changes made to source code files. (It may also be called version control). Since most development files are text, it is relatively easy for software tools to track changes between files, who made the changes, optional user-entered notes, and when the changes were made. Rather than keep track of this by hand, these software tools assist in automating the process. As a developer, you can still work with familiar filenames like `Program.cs` or `HelperClass.cs`, but to the tool, the changes are tracked as distinct versions. This allows you to compare the current file to its history, and if you make an unworkable change on the current copy, replace it with something from the source control's archive. Two of the more common tools for source code management, TFS and Git, are discussed in this chapter.

Creating a new TFS project

As this book focuses on VS2015 and not TFS administration, we are going to use VSTS to host a new development project that we can then connect to via any version of VS2015. Using VSTS will let us focus on project setup while Microsoft can handle the server administration and configuration. The concepts for creating a new project are similar whether you are using VSTS or standalone TFS. Since, in many cases, corporate users merely access a previously configured TFS environment, this example will let all readers follow along to focus on the bits that are pertinent to Visual Studio.

Getting ready

You will need a Microsoft account ID, and you can either create a new ID for this chapter, or use one of your existing IDs. You will also need a copy of VS2015 available. We will be using Visual Studio Community, but the concepts are applicable across all versions.

How to do it...

Perform the following steps:

1. Connect to VSO (http://www.visualstudio.com/), and create a VSO account. (If you already have a Microsoft account, you will be adding VSO capabilities.)

2. The account URL is something you will be using as the access point to your projects, so pick something meaningful—or, at least something you won't mind reading everyday. (Your URL will ultimately have a form similar to https://teamname.visualstudio.com.)

Multiple projects can be housed at the same URL, so you may want to avoid using a name that is project-specific.

3. After account creation, you can enter the details for a new project. Enter **Project name** of your choice. For the purposes of the recipe, select **Team Foundation Version Control**, and select **Agile** as your **Process template**; then click on **Create project**, as shown in the following screenshot:

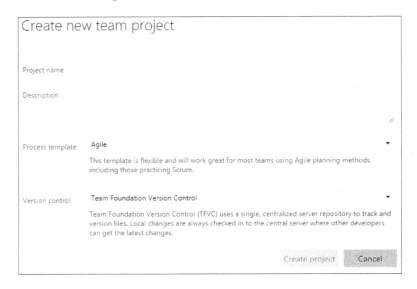

4. Once created, you will be able to connect to this project with Visual Studio. For easy access, you can have VSTS open your local copy of Visual Studio (2013 or newer) directly via the link on the lower-right side of the project page as shown in the following screenshot. However, for this recipe, we will continue by showing how to connect to a TFS/VSTS project from within Visual Studio.

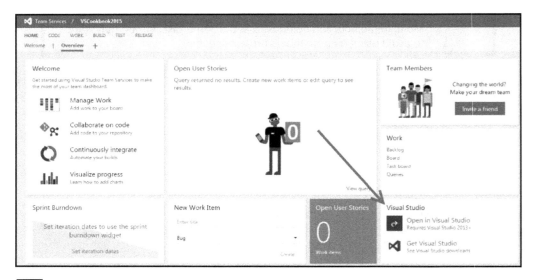

5. Open your copy of VS2015. The **Team Explorer** window should be on the right, but if it is not, you can open it through **View | Team Explorer** or *Ctrl + \\, Ctrl + M*. Once visible, click on Manage Connections, as shown in the following screenshot:

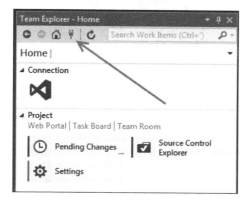

6. In the next screenshot, you will see that the **Team Explorer** window title has changed to **Connect**. As you will see, there is an ad-like prompt recommending **Visual Studio Team Services** and another option to **Manage Connections**. Click on **Manage Connections** (**1**) and then on the **Connect to Team Project** (**2**) menu option, as that will work for both VSTS and TFS connection types.

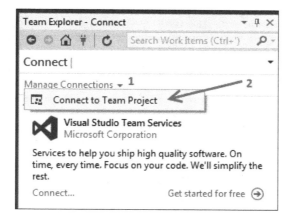

7. After completing *Step 6*, a new dialog box will appear, listing the available Team Foundation Servers and the Collections available from each server. The **Servers...** button allows you to add or remove the servers displayed. For our recipe, select the name of the Team Project you created in *Step 3*, and then click on **Connect**.

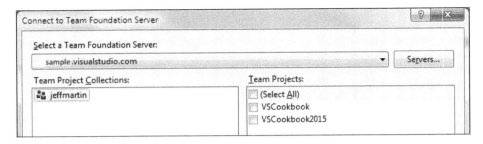

8. After making a Team Project selection, **Team Explorer** will update. Double-click on the name of your Team Project (in our example, it would be VSCookbook2015), and then you will receive a prompt to configure your workspace if it is a brand new TFS project, as is the case with our example. Click on **Configure your workspace**, as shown in the following screenshot:

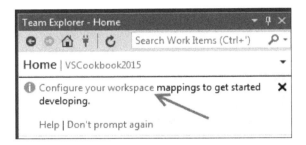

9. The **Configure Workspace** dialog area will then open. To complete the process, click on the **Map & Get** button, as shown in the following screenshot:

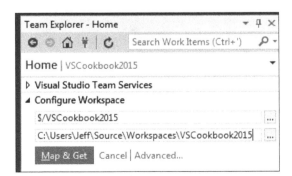

10. To add an existing solution or create a new one, you can either click **New...** or **Open...**, as shown in the following screenshot:

11. Let's continue by assuming you want to add a brand new solution. Click on **New...**, which will open Visual Studio's **New Project** window. For the purposes of this recipe, you can pick whatever project type you want, but the point is to make sure you select the **Add to Source Control** option before clicking **OK**, as shown in the following screenshot:

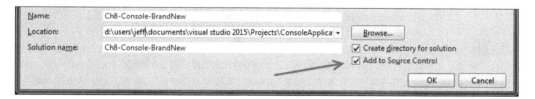

12. Visual Studio will then prompt you to determine where the solution should be stored. Typically, the defaults will suffice, but if you have reason to change them, you can do so now. We will continue with the defaults, as shown in the following screenshot:

13. At this point, your new solution is associated with your VSTS project, but it has yet to be committed. This means that, while version control information has been defined, none of your source files have been uploaded to the server, so nothing is actually protected yet. To commit your changes, click on the **Pending Changes** tile, as shown in the following screenshot:

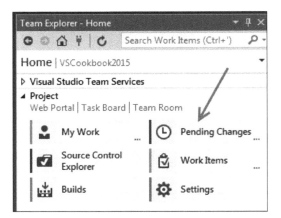

Clicking on the icon of the House at the top of the **Team Explorer** toolbar will always return you to the home page, where you can find the main functional areas such as **Settings** or **Pending Changes**.

14. On the **Pending Changes** screen, we are shown several key pieces of information. First, there is a **Check In** button (marked by **1** in the following screenshot), which will actually send our changes to the VSTS or TFS server associated with our project. Next, there is a field to enter comments that describe what has been done (marked by **2**). It is always a good idea to leave a brief, but informative, description of what has been changed and why so that both you and other developers can understand why the changes were made. Finally, the last section (marked by **3**) indicates the files that will be included with this check-in. You should review this list to ensure you have not modified something that you did not intend to.

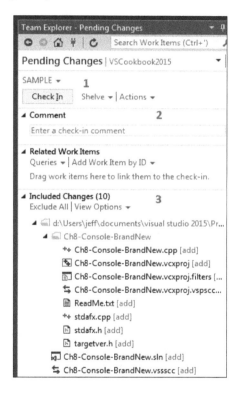

15. For the purposes of this recipe, enter a brief comment, and then click on **Check In**.

16. At this point, your project and its accompanying new files have been checked in, and are considered committed. This means they are safely stored on the VSTS server, and should something happen to your local computer, you will be able to retrieve a copy of your work. It is also at this point that fellow developers on your project could retrieve a copy of your changes.

17. To confirm the check-in was successful, you can open up your instance of VSTS and refresh to see the newly added files, as shown in the following screenshot:

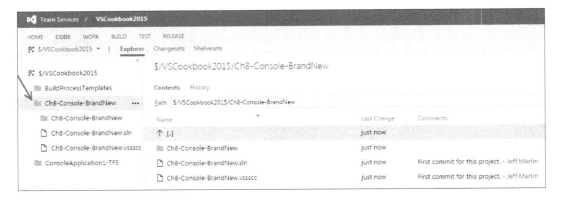

How it works...

VSTS provides all of the functionality of standalone TFS, but with the added benefit that the details of server management are handled by Microsoft. In our example, a new site and Team Project were created to hold your project's source code and work items. By using version control, you will benefit from the ability to track changes to your source code and simplify maintenance. Working with other developers on a common project is easier, as everyone involved can always obtain the most current version of the source code from a centralized location that doesn't require e-mailing zip files around. Better still, the details of your project are not going to be lost if your local developer machine crashes.

There's more...

Going back to *Step 10*, let's assume you have an existing project to add versus creating a new one as shown earlier. In this case, when you click on **Open,** you will be prompted to select an existing project on your local system. Choose the Visual Studio solution and/or project you wish to add. This may require you to reauthenticate with VSTS, so enter your Microsoft ID if prompted.

Once your existing solution has been opened, right-click on it in **Solution Explorer** and select **Add Solution to Source Control...**, as shown in the following screenshot:

⚙	Set StartUp Projects...
🗄	Add Solution to Source Control...

This will produce a dialog similar to the one in *Step 12*, and you can follow the remaining steps of the recipe to check-in and view the changes.

See also

▸ The *Using Git for source control* recipe in this chapter

Managing your work

Whether you work in a team or as an independent developer, the odds are good that you will have a lengthy list of requirements describing what you need to build. Scrum teams use product backlogs, traditional teams use functional specifications, and other teams will have their own variations of these. Even as an independent developer, you probably maintain, at minimum, a to-do list of features to add and bugs to fix. Using TFS, this information can be stored in the team project.

TFS provides several different ways you can classify your outstanding tasks, which are called **work items**, and include bug, feature, issue, task, and several more. As you may expect, these let you indicate the type of item being described. A minor bug (say incorrect font sizing) may be passed over in favor of a new feature to implement or a more serious bug (application keeps crashing).

You may recall that in the *Creating a new TFS project* recipe, you were able to select a **Process template** while creating a new team project (note that a **Process template** may also just be called **Process**.) The template choice indicates the type of work items that are provided.

Processes available and the work items provided:

▸ **Scrum**: Epic, feature, product backlog item, task, bug, and impediment

▸ **Agile**: Epic, feature, user story, task, bug, and issue

▸ **Capability Maturity Model Integration** (**CMMI**): Epic, feature, requirement, task, bug, change request, issue, and review

In this recipe, we'll show you how to manage your work using VS2015 and TFS.

Getting ready

You will need to have access to a TFS project like the sample one created in the *Creating a new TFS project* recipe, or another that you have access to.

The recipe also requires that your team project be based on the **Agile** process template. If your project uses a different process template, the work item types may be different from those in the recipe, but the concepts remain the same.

Once you have identified the connection to TFS or VSTS that you will be using, start your copy of VS2015, and you're ready to go.

How to do it...

Perform the following steps:

1. When you first connect to TFS, you will need to set up the connection if you have not already done so. From the Visual Studio menu, navigate to **Team | Manage Connections...**. Then click on **Manage Connections** within **Team Explorer** to connect to TFS. If your server is not already available in the drop-down menu (do note that the default can be blank), use the **Servers...** button in the connection dialog to add a new connection for the TFS. Then connect to the project collection and the specific team project you wish to use for this recipe.

 If the **Team Explorer** tool window isn't visible, open it by navigating to **View | Team Explorer** from the menu by pressing *Ctrl + \, Ctrl + M*, or by using the **Quick Launch** tool.

2. To ensure you are connected to TFS, navigate to the **Home** hub, and confirm that it is displaying the correct team project name, as shown in the following screenshot:

In the preceding screenshot, **1** marks the TFS project name, **2** marks both the project name and its corresponding URL, and **3** marks the location of any solutions for this project. Your **Home** hub may look slightly different if your team project has a team portal, or reporting is enabled.

3. This recipe needs some work for you to track, so start out by creating a new work item. Click on the **Work Items** entry in **Team Explorer** to navigate to the **Work Items** hub.

4. Click on the **New Work Item** drop-down menu from the **Work Items** hub, and click on **User Story** from the list, as shown in the following screenshot:

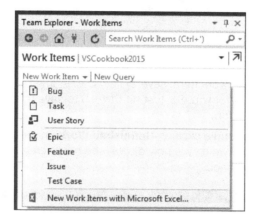

5. A new **Work Item** form will be displayed in the Visual Studio document area. Enter a title of your choice, and set the **Assigned To** user to yourself. You can set the value of any of the other fields as you wish, and when you are ready, click on the **Save Work Item** button in the form's toolbar, or press *Ctrl + S* to save the work item.

6. Right-click on the background of the **Product Backlog Item** form (that is, right-click on the white space), and select the **New Linked Work Item...** option (*Shift + Alt + L*).

7. In **Work Item Type**, select **Task** from the list, and enter a **Title** for the item before clicking on **OK**, as shown in the following screenshot:

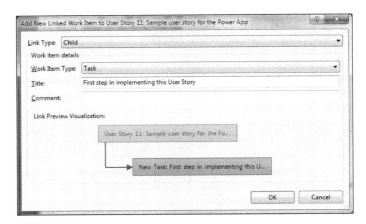

8. Since this is a linked work item, several fields, including the **Assigned To** field, will automatically be set for you. So, just hit *Ctrl* + *S* to save the work item, or click on the **Save Work Item** button.

9. In **Team Explorer**, double click on **Unfinished Work** under **Queries | Shared Queries | Product Planning**, which will now display the newly created work item, as shown in the following screenshot:

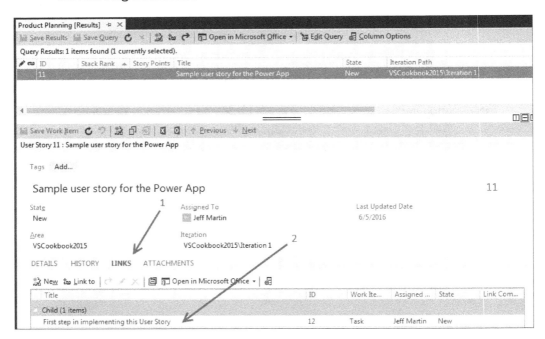

In this screenshot, the User Story we created in *Step 5* has been selected and is displayed. Within that User Story, we clicked on the **LINKS** tab (marked by **1**) to show the linked Task created in *Step 7* (marked by the **2**).

10. To start work, click on Task that you created in *Step 7*. Then, change the state to **Active**, and click on **Save Work Item**, as shown in the following screenshot:

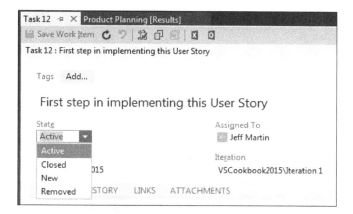

Something to remember about states under TFS

 Depending on the configuration, states are typically changed in sequence. That means, a newly created item cannot always be changed directly to **Closed**. Saving a work item after each state change will usually allow you to advance the choices for available states.

11. If you look at **Shared Queries | Current Iteration | Active Tasks query**, this task will now show as the result.

12. Open up one of the solutions you have previously checked in to TFS. (If using the Team Project from the first recipe in this chapter, the solution was titled `Ch8-Console-BrandNew`.) Solutions can be accessed from the **Home** hub under the **Solutions** heading.

13. Modify one of the files in the solution; for this example, a comment was added to `Ch8-Console-BrandNew.cpp`. (For this recipe, the exact changes made aren't important, just that the file has been modified.)

14. Navigate to **Pending Changes** by clicking on the House icon on the **Team Explorer** tab and clicking on the **Pending Changes** tile. (Also available under **View | Other Windows | Pending Changes**.)

15. To include this task with your commit, you can either drag it onto **Team Explorer**, or you add it by **ID** (both methods are highlighted in the following screenshot).

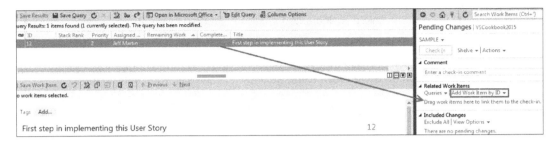

 If actual source code changes were made, these would be included by Visual Studio under the **Included Changes** heading. If they were missed for some reason, you could manually add them in the same fashion as this work item.

16. Once a work item and changed source file(s) are associated, you will be able to enter a **Comment** and click on **Check In**, as shown in the following screenshot:

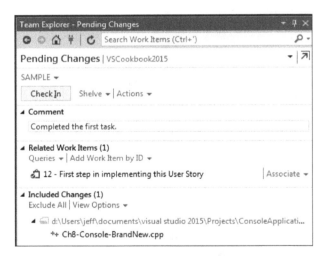

17. Visual Studio may prompt you when you click on **Check In**, and if it does, just click on **Yes**, as shown in this screenshot:

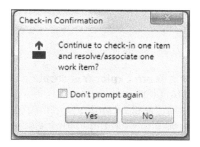

18. After making the check-in, Visual Studio will provide a message indicating the results, as shown in the next screenshot:

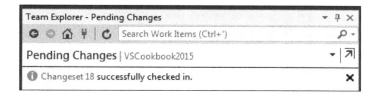

19. The changeset text is a link, and if clicked, it will show you the details of what was just checked in.

How it works...

The **Team Explorer** window provides an overview of the common tasks available for working with projects stored in TFS (regardless of if it is locally hosted, or part of VSTS). **Pending Changes** keeps track of outstanding modifications made since the last commit was made. **Work Items** keeps track of the work items available in TFS, with those marked In Progress appearing in the Work in Progress query.

You can check the details of a query by selecting the query, right-clicking on it, and selecting **Edit Query**. The task category doesn't have to be limited to just the **Task** work item type, but can also incorporate any custom work item types you include in the task category.

If you double-click on a work item in **Team Explorer** that isn't already open, it is opened, by default, in the preview pane in Visual Studio to prevent window clutter.

There's more...

A couple more areas of **Team Explorer** are available for use to increase the effectiveness of the tool for your development work.

Using Favorites

A key part to effectiveness in using **Team Explorer** is creating and using queries. Making a copy of an existing query and editing it to suit your needs is a quick way to customize the tool. Whether you use custom queries or the standard ones, drag your frequently used queries into **My Favorites** or **Team Favorites**, as shown in the following screenshot:

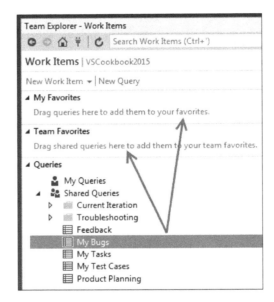

 My Favorites are queries that only appear to you, while **Team Favorites** are queries that are usable by anyone that is part of the project.

Shelving active work

Team Explorer generally encourages you to only have one logical task in progress at a time. This can help you limit the amount of work in progress you have, and push you towards finishing a task completely before starting the next one. If you want to improve your personal productivity and work smarter, not harder, then this is a good practice to follow.

Unfortunately, if you plan to only work on one thing at a time, then what happens when you have to pause what you are doing and deal with an unexpected issue? If you have used previous versions of TFS, you may be familiar with the concept of shelving and unshelving code. Shelving takes a copy of the changes you have made, stores them on the server, and then optionally resets your local workspace. Unshelving is just the reverse of that. This lets you deal with the emergency, and then return to your previous work without commingling the two separate items. Shelving is available in all editions of VS2015.

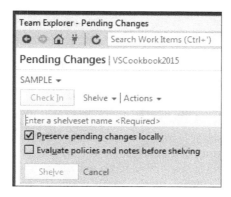

Suspending active work

With Visual Studio Community or higher, you also have the added ability to suspend work. This automatically shelves your current changes, and the current state of your Visual Studio windows when you hit the button. It then resets your workspace, clears the work items that were in progress, and puts you back in a state ready to start another work item.

To access this, click on **My Work**, expand **In Progress Work**, and then click on the **Suspend** button, as shown in the following screenshot:

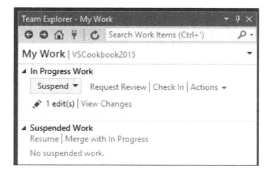

 You will notice that previously suspended work is also available under **Suspended Work**, allowing you to continue a previously suspended work item.

See also

- ▶ MSDN documentation on choosing a TFS process: `https://www.visualstudio.com/docs/work/guidance/choose-process`
- ▶ The *Using local workspaces for source control* recipe
- ▶ The *Performing code reviews* recipe

Using local workspaces for source control

Long-time users of TFS may recall an era where using it required that their development machine have constant contact with the TFS server, even for relatively benign operations. This was because the TFS server would track the files you had on your development machine, which meant that all check-in and check-out operations required communication with the server.

The consequence of this behavior is that it makes offline work very difficult. In areas of poor network connectivity (on a plane, café, and the like), it may even mean work is prevented. Since the use of source control is something to be encouraged, this behavior is very frustrating, especially when conflicts emerge during check-ins and "get latest" operations.

In an effort to mitigate this, TFS sets the read-only flag on all files that are under source control, which only frustrates developers more, since they can't easily edit files unless they use a tool that is aware of this behavior and can properly communicate with TFS.

While there can be valid reasons to the historical approach, it would be best if the tools fit your workflow rather than adjusting your behavior to fit your tools. Local workspaces provide that exact flexibility. TFS is still the sole source of truth for source control, and is the only place where check-ins can occur. However, the decision over which files have been changed now occurs on your development machine, not on TFS.

Another benefit is that Visual Studio no longer needs to ask TFS if it can open a file for editing or not. Also, you can use any program you want to edit files, because the read-only flag is no longer applied to files. This change also improves the offline editing scenario, and you no longer need to mess around with the "go offline" and "go online" operations.

In this recipe, we'll make some changes to the source code so that you can see how this refined approach to source control works.

Getting ready

As before, you will need to have access to TFS in order to follow this recipe. It would be best if you also had a sandbox team project—a project where you can try things and change data without worrying about it affecting your normal work.

Start VS2015, connect to your team project, and you're ready to go.

How to do it...

Perform the following steps:

1. Create a new Visual Basic-based **Class Library** using the default name. Ensure that the **Add to source control** option is checked.

2. You may be prompted to choose a source control system; if so, pick **Team Foundation Version Control**.

3. If you choose a local path for your project that is not already mapped to a folder in source control, you will be prompted for a location in TFS where it should be stored. Select a folder in your source control tree in which to store the project, and click on **OK** as shown in the following screenshot:

4. In **Team Explorer**, navigate to the **Pending Changes** tile. The files that will be added to source control are shown in the **Included Changes** section. Since this is a brand new project, all of the files are scheduled to be added, as shown in the following screenshot:

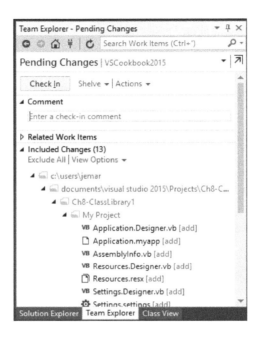

5. Enter a check-in **Comment** to describe what you are doing, and then click on **Check In** to submit the changes to TFS. If you are asked to confirm your check-in, click on **Yes**.

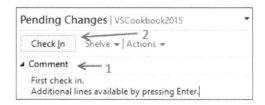

6. The files will be checked in and a confirmation of the changes will be displayed in **Team Explorer**. If you wish to look at the contents of the changeset, you can click on the changeset number displayed in the notification, as shown in the following screenshot (the changeset number will vary based on your particular TFS server history):

7. In **Solution Explorer**, right-click on the class library project, and select **Open Folder in File Explorer**.

8. Right-click on `Class1.vb`, and open the file with Notepad or a favorite text editor that is not Visual Studio.

9. Add some comments to the body of the class, save your changes, and then close Notepad. The following screenshot shows an example of some brief modifications made to `Class1.vb`:

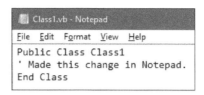

10. Switch back to Visual Studio, and, if prompted to reload any files, select **Yes to All**.

11. In **Solution Explorer**, you should now see that `Class1.vb` has been modified (it will have a checkmark next to it). Navigate to **Team Explorer** and within that, go to the **Pending Changes** tile. You should now see that `Class1.vb` is listed as a pending change, as shown in the following screenshot:

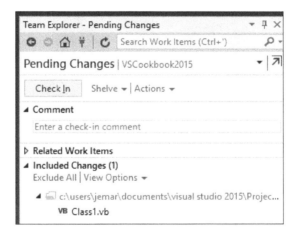

12. Before checking anything, switch back to **File Explorer** (formerly **Windows Explorer** in Windows 7), and make a copy of `Class1.vb`. Edit the file in Notepad and change the class name to `Class2`. Alter the comments in the body of the class to differentiate it further from the original before saving it and closing Notepad. Rename the copy as `Class2.vb`.

13. Switch back to Visual Studio, and navigate to the **Team Explorer | Pending Changes** tile. The new file you just added won't be listed as an included change, but it has been detected as a change. Since it's not part of the solution, you will only see it by looking at the **Excluded Changes** section and clicking on the **Detected** link. Instead of including the file into source control directly, you'll want to first properly add it to the solution. To do so, navigate to **Solution Explorer**, and click on the **Show All Files** button (marked by **1** in the screenshot succeeding *Step 14*) on the toolbar.

14. Right-click on `Class2.vb`, and click on **Include in Project** (marked by **2**), as shown in the following screenshot:

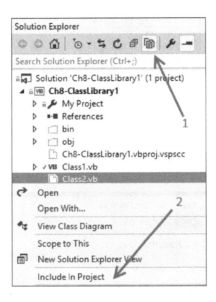

15. Navigate to **Team Explorer** and the **Pending Changes** tile again, and confirm that `Class2.vb` file is now included as a pending change. Add a check-in **Comment**, and then click on **Check In** to reflect the changes, as shown in this screenshot:

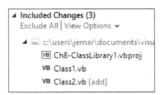

16. In the preceding steps, we renamed the file before we committed it. Let's look at what happens if you use Windows (File) Explorer to rename a file outside of Visual Studio. Rename `Class2.vb` to a name of your choice (our example will use `SecondClass.vb`).

17. Switch back to Visual Studio, and navigate to the **Pending Changes** tile in **Team Explorer**. The rename isn't detected automatically, since it wasn't made in Visual Studio, however, you may notice that there are two changes in the **Detected Changes** section (one add and 1 delete).

18. Click on the **Detected** link, and you will see that the rename is detected as a **delete** of the old filename and an **add** of the new filename. You can let Visual Studio know that this change is actually a rename by selecting both changes (*Ctrl* click on each item) in the add/delete pair, right-clicking on and choosing the **Promote as Rename** option. If prompted to rename all instances of `Class2`, click on **Yes**. When this is done, just click on the **Cancel** button to close the **Promote Candidate Changes** window. The following is the screenshot of the **Promote Candidate Changes** window:

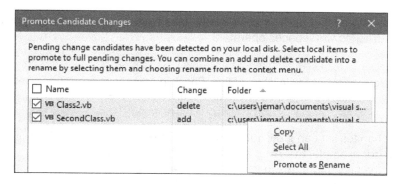

19. Not only is the rename now listed in the **Included Changes** section, but the solution file has also been updated to reflect the change and is also included as a pending change. The **Pending Changes** tile should now look similar to the following screenshot:

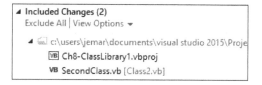

20. Check-in your changes when you have finished.

How it works...

When using a local workspace, Visual Studio creates a hidden local folder named `$tf`, and stores within it zipped copies of the workspace version of your source files. Visual Studio detects changes by comparing the contents of your local files and folders to the contents of the `$tf` folder, and adds any differences as pending changes.

It might be an obvious warning, but don't delete the `$tf` folder or any of its contents, not even if you are short on disk space. Doing so will cause significant problems. If you want to examine this folder, a typical location would be `C:\Users\username\Source\Workspaces\TFS_Repository_Name\$tf`. Change `username` and `TFS_Repository_Name` to reflect your specific situation.

You might have noticed that at no time during the recipe did you have to change the read-only flag on any of the files, nor did you have to check-out any files for edit. In fact, the only time Visual Studio communicated with TFS was during the check-in process. All other changes were managed and tracked locally.

This should alleviate a lot of pain for people who have been used to older versions of TFS and the way server tracked workspaces operated.

 You cannot check-in when offline. Check-in operations are still server-based, and require that you be online and connected to TFS.

The detected changes list can grow quite large over time, and you may want to ignore certain folders or files (for example, the `/obj` and `/bin` folders). You can either create `.tfignore` files to specify the files and paths to ignore, or in **Team Explorer**, you can open the list of detected changes and exclude files either individually, by extension, or by folder path. Doing so will create or alter `.tfignore` files for you, and add them to the Pending Changes list so that they can be checked in and shared with all the other developers on the team.

There's more...

Be aware that when using a local workspace, you will no longer have any real visibility on the server over who has checked out a file. The exception to this is locking files. If you lock a file, the server is notified and can report that you have locked it.

Unshelving a shelveset now merges any shelveset changes with your local edits. Any conflicts between the shelveset and your local version will cause a merge conflict, and you will need to resolve it in the normal manner.

When might a local workspace not be appropriate? For many users, it is a good choice. But sometimes, you may have a large number of files in your TFS project (100,000+), or your personal workflow might be such that you use two or more open instances of VS2015 with the same project. In those situations, you will not want to use a local workspace.

Viewing or changing local workplace settings

By default, the partnership of VS2015 and TFS/VSTS will be set such that you are using a local workplace as described in this recipe. But if you would like to change your workplace setting for your project, or verify that it is in fact configured as you intend, you can take the following quick steps to view the settings.

1. Select **Team Explorer**. Then select the active workspace title and click on **Manage Workspaces...**, as shown in the following screenshot:

2. In the resulting **Manage Workspaces** dialog, select the workspace you would like to view and/or change, and click on **Edit**.

3. The **Edit Workspace** dialog will then appear. Select your folder from **Working folders**, and then click on **Advanced** to see full details. An excerpt of this dialog is shown in the following screenshot:

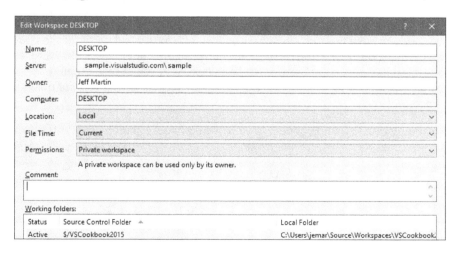

4. From this dialog, **Location** can be changed to indicate whether the workspace should be **Local** or **Server**. Other options include setting the **File Time** and **Permissions** for the workspace.

See also

▶ The *Managing your work* recipe

Performing code reviews

When developing in a team, one of the more widely recommended practices for improving code quality and overall consistency is to conduct code reviews. VS2015 combines with TFS to support the code review process and make it as efficient as possible.

In this recipe, you'll see just how this works.

 What are code reviews? By default, it is common to let any developer with access to a source code repository check-in whatever changes they would like, whenever they like. In an effort to improve code quality, a code review can be used where a second developer reviews what has been changed by the first. In this way, the odds of committing broken or poorly thought-out code is minimized, if not eliminated.

Getting ready

You will need to have access to TFS in order to follow this recipe. It would be best if you use a sandbox team project, a project where you can try things and change data without worrying about it affecting your normal work.

You will also need to have two accounts you can use: one for the submitter of the code review and one for the reviewer. If you don't personally have two accounts, that's okay. Create a test account or get a colleague to act as your reviewer. Note that you should create this second account before beginning the recipe, and ensure it can access VSTS if you are not using a local TFS account.

Open your copy of VS2015, and connect to your team project using the submitter's account.

 Starting with VS2015, code review is available in Visual Community, Professional, and Enterprise.

How to do it...

Perform a code review using the following steps:

1. We need to make sure the test account that you have created has access to our sample project. Your local TFS administrator can assist you with this if you are using a local server, but for those using VSTS (as we are, in this example), proceed to login to VSTS with your primary account.

2. When you have logged in, select the VSTS project that you will be working with. Add your second account to the project by navigating to your project's **Overview** page, then click on **Invite a Friend,** as shown in the following screenshot:

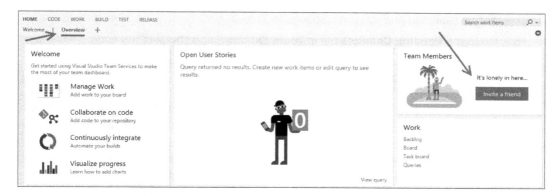

3. In the ensuing dialog, add the user by clicking on **Add...** and then entering the name of that user; click on **Save changes** when complete:

4. Returning to VS2015, start a new C# **ASP.NET Web Application** project using the **ASP.NET 4.6.1 MVC** template, and add the solution to source control (**Team Foundation**). Refer to the *Using local workspaces for source control* recipe if you're not sure how to do this.

 If you are not currently connected to TFS, you can re-establish your connection under **Team | Manage Connections,** and then select the appropriate TFS instance on **Team Explorer**.

5. Ensure that your new solution is part of TFS by right-clicking on the solution in **Solution Explorer** and selecting **Add Solution to Source Control**. The suggested defaults are acceptable. (If the solution is already part of TFS, this option will not be available and you may proceed to *Step 3*.)

6. Go to the **Pending Changes** tile in **Team Explorer**, and check-in the code.

7. Open the `HomeController.cs` file under the `Controllers` folder, change the contents of the message text for `About()` and `Contact()`, and change the name of the `About` method to `AboutUs`. (VS2015 will suggest further edits for the renamed method, but for the sake of this recipe, do not accept the recommendations even though under normal circumstances you would want to take advantage of them.)

8. Open the `Index.cshtml` view under the `Views\Home` folder, and alter the text of the page to something you like. Then switch to the **Pending Changes** tile, which should now look similar to the following screenshot but don't make a check-in just yet:

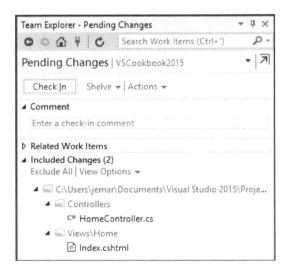

9. Click on the **Actions** drop-down menu, and select **Request Review** as shown in the following screenshot:

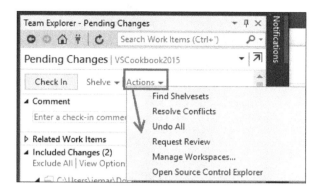

10. In the **New Code Review** pane, enter the name of your reviewer and press *Enter*. The reviewer should be the second user account you are using in this recipe, as mentioned in the *Getting ready* section. Add a subject for the code review, and then click on **Submit Request**, as shown in the following screenshot:

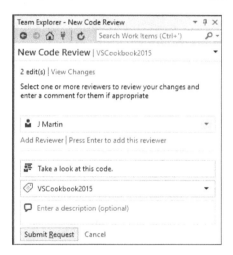

11. **Team Explorer** will then switch to the **My Work** display and show the code review request as an outgoing request.

12. Now we will handle the code review with the second account. Log out of VS2015 with your current account, and restart VS2015. Restart VS2012 and login with the second user account that you assigned to the Code Review, and connect to your TFS/VSTS project.

13. In **Team Explorer**, open the **My Work** tile. You should see a code review request displayed. Note the arrow next to the review indicating it is an incoming request for you to look at. This is shown in the following screenshot:

14. Double-click on the code review task to begin the review process. **Team Explorer** will switch to the **Code Review** pane, and display the details of the review and information on the files that have been modified.

15. Click on the `HomeController.cs` file in the **Code Review**, as shown in the following screenshot:

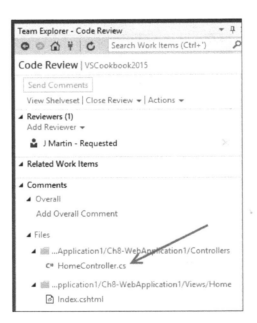

16. You will see both the original and modified versions of the file displayed using Visual Studio's **diff** viewer as follows:

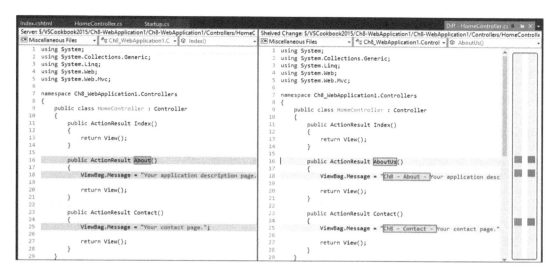

17. As noted earlier in *Step 7*, we renamed `AboutUs()` in `HomeController.cs` but not in `View`. So we will make note of that in the comments.

 A diff tool (short for differences) is used to compare the changes between the two text files. They are a popular way to easily see the differences between files.

18. Select the entire `AboutUs` method from the right-hand side pane, right-click on the selection, and then choose **Add Comment** from the context menu, as shown in the following screenshot:

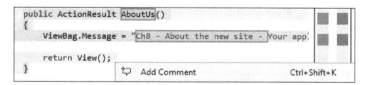

19. The focus switches to the comment box in the **Code Review** pane. Enter a comment, as shown in the following screenshot, and then click on **Save** (*Ctrl + Enter*):

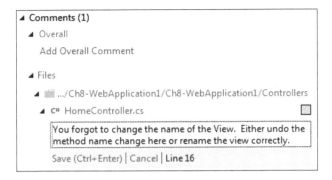

20. Click on the checkbox next to the `HomeController.cs` file in the **Code Review** pane to indicate that there are no further comments to make on that file.

21. Click on the **Add Overall Comment** link in the **Code Review** pane, and supply a general comment on the code review; then click on **Save** (*Ctrl + Enter*).

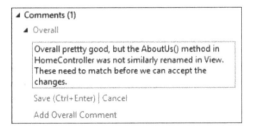

22. After saving the comment, a checkbox will appear to the right of your comment. Be sure to check this.

23. Make further comments on the review as you wish and, when you are done, click on the checkbox next to `Index.cshtml`. When you have entered all the comments that you wish to make, click on the **Send & Finish** link, choosing the **Needs Work** option from the drop-down menu that appears.

24. Switch back to the first user's account that submitted the request for a **Code Review**. In **Team Explorer**, go to the **My Work** tile, and click on the refresh button (assuming you left Visual Studio running). Click on the arrow next to the review request to see the status of the review, and if the review is complete, double-click on it to display the **Code Review** hub.

25. Click on the `HomeController.cs` file in the **Code Review** hub and the diff viewer will be displayed.

26. As the submitter, you would then take action on the review comments as appropriate, but for the purpose of this recipe, you're going to close the code review. Click on the **Close Review** drop-down link, and select **Complete** from the list of options to close the entire code review request.

How it works...

If you noticed, the code review occurred on code that wasn't even checked in to source control. The advantage of doing so is that this allows for code to be shared for reviewing purposes before it is entered into the main repository. Behind the scenes, asking for a code review automatically creates a shelveset for the reviewer to look at. Unlike the **Suspend** and **Shelve** operation, requesting a code review doesn't reset your workspace or clear any of the work items you have marked as "in progress".

You can also request reviews for changesets that have already been checked in and other shelvesets that have been manually created.

See also

▸ The *Managing your work* recipe

▸ The *Using local workspaces for source control* recipe

Getting feedback from your users

When working on a product, one of the most valuable things you can do is get feedback from your users as to whether the software you have built meets their requirements or not, and their opinions about the software. You will notice that in TFS terminology, the word "stakeholder" is used over "user", representing the diverse sources of feedback that exist. Besides traditional end-users, several additional groups should have their voices heard—including design, QA, and the product owners funding development.

Even if you have a process that defines clear acceptance criteria for requirements, and you have a clear definition of what it means to be done with a piece of work, you still want feedback from these stakeholders to determine whether there are any other points that may have been missed when the requirement was first discussed, or if new ideas have occurred now that they have seen the latest build of the software running.

A normal feedback process involves telling your users that the software is available, asking them to please go and try it, and let you know what they think. The feedback you get can often be incomplete, verbally reported, and hard to turn into actionable items for improving the software. Fortunately, there are steps that can be taken to improve communication and reduce confusion.

Let's take a look at how gathering feedback can be improved by using TFS.

Getting ready

Just make sure you have access to TFS and a team project. As before, we will be using VSO for our demonstration screenshots.

How to do it...

Gather feedback from people by following these steps:

1. Go to the **Web Portal** site for your team project, and look for the **Other Links** widget on the dashboard. If it is not present, you will first need to add it. There is a blue pencil icon in the lower-right corner of the dashboard. When you hover your mouse cursor over it, a green plus sign appears. Click on this green icon, as shown in the following screenshot:

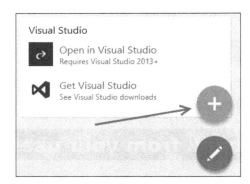

2. After clicking on the plus icon, an **Add Widget** dialog box will pop up. Search for the **Other Links** widget and it to your dashboard by clicking on **Add**, as shown in the following screenshot:

3. After clicking on **Add**, click on **Close** (as each time you click **Add**, another copy of the widget is added.) Your dashboard will still be in an editable state once the widget has been added, so, to save changes, click on the blue checkmark icon in the lower-right corner.

4. Now you should see a **Request feedback** link under the **Other Links** widget we just added. Click on this link to start the feedback gathering process, as shown in the following screenshot:

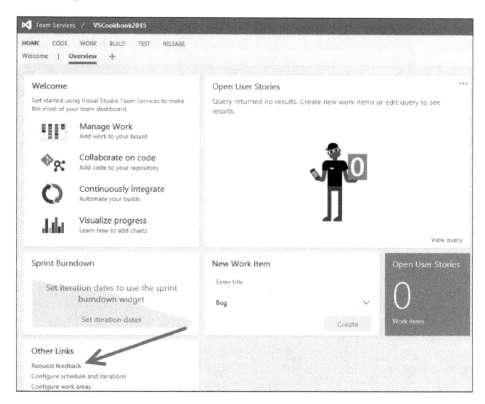

5. A dialog will appear asking you to fill in the information in three distinct sections. Section **1** is named **Select Stakeholders**, and you must enter the details of the people you want feedback from. They must be valid TFS or VSTS users in order to be selected. For this recipe, you can just enter your own account here.

6. In section **2**, supply the details of how users should access the application. This would typically be the details of a test site or application to install and run. For example, enter `www.packtpub.com` as the address of the web application/site.

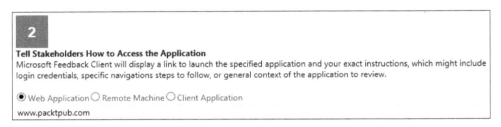

7. In section **3**, add details for the specific feedback you want from your users. Note that the **Add feedback item** link is available to add extra items for feedback, as shown in the following screenshot:

8. After completing all three sections, you can either send the request immediately, or you can preview the message that will be sent. Feel free to view the preview message on your system, but for this recipe, we will just go ahead and hit **Send**.

9. You should then receive an e-mail similar to the following:

10. Depending on how your system is configured, you may need to install the feedback tool. Fortunately, a link to this tool is included in the e-mail. After installing the tool, you can just click on the **Start your feedback session** link in the e-mail. The **feedback** client will then launch.

11. Click on the application link to launch the website, and then click on the **Next** button in the feedback client.

12. The feedback client is now ready to accept feedback from the users, and the specific instructions you entered for the feedback session are shown to the recipient. The next screenshot shows our sample question to the reviewer, and provides a rich text editor. This allows the reviewer to clearly document their work and provide screenshots or other attachments.

13. In the comments section, enter some text and then click on the **Screenshot** button. Select a section of the screen for your snapshot by dragging the mouse to create a rectangle. Notice that the screenshot you take is inserted wherever the cursor is in the comments box. Click on the **Next** button to continue.

14. A summary of the feedback will be shown, and you can rate each item using a five star approach. If you are happy with the feedback you have provided, click on **Submit and Close** to complete the feedback session.

15. Switch back to Visual Studio and, in **Team Explorer**, navigate to the **Work Items** tile and double-click on the `Feedback` query (under **Shared Queries**) to run it, as shown in the following screenshot:

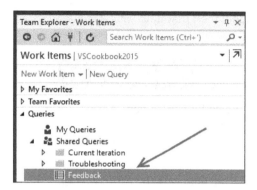

16. The query results will display all the feedback responses received from your users. Select one of the items in the list to view the specific details of the feedback along with any images and attachments that may have been created by the feedback tool. This screenshot shows the results of the query for our sample project:

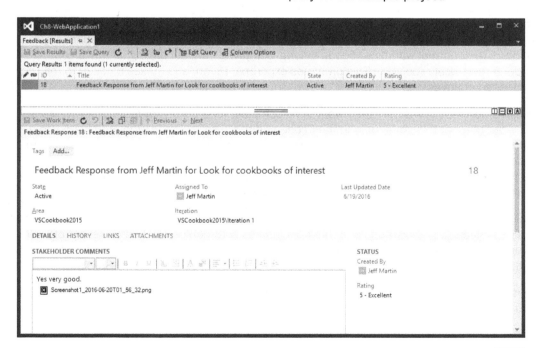

17. At this point, you can create new work items based on the feedback or close the items, just as you would for any other work item.

How it works...

Under the hood, all feedback requests are stored as work items in TFS. The feedback client adds all the responses as child work items linked to the feedback request. If your users record feedback using audio or video, then that data will be included as an attachment to the work item so that you can replay it when you review the responses.

Using Git for source control

Git has become a popular choice for source control as an alternative to the classical centralized source control approach. Originating in the open source world for use in development of the Linux kernel, it has since spread in the software development world to be used on a variety of platforms.

While nothing prevents one from installing the Git toolset on their Windows system, a few years ago, Microsoft decided to add native Git support to Visual Studio. Since its arrival in VS2012 Update 2, Microsoft has continued to refine their offering, and given Git a prominent role within Visual Studio.

The basic concept of Git is that it takes the approach of decentralized source control—rather than having a central server that serves as the sole repository, Git facilitates distributed repositories. In practice, this means that each developer can have a full copy of the repository on their local developer machine that contains the entire project history. Developers can perform their normal workflow of code editing, compiling, and debugging, all while committing code to their local repository. This promotes experimentation, and makes it easier to roll back undesired changes.

When a developer considers their work to be complete for a particular feature or milestone, they can then, at this point, upload their code and the associated development history to a remote Git repository as needed. This repository can be anything from a fellow developer to a designated corporate source control server. It also facilitates multiplatform development, as Git clients exist for Mac and Linux. So, you can easily interact with developers on those platforms while still using your familiar Visual Studio tools.

Unlike TFS, you can use Git on your local development workstation without any other server or online service. Git is very popular in the open source community, and has a vast set of tools available for most mainstream operating systems, ensuring that you can easily share code with these developers without requiring them all to have Windows or Visual Studio.

This recipe will show how Git can be used with your projects, and will be a useful tool even if you are a solo developer.

Getting ready

For this recipe, we will be using Visual Studio Community 2015 Update 2, but any of the premium editions may also be used. The concepts are applicable to any version of Visual Studio Version 2012 Update 2 or later.

To keep things simple, we will not involve TFS for this recipe. If you have been following along with the previous recipes in this chapter, make sure you are not still connected to TFS or VSTS by clicking on **Disconnect from Team Foundation Server** under the **Team** menu before starting this recipe.

How to do it...

Take advantage of Git by following these steps:

1. We will begin by creating a new C#-based **Console Application**. The default name may be used, but before closing the **New Project** dialog box, be sure that the checkbox for **Create new Git repository** has been checked, as shown in the following screenshot:

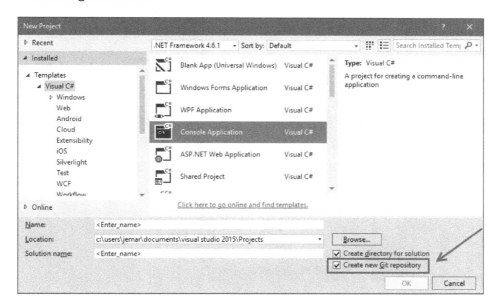

2. After clicking on **OK** on the **New Project** dialog box, Visual Studio may then prompt you to choose a source control system (depending on your particular Visual Studio configuration). If this dialog appears, pick **Git** as shown in the following screenshot, and click on the **OK** button:

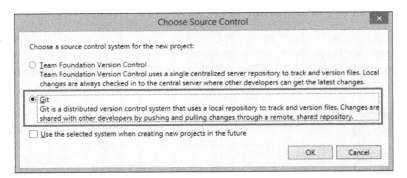

3. Visual Studio will set up your project, and then present you with the familiar main editing screen. If it is not already open, click on the **Team Explorer** tab. Alternatively, you may open it via **View | Team Explorer**.

4. Once **Team Explorer** is open, click on the **Settings** tile, as shown in the following screenshot:

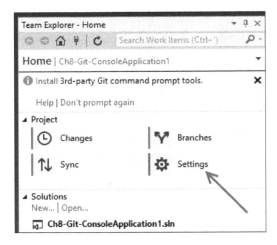

5. The resulting screen will provide two main choices: **Global Settings** and **Repository Settings**. We will start with **Global Settings**, so click on that first.

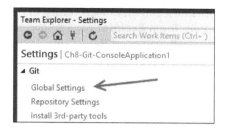

6. As you may surmise, **Global Settings** are applied to all Git based projects that you are using. For proper operation and as a matter of best practice, ensure that your name and e-mail address are entered here. They will be used to identify all of your commits (check-ins) to Git. If you have a specific diff or merge tool installed that you would like to use instead of VS2015's built-in tools, you can also choose those here. Before proceeding, be sure to enter your **User Name** and **Email Address,** and then click on **Update**. The following screenshot illustrates all of these fields:

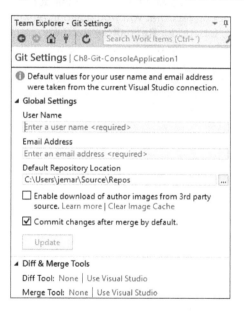

 You may have noticed the **Default Repository Location** field in the preceding screenshot . By default, VS2015 will use your C: drive for this, but if you would like to pick a different drive, perhaps one with more space, you can make that change here.

7. After entering your name and e-mail, you will return to the prior **Git** settings screen. Navigate back to the main **Team Explorer** page by clicking on the back arrow or home icon on the toolbar. Then choose **Repository Settings,** as shown in the following screenshot:

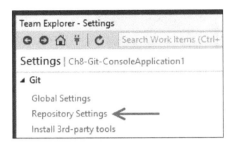

8. **Repository Settings** are specific to each Git based project that you have. They allow you to make customizations that best suit the task at hand. For example, you may be working on a personal project that you would like to associate with a separate identity from that of your day job. Under **Repository Settings**, you can set a specific **User Name** and **Email Address**. For our purposes, we will stick with the defaults, but this is where to find them should you need to change them. The following screenshot shows what is available:

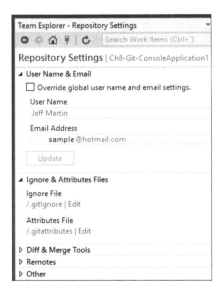

You may also have noticed the presence of the fields **Ignore File** and **Attributes File** in the preceding screenshot . By default, each Git repository has these two files, and they allow for project-specific customization. The **Ignore File** is used to indicate files that should be ignored by Git, such as temporary files or private user data. The **Attributes File** is used to configure how Git handles line endings and what files should be treated as binary objects (versus text). Both are simple text files that can be edited within VS2015.

9. With VS2015, a new project using Git will automatically check-in your initial project files as part of its setup process. You can see this default setup by clicking on **Team Explorer,** and then clicking on the **Changes** tile. On the **Changes** screen, click on the **Actions** menu and select **View History...,** as shown in the following screenshot:

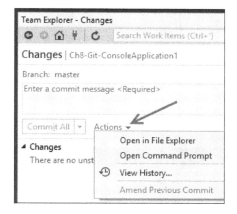

10. This brings up the **History** for the entire project, showing all commits for the entire project and not just a specific file. You can see in the following screenshot that this project has the initial two commits made, and includes the author, date/time stamp, and a brief description of what was done:

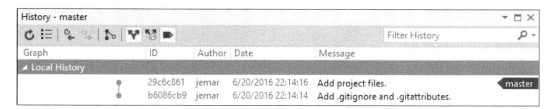

> Commit is the term used in Git to describe the action of your recording changes to the repository. This can be considered as similar to the TFS check-in command.

11. Now that the required settings have been configured, let's see what happens when we make some changes and add a commit of our own to the project.

12. Switch back to the VS2015 main editor window, and open your project's `Program.cs` file. We're going to make a small edit so that we have something to commit to the repository. Update the main method as shown:

```
static void Main(string[] args)
{
    int x = 2;
    int y = 16;
    Console.WriteLine("The original Pentium CPU is "
    + x * y + " bits.");
}
```

13. After this change, be sure to save your work and then open **Team Explorer**. There you should see that Git has noticed the change to `Program.cs`, and it will be included with the next commit. Before continuing, enter a commit message and then commit the changes as shown in the following screenshot (note that **Commit All** will be active once a message is entered):

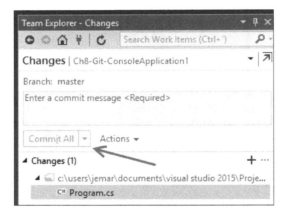

14. After making the commit, you will then see the **Commit Details** appear on **Team Explorer**, as shown in the following screenshot:

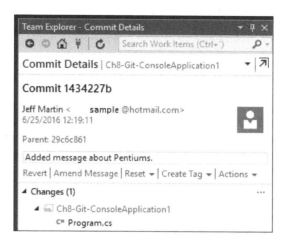

15. The **Commit Details** shows us the name of the committer, date and time stamp, commit message, and the files that were part of the commit. If you made a mistake in committing, note that you can also undo the commit by clicking on the **Revert** link. Also available under **Actions** is the ability to copy the full commit ID to the clipboard should you need to use it elsewhere (that is, —for a search or with a command-line tool).

 Every commit made to a Git repository is assigned a unique ID string generated by an SHA-1 hash. Rather than showing the full ID, Visual Studio displays a portion for easy reference.

16. Now navigate to home on the **Team Explorer**, select the **Changes** tile, click on the **Actions** link, and select **View History** (repeating the steps taken in *Step 9*). Now we can see that our **Local History** has been updated to reflect the changes. Selecting a given commit will present the details of the commit on **Team Explorer**. The following screenshot shows this updated history:

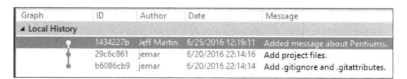

 Hovering over a given row will provide all details of the commit, including its full commit ID.

17. Clicking on one of these commit messages will provide more details about what the commit included. When the project is fresh in your mind, the details are easy to remember, and the changes are obvious. When working with multiple contributors or when dealing with long-term projects, Git's organized recording of changes can make new development much easier.

How it works...

Git is an advanced piece of software that provides many powerful features in exchange for its complexity. It uses the SHA-1 algorithm to provide a checksum of the data header being committed. Using this algorithm provides for accurate tracking while continuously ensuring the integrity of your repositories, since discrepancies in checksums will alert you to inconsistencies. They also provide a unique way to identify each commit made.

There's more...

Staging files

Prior to VS2015 Update 2, using Git on Visual Studio also meant that pending changes had various states: **Included Changes**, **Excluded Changes**, and **Untracked Files**. With VS2015 Update 2, everything is just listed under **Changes**, as this recipe showed. Those of you familiar with the old way may then wonder if it is possible to only commit a subset of the files changed. Fortunately, the answer is yes, and one of the benefits is that you can use a specific commit to highlight changes.

The way to do this is via **Staging**. After you have made a series of changes/additions to your source code, the changed files will appear in **Team Explorer** under **Changes**. To only commit a portion, select those that you would like to have committed, and then click on **Stage**. This will separate the changed files, allowing you to commit only the ones you want. The following screenshot shows files in these two states:

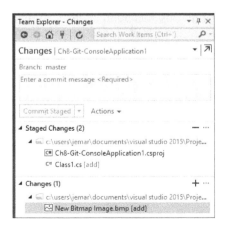

In this case, the `Class1.cs` and the project file will be committed while the new bitmap file won't. Prior to making a commit, you can always change your mind, and add more files to the staging or remove existing ones.

Looking ahead

We have only scratched the surface of what Git can do and the value it can provide in your software development efforts. You can use these tools to clone (make a local copy) of a remote repository into your local development environment. For example, the Bootstrap framework described in *Chapter 3, Web Development*, maintains its project files in a Git repository at `https://github.com/twbs/bootstrap`. This project is hosted on GitHub, which offers an alternative to TFS for code sharing and team collaboration.

Git also has a multitude of features for branching and merging. Branching has many uses, and is almost a necessity when supporting existing software. For example, you can create a development branch that lets you work on the next version of your application while keeping the current branch available for the version currently in production use. Exploring new concepts or making risky changes can be done in the development branch, allowing the release branch to remain in a bug-free, buildable state.

See also

- Git has an extensive online manual available at `https://git-scm.com/`
- If you would like to use Git on your development machine, but still need to interact with external TFS severs, consider visiting `http://gittf.codeplex.com/` or `https://github.com/git-tfs/git-tfs`
- The recipe *Taking Advantage of Git's command line*

Taking Advantage of Git's command line

Using Git directly through VS2015 is one of the most common ways for you to incorporate it into your daily workflow to easily accomplish your most frequent tasks. However, at its roots, Git is a command-line tool, and in some cases, it can be advantageous to access Git in this manner.

Throughout the previous recipe *Using Git for source control*, you may have noticed that VS2015 was prompting you to install the 3rd-party command-line tools. In this recipe, we are going to do just that so that all of Git's functionality is available to you when Git is used with your projects.

Getting ready

This recipe will pick up directly from the previous one, but feel free to substitute your own Git-based project should you have one available. This recipe will assume you are using Visual Studio Community 2015 Update 2, but the important thing is for you to be using a version of VS2015 with Update 2 or newer applied.

How to do it...

To use Git on the command line, take the following steps:

1. Start your copy of VS2015. Under **Team Explorer**, you will see a prompt to install **3rd-party Git command prompt tools**, as shown in the following screenshot:

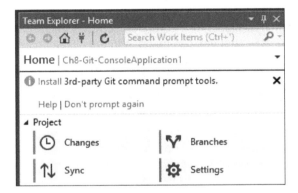

2. Click on **Install**. On the next screen, you will be prompted to read a short license agreement. Again, click on **Install**. This second click will then take you to the official Git webpage where the download of the latest Git tools will be installed. If you are looking for them outside of VS2015, go to `https://git-scm.com/download/win`.

3. After downloading the tools, run the installation program. The default options are okay, and no changes are needed. Restart VS2015.

4. While you can open Git outside of VS2015, this recipe will explore how to do so from within Visual Studio. Using the project from the previous recipe or a similar Git-based project, click on the **Changes** tile under **Team Explorer**. Then click on the **Actions** menu, and select **Open Command Prompt**, as shown in the following screenshot:

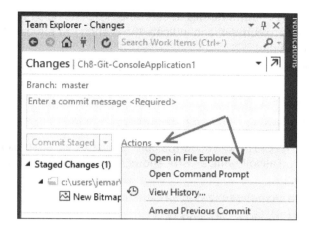

 Alternatively, you can select a local repository to work with from **Team Explorer – Connect**. Click on the menu **Team | Manage Connections** or use the hot key *Ctrl + 0, C* (that is, the number zero, followed by the letter *C*). Once that is open, right-click on the desired Git repository and select **Open Command Prompt**, as shown in the following screenshot:

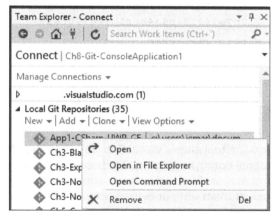

5. Once you have opened the Git command prompt, you will find that you are currently located in the base directory of the solution you have selected. From there you have access to all of Git's commands, and we will take a look at some of the common ones.

6. The command `git status` will indicate whether or not you have any outstanding files to commit, and indicate the branch you are on. The following listing is an example:

    ```
    c:\users\jemar\documents\visual studio 2015\Projects\Ch8-Git-
    ConsoleApplication1>git status

    On branch master

    nothing to commit, working directory clean
    ```

7. The command `git log` will show the commit history for the project you are working on. The following excerpt shows a portion of the history from our previous project:

    ```
    commit 5ac2388506970f3283c2a364c620f6537534f4ae

    Author: Jeff Martin <jemartin>

    Date:    Sat Jun 25 13:07:16 2016 -0400

        Adding new class

    commit bf162194b618b5a7c3166655be72d5c5dbe47c8f

    Author: Jeff Martin <jemartin>

    Date:    Sat Jun 25 13:04:05 2016 -0400

        Revert "Just project file"

        This reverts commit 2494dc217b7e752124b5a4bcf3b144720fea7248.

    commit 2494dc217b7e752124b5a4bcf3b144720fea7248

    Author: Jeff Martin <jemartin>

    Date:    Sat Jun 25 13:03:35 2016 -0400

        Just project file
    ```

How it works...

Installing the Git command-line tool allows VS2015 to work with the official project tools, and provide you with an additional option beyond the GUI based approach provided in VS2015. Since Git is a multiplatform tool, various tutorials and scripts will assume it is present, and this allows you to make use of them without being constrained by VS2015.

 Not all of the Git commands are available through VS2015. There are a few that require you to use the command line, including `stash` and `reset`. For a complete list, go to `https://www.visualstudio.com/en-us/docs/git/command-prompt`.

There's more...

While Microsoft recommends that you start the Git command prompt from within VS2015 as we have shown in this recipe, that isn't the only way. As part of the Git tools installation, you may also use the included Git Bash program. Git Bash is accessible through your Windows Start menu. This uses the familiar Bash shell environment to interface with your file system. The biggest immediate difference to using this via the approach in the recipe is that you will start in your Windows user's base directory rather than within your VS2015 project folder. Those of you familiar with Bash and its associated commands may prefer this method.

9
Languages

In this chapter, we will cover the following recipes:

- ▶ Fortifying JavaScript applications with TypeScript
- ▶ Integrating Python into Visual Studio
- ▶ Integrating Python with .NET
- ▶ Targeting Linux with Visual Studio 2015

Introduction

Historically, Visual Studio has focused on specific Microsoft-centric languages, including C++, C#, and Visual Basic. Between the Internet, mobile devices, and the ever-increasing rapid pace of change, new computer languages are being created in an effort to ease development, and present new solutions to problems. In view of these changes, it is easy to see that Microsoft seeks to position VS2015 as the tool of choice for any development work taking place on Windows, regardless of the ultimate target platform.

The benefit to us as users of VS2015 is that as we improve our understanding and usage of this platform, we can then make use of it in a greater number of situations. In this chapter, we will look at TypeScript, Python, and IronPython, a few languages that offer some unique capabilities when compared to the traditional languages offered in Visual Studio. Then we will conclude this chapter by learning about VS2015's capability to target non-Windows platforms when writing C++ code, giving you the ability to use your VS2015 skills in a new environment on devices ranging from the Raspberry Pi to powerful Linux supercomputers.

Fortifying JavaScript applications with TypeScript

JavaScript's role in web development has gone from being considered a starter language for hobbyist programmers to being regarded as a serious tool for building modern web applications on both the client and the server. This change means that the size and scope of JavaScript applications has grown tremendously, and with that growth, the costs of managing the complexity have also increased. To address this, Microsoft has developed the open source project TypeScript, which is a superset of JavaScript that adds static type checking.

 TypeScript is not limited to Windows, and is a fully open source project that is capable of running on any JavaScript engine that supports ECMAScript 3 or greater.

VS2015 includes integrated support for TypeScript projects, making it easy to get started with the language. Let's take a look at how TypeScript can benefit your web application.

Getting ready

For this specific recipe, we will be using Visual Studio Community 2015.

How to do it...

Let's perform the following steps to see how TypeScript can fortify your JavaScript applications:

1. Open VS2015, and create a new **HTML Application with TypeScript** project, as shown in the following screenshot:

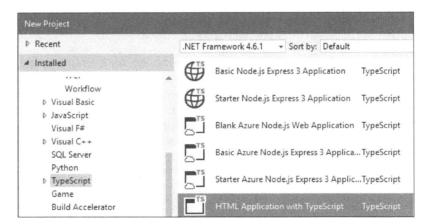

2. Accept the default project name, and create the project.

3. The default project will open with a small sample that, when executed, will produce a web page that shows a simple clock. When you look at the source, it is pretty sparse, as shown in the following screenshot:

```
1  <!DOCTYPE html>
2
3  <html lang="en">
4  <head>
5      <meta charset="utf-8" />
6      <title>TypeScript HTML App</title>
7      <link rel="stylesheet" href="app.css" type="text/css" />
8      <script src="app.js"></script>
9  </head>
10 <body>
11     <h1>TypeScript HTML App</h1>
12
13     <div id="content"></div>
14 </body>
15 </html>
```

4. As you can see, beyond some HTML, there is not much except for a reference to a file called `app.js`. Returning to Visual Studio, the most closely related source file is `app.ts`. So where did the `app.js` file come from?

5. Going back to our original explanation of TypeScript, remember that it is a superset of the JavaScript language. This means that all valid JavaScript code is also valid TypeScript code. When TypeScript is compiled, JavaScript is generated. In this case, our file `app.ts` is compiled by Visual Studio to `app.js`. You can find the `app.js` file if you look inside your project folder, as shown in the following screenshot:

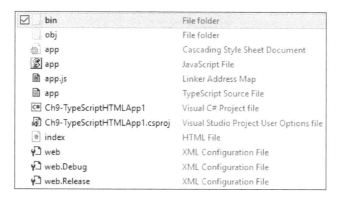

6. At this point, you are ready to start writing your application, and can use NuGet to add TypeScript aware packages such as jQuery.

How it works...

Since TypeScript ultimately compiles down to JavaScript, you may be wondering about the advantages of using it. Firstly, using TypeScript allows meaningful IntelliSense support. For example, examine the `app.ts` file that is part of our project. The following screenshot shows one of the available IntelliSense menus that can appear while editing:

Secondly, TypeScript (as its name suggests) allows type checking. Consider the `greeter` class, and how Visual Studio is able to help by comparing the differences, as shown in the following screenshot:

```
var greeter = new Greeter(el);
greeter.element = 16;

    (local var) greeter: Greeter

    Type 'number' is not assignable to type 'HTMLElement'.
```

Since TypeScript is being used, Visual Studio detects an error with the assignment, as shown in the preceding screenshot. Conversely, in the JavaScript code (shown in the following screenshot), Visual Studio did not detect the error:

```
var el = document.getElementById('content');
var greeter = new Greeter(el);
greeter.start();
```

This creates a bug that is easy to overlook. In smaller applications, the lack of type checking can usually be managed by the programmer. However, with larger applications or unfamiliar code bases, it becomes much more difficult. Catching the error immediately saves debugging time later.

The third and perhaps the best advantage of using TypeScript is that the TypeScript compiler (`tsc.exe`) produces valid JavaScript that works on any browser or platform that supports JavaScript. This compatibility means you can use TypeScript in your projects without requiring your users to install something new. Since the nature of the TypeScript language is more specific than JavaScript, you can catch errors sooner, and increase the power of IntelliSense. This allows you to keep the good parts of JavaScript (fast and powerful design capabilities) while increasing its safety and usability in large projects.

There's more...

You don't have to create a brand new project just to take advantage of TypeScript; it can be easily added to your existing web projects. From within an existing web project, add a new item (*Ctrl* + *Shift* + *A*) or right-click on your project name or directory within the **Solution Explorer** window, and select **TypeScript File**. Similarly, you can use NuGet to add TypeScript aware packages to both new and existing projects, allowing you to phase in a manner that fits your development schedule.

If you would like to try TypeScript, but are wondering about all the existing JavaScript code that would have to be converted, don't worry. Library types for many popular JavaScript projects, including Backbone.js, Node.js, and jQuery, are available at DefinitelyTyped (`https://github.com/DefinitelyTyped/DefinitelyTyped`).

Integrating Python into Visual Studio

Python was created by Guido van Rossum in the early 1990s, and quickly developed a following among developers across the world. Python is a dynamic, general purpose language, well suited for all types of projects. Among its many features are support for multiple paradigms (object-oriented, functional, and so on), a rapid development cycle (thanks to its interpretive nature), and its structured approach to syntax.

Microsoft has released **Python Tools for Visual Studio** (**PTVS**) so that those of us on the Microsoft platform can easily try and use Python within Visual Studio. Whether you would like to sample Python or create a new application from the ground up, you will be able to do so while using tools with which you are already familiar. In this recipe, we will see how Visual Studio can become a highly tuned Python development environment.

Getting ready

For this recipe, we first need to install PTVS. A link to the PTVS installer is included in VS2015. Open **New Project**, and select **Python | Install Python Tools for Visual Studio**. VS2015 will then prompt for confirmation, so grant it by clicking on **Install**. During installation, you will be prompted to close Visual Studio, which you should do to provide for an orderly upgrade. The latest available version of PTVS will then be applied to your system.

 If you are installing Visual Studio from scratch, you can also opt to install PTVS in the installation program, saving time later.

Next, you need to install a version of Python for PTVS to work with. You can find the latest versions of Python at `https://python.org`. There, you will find the two main releases (at the time of writing), 2.7.11 and 3.5.1. The Python home page provides a good description of the differences between the two versions. For this recipe, choose 3.5.1, and install it with the default options. After both PTVS and your copy of Python has been installed, load VS2015. For this recipe, we will assume that you are using Visual Studio Community 2015.

How to do it...

Once you have installed PTVS and Python, open Visual Studio, and perform the following steps:

1. We will begin by ensuring that everything is installed correctly. Open the menu item **View | Other Windows | Python Environments**.

2. A new window will appear in the **Solution Explorer** area. This provides information on the installed **Python Environments** that VS2015 finds. You should see the version of Python that you installed is present. While you are there, click on the refresh button, as shown in the following screenshot, to update the Completion Database for IntelliSense:

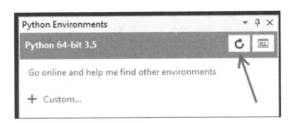

3. Let's take a look at the new project types that are available. Open the **New Project** dialog box (*Ctrl + Shift + N*). Under **Templates | Python**, you will see several Python-based options, as shown in the following screenshot:

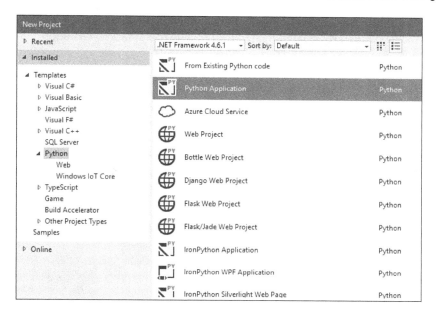

4. Proceed by selecting the **Python Application** project type and accepting the default name.

5. Now that this project is open, let's explore what other Python tools are available. One very helpful window is the interactive prompt. One of Python's strengths is **read-evaluate-print-loop** (**REPL**). PTVS provides an easy way to access this from within Visual Studio. Activate this by navigating to **View | Other Windows | Python 3.5 Interactive,** as shown in this screenshot:

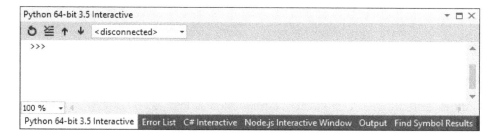

6. This window shown in the preceding screenshot lets you enter Python code directly for immediate execution. If you need to test a command or run a quick experiment, you can do so from within your editor. Also, because you are within the VS2015, you get all of the IDE features that you are familiar with: the navigation scroll bar, IntelliSense, and the ability to easily cut and paste results back into your main editor window.

7. Let's explore how this interactive window provides these benefits. Add the following code to your blank Python file (if using the defaults, it is titled `PythonApplication1.py`):

```python
print('Hello World')

a=32

b=64

print("Results: " + (b+a))
```

8. After entering the code, run the program using *F5* or through the **Debug | Start Debugging** menu. As you will see, this code displays the following **TypeError** error: **Can't convert 'int' to str implicitly.**

9. Now we will see how the **Interactive Window** can help solve this. Highlight the added lines of code, right-click on them, and choose **Send to Interactive**, as shown in the following screenshot:

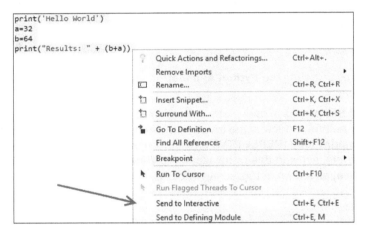

10. Once sent, the **Interactive Window** will rerun the code, and you will see the same error again. We can use this window to quickly work through solutions. With your cursor at the `>>>` prompt, just press the up arrow key to cycle through the program's lines. Edit the `print` line so that it now reads as follows:

```python
print("Results: " + str(b+a))
```

 When you add the `str` type, your cursor will still be in the middle of the line, so be sure to get to the end of the statement before pressing *Enter*.

11. Now that we are explicitly declaring the type, the correction will produce the following code:

```
>>> print("Results: " + str(b+a))
Results: 96
```

12. This solved the problem, so we can now add the `str` type to our source file, and continue with development.

How it works...

PTVS turns Visual Studio into a real, fully fledged developing environment for Python. In conjunction with the Python interpreter, PTVS allows you to use Python in a familiar setting without having to learn new tools.

There's more...

Since PTVS integrates the full Python language, covering all of the benefits it provides cannot be accomplished in a single recipe or even in a single book. Some of the additional features that PTVS supports include integration with the test runner, profiling, and remote debugging. As is the case for many of their open source tools, Microsoft uses GitHub to host the Python Tools for Visual Studio's home page (`https://microsoft.github.io/PTVS/`), which is a great source of information.

Integrating Python with .NET

We've just explored how PTVS can easily integrate Python into VS2015. Now we will look at **IronPython**, which integrates Python with the .NET and Mono platforms.

IronPython provides the ability to write applications that use WPF and WinForms as well as easily call the .NET code from within your Python program. Whether you want to do some rapid prototyping using IronPython as a glue language or build a full application, IronPython can be a useful addition to your developer toolbox.

Getting ready

IronPython is available for download at `http://ironpython.net/`, and should be installed before opening Visual Studio. This recipe assumes you have installed PTVS as described in the *Integrating Python into Visual Studio* recipe.

 The Python 2.7 series is different than the IronPython 2.7 series. Make sure you have the correct version installed!

How to do it...

Once you have installed PTVS and IronPython, open VS2015, and perform the following steps:

1. Create a new project using the **IronPython Windows Forms Application** template under **Python**.

2. The project will open with a Python listing in the editor window. This gives us an application skeleton that we can easily extend. Press *F5* to see what it looks like in its initial form. Once compilation has finished, a simple plain Windows form appears. After verifying it's presence, close the window, and return to the VS2015 editor.

3. Now, we are going to add some code to show a little bit more interactivity. Edit the `MyForm` class so that it matches the following code:

```python
class MyForm(Form):
def __init__(self):
# Create child controls and initialize form
  self.Text="Iron Python"
  goButton = Button()
  goButton.Text = "Go"
  goButton.Click += self.goButtonPressed
  self.label = Label()
  self.label.Text = "Ready to go!"
  self.label.Location = Point(40,40)
  self.label.Height = 25
  self.label.Width = 200
  self.Controls.Add(goButton)
  self.Controls.Add(self.label)
  pass
  def goButtonPressed(self, sender, args):
  self.label.Text = "Go button pressed"
```

 As with any Python program, whitespace is significant. If you have difficulty running the code sample, verify your formatting (including indentation).

4. Once entered, view the results by running the application again (press *F5*). The result is shown in the following screenshot:

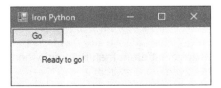

5. As mentioned in the introduction to this recipe, one of the advantages of using the integration that PTVS and IronPython provides is the ability to rapidly prototype the .NET code. We will continue this recipe by showing how this can work with a C# DLL.

6. Right-click on your open solution, and select **Add | New Project**. Select the **Class Library** template under **Visual C#**. Use the default project name of ClassLibrary1.

7. Add the following method to the Class1 body of your new class library:

```
public static int generate(int a, int b)
{
    Random rand = new Random((int)DateTime.Now.Ticks);
    return (rand.Next(a)+b);
}
```

8. Build the library through **Build | Build ClassLibrary1**. This will produce a DLL that includes our method, and makes a pseudo-random number available for our use. Now, we will use the next couple of steps to update our Python code and make use of it.

9. In the Python file, add the highlighted line in the following code snippet:

```
clr.AddReference('System.Drawing')
clr.AddReference('System.Windows.Forms')
clr.AddReferenceToFileAndPath(r"..\ClassLibrary1\bin\Debug\
ClassLibrary1.dll")
```

 If you have changed the default project names, you will need to adjust the reference to the DLL file path accordingly.

10. Similarly, add the following highlighted import statement:

```
from System.Drawing import *
from System.Windows.Forms import *
from ClassLibrary1 import *
```

11. Change the method for the button press action, as shown in the following code:

```
def goButtonPressed(self, sender, args):
classy = Class1()
self.label.Text = "Random number received: " +
str(classy.generate(10,4))
```

12. Run the application, and click on the **Go** button. You should see something similar to the following screenshot:

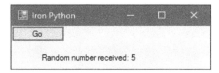

How it works...

By directly targeting the .NET and Mono runtimes, IronPython offers a different way to take advantage of Python. IronPython is able to do this as it runs on a **Dynamic Language Runtime** (**DLR**), which, in turn, runs on the CLR used by .NET languages. The conventional **CPython** interpreter (the Python environment that is the most widely used) is written in C, and typically runs standalone.

In our example, we first demonstrated how IronPython lets you build a WinForms application easily. Then, we created a proof of concept C# library to show how the resulting DLL can be accessed from Python with very little cost of time and effort. This gives you a lot of freedom, whether you want to add more functionalities to your Python-based programs or test the .NET code without having to spend a lot of time writing routine setup code.

Targeting Linux with Visual Studio 2015

The Linux operating system has been a popular alternative to Windows for many years. It has found great popularity in server environments, as well as powering many familiar systems, such as Google's Android. With the rise of new devices such as the Raspberry Pi and the staying power of non-Windows operating systems, many developers have found themselves looking for a way to pair their experience with Visual Studio onto these other systems.

Thanks to a new component of VS2015, it is now possible to use Visual Studio to write C++ code that can be compiled and debugged on a Linux- or UNIX-based system. The Visual C++ for Linux extension opens up the world of Linux development while enabling you to use the VS2015 tools you are already familiar with.

In this recipe, you will see how easy it is to use your copy of VS2015 to develop for Linux.

Getting ready

For this recipe, you need to make sure that you have a copy of Visual Studio Community 2015 (or higher) with the most recent update. Then you need to install the Visual C++ for Linux extension, which is available for download at the Visual Studio Gallery. At the time of writing, we will be using version 1.0.3, which is found at `https://visualstudiogallery.msdn.microsoft.com/725025cf-7067-45c2-8d01-1e0fd359ae6e`.

 This extension is undergoing rapid development, so despite being labeled a technical preview, it is still possible to use it today to accomplish useful work.

You will also need access to a system or virtual machine running Linux. These can be created on Azure or another system that you have access to. Our recipe assumes that you have a Debian- or Debian-based system (such as Ubuntu). If the necessary utilities are present, root access is not needed.

The extension supports most Linux and UNIX systems as long as they have the following programs installed:

- OpenSSH server (sshd)
- The g++ compiler (GNU C++ compiler)
- gdb (GNU Debugger)
- gdbserver (remote server for the GNU Debugger)

If you have root (administrator) access, you can usually install these on your Linux system with the following command: `sudo apt-get install openssh-server g++ gdb gdbserver`.

 Other Linux-based systems (RedHat, SUSE, and so on) as well as UNIX-based operating systems (FreeBSD, Mac OS X, and the like) should also work with this extension as long as you have the previously described tools installed.

Be sure to make note of the username and password for your account on the Linux-based machine before proceeding. After installing the extension, start Visual Studio.

How to do it...

With the successful installation of the extension, we can begin developing for Linux by taking the following steps:

1. The extension has provided some new project types. Create a new project using the **Console Application (Linux)** template, which is located under **Visual C++ | Cross Platform | Linux**, as shown in the following screenshot. You may use the default project name or one of your choice.

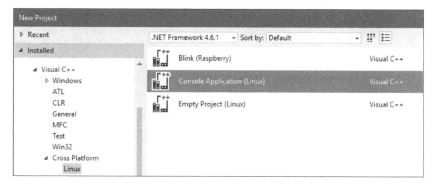

2. Open the `main.cpp` file to see the default skeleton file that will be used. You will see that it is a basic `HelloWorld` type program, but it will be sufficient to test our connections.

3. Clicking on **Remote GDB Debugger** in the toolbar (or pressing *F5*) will start a new build for your application.

4. If you have reinstalled the extension, your settings will remain on your VS2015 system and be reused. If you are running the extension for the first time, you will be prompted to set up a new connection to your Linux machine. To view or set up a connection, navigate to **Options | Cross Platform | C++ | Linux | Connection Manager**, and then click on **Add**, as shown in the following screenshot:

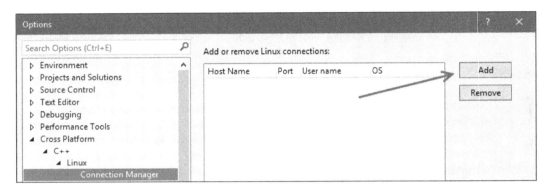

5. After clicking on **Add**, the **Connect to Linux** dialog appears. This lets you define the **Host name** (domain name or IP address of the machine you would like to connect to), the **Port** to use (typically, the default SSH port of 22 is correct), and the **User name** and **Password** of your user.

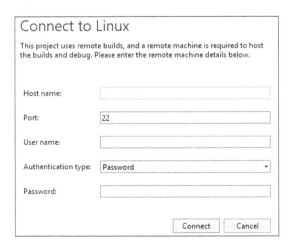

6. Complete the prompts for your system, and click on **Connect**. When you do so, VS2015 will test the connection to confirm that everything works. After successfully entering a connection, the **Connection Manager** updates to include the entry, as shown in the following screenshot:

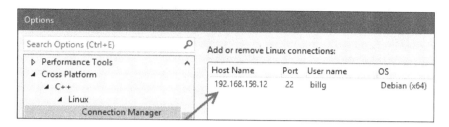

 Be sure to use the **Host Name** and **User name** for your environment.

7. Now when you build the application, it should connect to the remote machine you have specified, copy over your code, compile it, and then execute the resulting binary. Initially, a successful build may not look very exciting, as you can see in this screenshot of the **Output** window:

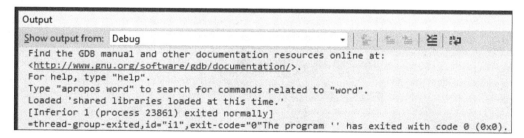

8. To view something more useful, we will check out **Linux Console**. This can be found under **Debug | Linux Console**, and you can see its output in the following screenshot:

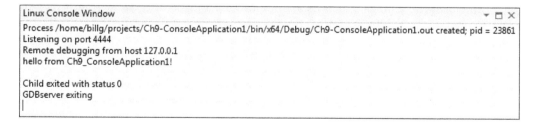

9. You can view the name of the executable created (`Ch9-ConsoleApplication1.out`) in the Linux Console window. You can also view the output from both the program and the debugger as it runs on the remote machine.

10. This **Linux Console** is not limited to output—it can also accept input and give that input to your running program. Rewrite the code in your `main.cpp` as follows:

```cpp
#include <cstdio>
#include <iostream>
int main()
{
    char str[128];
    printf("hello from Ch9_ConsoleApplication1!\n");
    std::cout << "Enter string: ";
    std::cin.get(str, 128);
    std::cout << "You entered: " << str;
    return 0;
}
```

11. Run your program again (*F5*). Return to **Linux Console Window**, where you will be prompted to enter some text. Enter some characters, and then hit *Enter*. The program will then repeat your text back to you, as shown in the next screenshot:

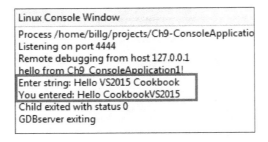

12. If you would like to view the settings for your application, you can do so by opening the properties for your project. There, under **Configuration Properties**, you can view or modify several changes including file paths or the remote machine you wish to use. The following screenshot shows a few of these settings:

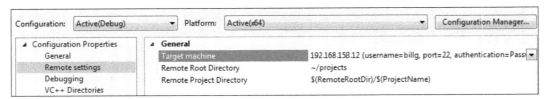

How it works...

The Visual C++ for Linux extension makes VS2015 aware of non-Windows environments, and of how to interact with their development tools over SSH. SSH is a popular protocol in the Linux and UNIX environments that provides secure connections. For more information on SSH, check out the multiplatform open source implementation, OpenSSH at `http://www.openssh.com/`.

To compile your code, VS2015 copies it over to your remote machine, runs that machine's compiler, and then shows you the output. For larger and more powerful systems, this extension gives you a way to harness their CPU cores and large amounts of memory from the comfort of your familiar VS2015 toolset. For smaller systems, such as the Raspberry Pi, you are able to develop for the device without having to worry about manually deploying files and connecting a display or keyboard.

There's more...

Our recipe demonstrated how the extension works by generating a 64-bit code for the x64 architecture, but you are not limited to this CPU type. You can also target different CPU types, such as the ARM based processors found in the Raspberry Pi family of devices, since the extension uses common open source tools and connections, allowing you to target several different major operating systems today, with more sure to follow.

10
Final Polish

In this chapter, we will cover the following recipes:

- ▸ Creating installer packages with InstallShield LE
- ▸ Creating custom installer packages
- ▸ Submitting UWP apps to the Windows Store
- ▸ Creating Visual Studio add-ins and extensions
- ▸ Creating your own snippets

Introduction

There are many little details that contribute to the success of a program. In this chapter, we will look at several different topics that don't fit into a specific category, but are useful to many different projects, and could be the missing ingredient your application needs. The first few recipes deal with some ways of getting your application ready for distribution to your end users, while the remainder provide some ways to improve your productivity with the Visual Studio IDE.

Creating installer packages with InstallShield LE

The need for an installer depends on the type of application you are working on. If you are creating a **Universal Windows Platform** (**UWP**) app, then you don't need an installer, as the new deployment model makes installers obsolete. If you are creating a web application, then Microsoft suggest you either use **XCopy** deployment or the **MSDeploy** web deployment technology.

But when it comes to traditional Win32-style applications, Microsoft seems to be in a conflict over whether to include a project for creating installer programs with Visual Studio. The release of VS2012 marked the removal of the popular Visual Studio Installer project type, which continues to remains absent in VS2015. There is still a way to construct an installer though, as the third-party publisher **InstallShield** has an arrangement with Microsoft to make the InstallShield Limited Edition available to developers using VS2015 Professional or greater.

In this recipe, we will use InstallShield to create an installer package for a simple application.

Getting ready

The recipe assumes you haven't yet installed InstallShield Limited Edition. If you have, then some of the early steps in this recipe will be different.

Simply start VS2015 (Professional or higher), and you're ready to go.

How to do it...

Create an installer using these steps:

1. Create a new **Visual C# | WPF Application** project, and name it `Basic WPF Application`.

2. Go to the project properties page by right-clicking on the project in **Solution Explorer** and selecting **Properties**. In the **Application** tab, set the icon for the application to either an icon of your choice, or to the icon located at `C:\Program Files (x86)\ Microsoft Visual Studio 14.0\Common7\IDE\ItemTemplates\CSharp\ General\1033\Icon.ico`.

3. Build the solution to make sure it compiles and executes properly. If you have already installed InstallShield Limited Edition, you can jump down to *Step 7*.

4. Right-click on the solution, and add a new project using the **Other Project Types |** **Setup and Deployment | Enable InstallShield Limited Edition** template, as shown in the following screenshot:

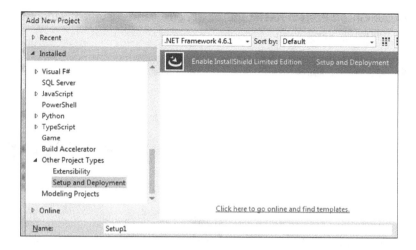

5. A browser window will appear with instructions on how to enable InstallShield in VS2015. Click on the link to redirect to the InstallShield website, register your details, and download the file as directed. When the download completes, save your solution, close VS2015, and then run the InstallShield setup executable.

6. Restart VS2013, and open the solution you created in *Step 1*.

7. Right-click on the solution in **Solution Explorer**, and choose **Add | New Project** from the context menu. In the **Add New Project** dialog, choose **Other Project Types |** **Setup and Deployment | InstallShield Limited Edition Project**, give it the default name, and then click on **OK**.

8. If this is the first time you have used InstallShield since it was installed, you will be asked whether you wish to evaluate or register. Choose to register, and activate the product using the serial number you should have received in your e-mail.

9. The InstallShield **Project Assistant** will appear in the document window, as shown in the following screenshot:

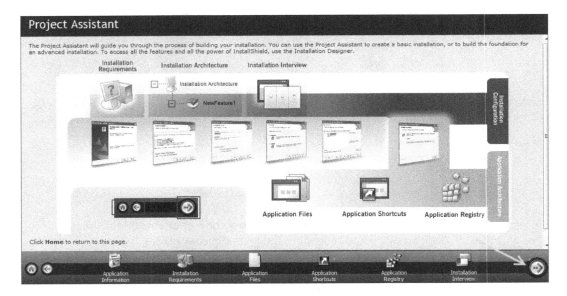

10. Click on the right arrow (the next button) at the bottom of the project assistant to advance to the **Application Information** page. On this screen, you may enter values for company name, application name, and so on. For our purposes, the defaults are acceptable. Enter a company web address, such as www.company.com, and then click on the next arrow.

11. Advance through the project assistant until you get to the **Application Files** page. Select the **My Product Name** node from the tree, and then click on **Add Project Outputs**:

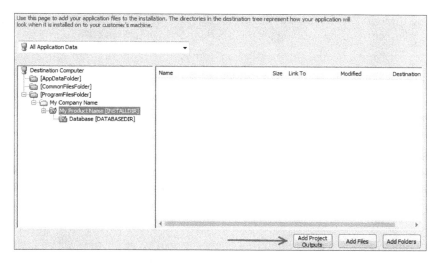

12. In the **Visual Studio Output Selector** dialog, select the **Primary output** item and click on **OK**:

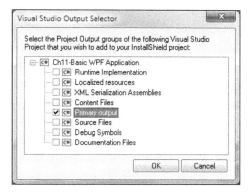

13. Click on the next button to go to the **Application Shortcuts** page. Click on the **New** button to add a shortcut to your application. Choose the [Program FilesFolder]\My Company Name\My Product Name\Simple WPF Application.Primary output from the dialog, and click on **Open**.

14. The shortcut is named Built by default. That's not very useful, so click the shortcut name to edit it and rename it to Simple WPF Application.

15. Additional menu options are available to make changes to the Registry or display a license agreement to the user, but we will skip them in this example. The required settings are now entered, so right-click on the Setup1 project in **Solution Explorer**, and select **Install** from the menu. If prompted to build out-of-date projects, click on **Yes**.

16. Step through the setup wizard to install the program. Verify that the program is installed correctly by looking for the application in your **Start Menu** or **Start Page**.

17. After verifying a successful installation, remove the program from your system by right-clicking on the `Setup1` project (from within Visual Studio) and selecting **Uninstall**.

How it works...

InstallShield reduces the complexity in creating installers by providing a set of sensible default configuration options and an easy-to-use user interface. It also understands exactly how the Windows installer system works, and warns when there are problems in how the installation process is configured. Any discrepancies can then be fixed so that your end users have a trouble-free installation.

A license for Limited Edition is provided free of charge with VS2015, and will be sufficient for basic installation purposes. If you need a heavily customized installation process, then you should investigate the more advanced versions of InstallShield, or competing offerings such as Nullsoft's NSIS or WiX (Windows Installer XML toolset) available at `http://wixtoolset.org/`.

See also

▶ The *Creating custom installer packages* recipe in this chapter.

▶ Microsoft has developed **ClickOnce**, which can also be used to deploy Windows-based applications. More information is available at `http://msdn.microsoft.com/en-us/library/t71a733d.aspx`. Developers using writing application in C++ should also review the ClickOnce information at `http://msdn.microsoft.com/en-us/library/ms235287.aspx`.

▶ **Nullsoft Scriptable Install System** (**NSIS**) at `http://nsis.sourceforge.net/Main_Page`.

Creating custom installer packages

The previous section detailed how to get started with the freely available InstallShield LE software. While this approach can be helpful in some cases, for users of the Visual Studio Community, it is not an available option. Another consideration is for those projects where greater control of the installation process is required over what is available in Limited Edition. Finally, developers just may not want to rely on a third-party vendor for their project to be successful.

For these reasons and any that you may have, it is good to know that an alternative exists. Thanks to the freely available VS2015 Installer Projects extension provided by Microsoft, there is a way to develop your own custom installer with VS2015.

Getting ready

For this recipe, you can use Visual Studio Community 2015 or one of the Premium editions. If you have an existing project with an executable, you can use that with the recipe, or follow along as we create a sample one to help illustrate the concepts.

How to do it...

Perform the following steps to create a custom installer for your project:

1. Download the Microsoft VS2015 Installer Projects extension from the Visual Studio Gallery or directly via the following URL: `https://visualstudiogallery.msdn.microsoft.com/f1cc3f3e-c300-40a7-8797-c509fb8933b9`.

2. After installing the extension, restart VS2015.

3. Create a new project that will represent the program you wish to install. If you have one of your own, feel free to use it. For the purposes of this recipe, we will create a new project using the **Visual C# | Console Application** template.

4. To provide us with something to look at, add the following code to the existing `Main` method as shown:

```
static void Main(string[] args)
{
  Console.WriteLine("Hello Cookbook");
  Console.WriteLine("Press any key to exit...");
  Console.ReadKey(true);
}
```

5. Build your project to ensure everything is in working order before continuing.

6. Now we will see what the Installer Projects extension can do for us. Right-click on your solution in the **Solution Explorer**, and select **Add | New Project**. Under **Other Project Types**, look for the **Visual Studio Installer** group, as shown in the following screenshot. Select the **Setup Wizard** template, accepting the default project name, or using one of your own choice:

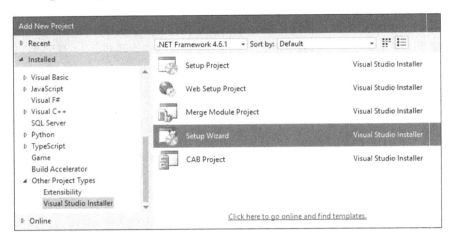

7. A **Setup Wizard** will then appear. The first screen will be introductory, so after reading it, click on **Next** and proceed to the second.

8. The second screen offers four available choices that correspond to the various project types that we saw in *Step 6*. For this recipe, choose the default option and click on **Next**, as shown in the following screenshot:

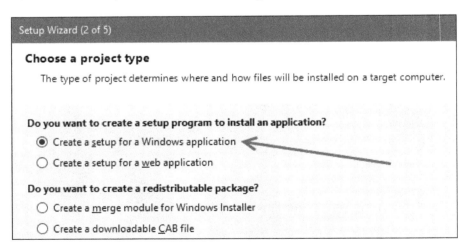

9. The third screen lets us select the files or groups that should be part of the installer. For our project, we will select Primary output (which includes our project's executable) as shown in the following screenshot, and click on **Next**:

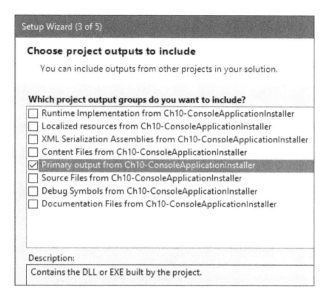

If you are adding an installer to one of your own projects, you may want to add additional groups such as **Content Files** or **Documentation Files**.

10. The fourth screen of the wizard allows you to install any extra files that you may require for your project. For this recipe, we will proceed as is, so click on **Next** to continue.

11. The fifth screen of the wizard provides a summary of your selections, and the opportunity to turn back and make any changes. For our recipe, we are ready to continue, so click on **Finish**.

12. The wizard will now create a new Setup project, and add it to your solution. A new screen appears with details about the project. The following screenshot shows the outcome of this recipe:

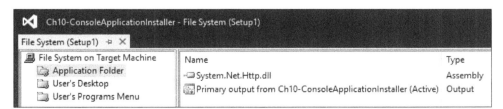

13. While the wizard has produced a valid installer for us, there are a few more things we should configure for best results. Let's create a shortcut for our program. Click on the `User's Programs Menu` folder for your Setup project, and then right-click on the right menu pane. Then select **Create New Shortcut**, as shown in the following screenshot:

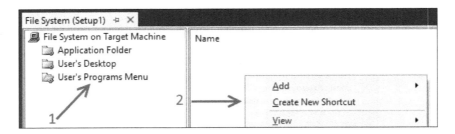

14. In the resulting dialog, select **Application Folder** and then **Primary Output...**, as shown in the following screenshot. Then click on **OK** to proceed:

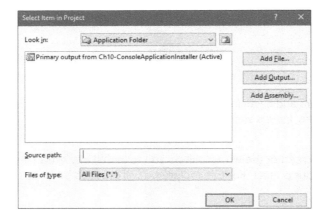

15. When using an installer, it is important for the installer to be aware of the requirements for the executable that you are deploying. Since C# projects default to **.NET Framework 4.6.1**, let's make sure that our installer is aware of this. Right-click on the Setup project in **Solution Explorer**, and select **Properties**.

16. In the project's **Property Pages** dialog, click on **Prerequisites...**, as shown in the following screenshot:

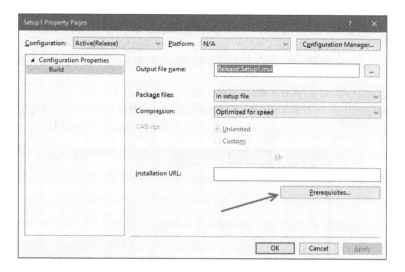

17. In the **Prerequisites** dialog, uncheck the currently selected Microsoft .NET Framework, and instead, select the one corresponding to your project, which, in our case, is **Microsoft .NET Framework 4.6.1**, as shown in the following screenshot:

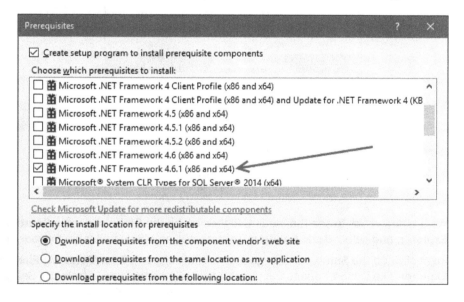

18. After making the change in **Prerequisites**, click on **OK** to return to the **Property Pages**. Then click on **OK** again.

> In our example, the build **Configuration** in *Step 16* was set to **Active(Release)**. When modifying **Prerequisites**, you will have to repeat Steps 16 through 18 for each target you are working with.

19. Finally, double-click on the **Microsoft .NET Framework** under Detected Dependencies in the **Solution Explorer**. Change the **Version** setting to reflect the proper .NET Framework, as shown in the following screenshot:

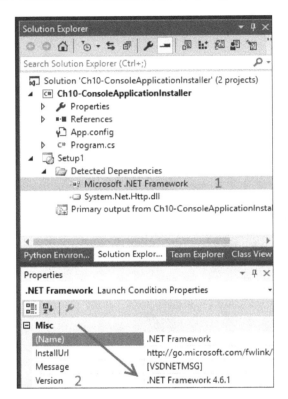

20. We are now ready to see the results. Right-click on the Setup project in **Solution Explorer**, and select **Build Solution**. This creates an MSI installer file for your project.

21. Right-click on the Setup project again, this time selecting **Open Folder in File Explorer**. File Explorer opens the directory containing the output from the Setup project. Depending on whether you selected a **Debug** or **Release** build, choose the appropriate folder. You will find the installer that you just built for your application within, ready for you to install.

How it works...

The Installer Project's **Setup Wizard** provides a guide through the various options available to us. Thanks to the wizard, it is easy to get started with a working installer. The resulting file packages our project's application, and assists with any required files that are needed.

There's more...

This extension has more than just the Setup project that we chose in this recipe. Based on the application you are developing, it is also possible to create a web application installer or redistribution packages for either a CAB file or a merge module, as shown in the screenshot accompanying *Step 8*.

> For more information on *Merge Modules*, visit `https://msdn.` `microsoft.com/en-us/library/windows/desktop/` `aa369820(v=vs.85).aspx` on MSDN.

Submitting UWP apps to the Windows Store

While existing legacy desktop-style applications can be distributed using the traditional methods (as described in *Creating installer packages with InstallShield LE*), the only way to distribute Windows Store apps will be via the Windows Store, and they must pass a certification process for that to happen.

Certification is the process by which Microsoft ensures that apps available in the Windows Store will meet certain performance and quality standards. As a developer, the Store makes it easy for customers to obtain and install your app. In this recipe, we'll look at how the certification process works. Since apps for Windows 8 can only be maintained at this point, we'll focus on creating a new app for Windows 8.1.

Getting ready

Since we will be working with UWP apps, you will need to use Windows 10 with Visual Studio Community 2015 or one of the Premium editions. We will use a blank UWP app for this recipe, but feel free to substitute one of your UWP apps if you have one available.

How to do it...

Perform the following steps to submit your UWP app:

1. Start a new **Visual C# | Windows | Blank App (Universal Windows)** project.
2. From the menu, select **Project | Store | Open Developer Account**.

3. A browser window will open, and you can apply for a developer account using the process as outlined on the page. Establishing a developer's account may require a payment of a small license fee, so have a supported payment method available (credit card, PayPal, or any other) when you perform this step.

4. Once you have an account, switch back to Visual Studio, and from the menu, choose **Project | Store | Reserve app name**.

5. Again a browser window will open, and you will be directed to the **Windows Dev Center** dashboard where you may register the name for your application. Follow the process as described on that page.

6. From the Visual Studio menu, select **Project | Store | Edit App Manifest**, and use the information from the app name reservation to populate the appropriate fields. Take particular note of the fields on the packaging tab.

7. Alternatively, you can select the **Project | Store | Associate App** with the Store menu entry, and follow the steps of the wizard to automatically populate the packaging tab with the appropriate values as shown in the following screenshot. This is helpful if you have started entering the metadata for your app online outside of Visual Studio:

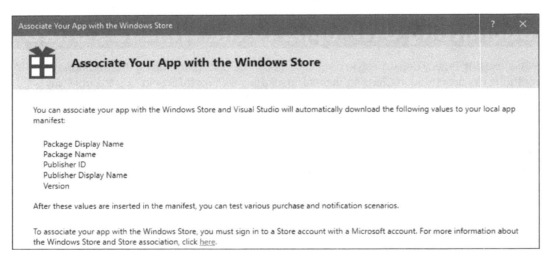

8. At this point, you are ready to write your application.

 Current Microsoft guidelines allow an app name to be reserved for a year. If your app is not submitted by this deadline, the reservation expires.

9. Verify your application using the **Windows App Certification Kit**. Refer to the *Validating your Windows Store app* recipe in *Chapter 2, Getting Started with Universal Windows Platform Apps*, to do this.

10. Package your application for uploading to the store by choosing **Project | Store | Create App Package**.

11. Then, upload the resulting package to the store by selecting **Project | Store | Upload App Package** from the menu. This will open a new web browser window and take you to the **Windows Dev Center** where you can complete an app submission form. This form allows you to enter details on your app's pricing, description, properties, and so on.

12. After completing the submission form, you can upload your app package. Once the upload completes, you can monitor the progress of your package through the approval process using the tools provided by the **Windows Dev Center** dashboard.

How it works...

The Store submenu is only available when running Visual Studio in Windows 10, and when you have opened the solution for a UWP app. When you upload a package to the store, there are a number of basic sanity checks to verify that your package is acceptable and meets the requirements of the Windows Store. These checks include running the certification toolkit on your app, and verifying the manifest information against the information you supplied when you registered the app name. Using Visual Studio's Associate app with the store wizard is an easy way to make sure you don't have any errors in your manifest, and it improves the chances of a successful first-time submission.

There's more...

Earning money with Windows Store apps is not limited solely to upfront purchase revenues. You may also distribute your app using a trial mode that encourages a try-before-you-buy approach. Apps may include the ability to support in-app purchases, in-app advertising using your choice of ad platforms, and it may implement a custom transaction system if you so desire.

> For in-app purchases and trial versions of your product, Microsoft bundles supporting functionality in the `Windows.ApplicationModel.Store` namespace to make it easier for you to build applications with these features. A sample UWP app is available using these features at `https://github.com/Microsoft/Windows-universal-samples/tree/master/Samples/Store`.

If you want to confirm the requirements for App certification, refer to the Microsoft documentation on the subject at `https://msdn.microsoft.com/en-us/library/windows/apps/dn764944.aspx`.

 ▶ The *Packaging your UWP app* recipe, *Chapter 2, Getting Started with Universal Windows Platform Apps*

 ▶ The *Validating your Windows Store app* recipe, *Chapter 2, Getting Started with Universal Windows Platform Apps*

Creating Visual Studio add-ins and extensions

When Microsoft released Visual Studio 2010, they changed the approach to extensibility by introducing the VSIX format, and the number of extensions in the Visual Studio gallery is a testament to how successful this change has been.

Thanks to this accessible framework, you can make your own add-ins and extensions in Visual Studio to fill in any missing functionality that you want for your particular workflow. This recipe will show you how to configure your copy of VS2015 for extension development.

Getting ready

To create extensions, you will need to have the VS2015 SDK installed. In prior versions of Visual Studio, this was a standalone product, but it is now available from the main VS2015 installer. Even better, the Professional edition is no longer required, so you can create extensions using Visual Studio Community.

To verify that you have the SDK installed, and to install it if necessary, you will need to run the installer for your copy of VS2015. This can be found by going to the **Control Panel** for **Add / Remove Programs**. In Windows 10, you can find this in **System Settings**, under **Apps & features**. Once the installer is open, you will need to install the **Visual Studio Extensibility Tools Update** (the exact version, appropriate to your copy of Visual Studio) as shown in the following screenshot:

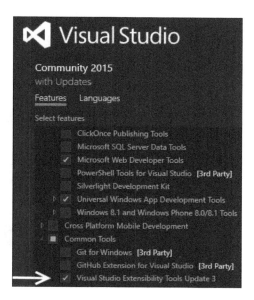

Once the SDK is installed, start VS2015, and you're ready to go.

How to do it...

Perform the following steps:

1. Start a new project using the **Visual C#** | **Extensibility** | **VSIX Project** template and the default name.

   Additional extensibility templates exist for Visual Basic and C++ too.

2. Pressing *F5* will start a new instance of Visual Studio in the debug mode (it may take a while to start), where you can use the Add-in manager (**Tools | Add-in Manager...**) to enable your add-in and check its functionality. For this recipe, no changes are needed. The following screenshot shows our recipe's extension installed and enabled:

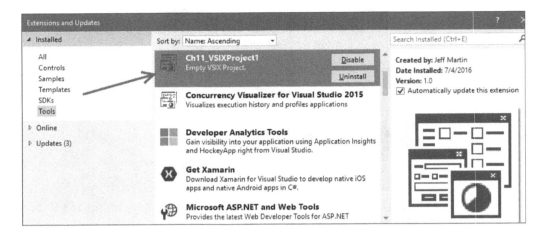

 Because a debugger is attached, starting the experimental instance of Visual Studio may take longer than you are used to. It will have **Experimental Instance** in the title bar to help distinguish it from your regular instance of Visual Studio.

3. Close the **Experimental Instance**, and return to your original instance of Visual Studio.

4. From the **Solution Explorer**, open the `source.extension.vsixmanifest` file, and populate the **Author** field with your name. You can also use this file to provide a **Description**, **Product Name**, and set a custom icon for your extension. When preparing an actual extension, you will want to ensure that these are filled in to be helpful for your users.

5. Now we will see how to add an item to our extension, and make it do something. Right-click on your project in **Solution Explorer**, and select **Add | New Item** (*Ctrl + Shift + A*). Under **Visual C# Items | Extensibility**, select **Editor Viewport Adornment**.

6. You can see the code for this adornment in the file `ViewportAdornment1.cs`. This is now part of our extension package, so execute the project to see the results.

7. When Visual Studio has finished loading, it will automatically instantiate the extension making it active and available. From the Visual Studio menu, select **File | New File | File**, select **General | Text File**, and click **Open**. You should see a purple box in the top-right corner of the editor surface, as shown in the following screenshot; this proves that the extension is working as expected:

8. Close the experimental instance of Visual Studio to return to your project.

How it works...

The **Experimental Instance** of Visual Studio is launched using an experimental hive. The experimental hive is a separate set of Visual Studio settings you can use when testing extensions that won't affect your normal development settings. You may have noticed proof of this separation when it launches, as you are prompted to set your settings, just as you did the first time you launched VS2015 after installing it.

With VS2015, extensions are now the official way to extend Visual Studio, as add-ins have been deprecated. An extension implements a **Managed Extensibility Framework** (**MEF**) contract, and is not as restricted in the APIs it can access or in the way it is implemented.

There's more...

There is a lot more flexibility in building extensions over add-ins, and this also applies to the update and distribution mechanism. Beyond the template we looked at in this recipe, there are many areas of Visual Studio that can be customized, including defining custom commands, tool windows, and so on. This provides you with the opportunity to reshape Visual Studio to fit your needs.

The **Extension Manager** complements the NuGet package system described in the *Managing packages with NuGet* recipe in *Chapter 3*, *Web Development*. The difference is that **Extension Manager** focuses on enhancements to Visual Studio, while NuGet is used to obtain libraries to be distributed with your application.

Creating your own snippets

Visual Studio snippets are a great way to quickly write repetitive chunks of code that follow the same basic structure—potentially, saving you from a lot of time and typing. Snippets have been extended to work on more than just standard code files, and should be considered whenever you find yourself writing similar code over and over. Using snippets can save time and reduce the possibility of bugs—simply write the code correctly once, and then reuse.

For example, you may want to generate a class signature that inherits from a specific base class you use in your application, or you may have a certain attribute that needs to be placed above method calls to enable logging, or you may have specific IDs you want to use in HTML elements to ensure CSS styles can be consistently applied to your web pages. Unfortunately, out-of-the-box Visual Studio still doesn't have an inbuilt way of authoring snippets, so you will have to write some XML. Fortunately, it only takes a few minutes to create a snippet and the time you can save once it exists makes it worth doing.

This recipe will show you how to create your own snippets, and then utilize them from inside Visual Studio.

Getting ready

Simply start VS2015, and you're ready to go.

How to do it...

Create your own snippet using the following steps:

1. From the menu, choose **File** | **New** | **File**, select **XML File**, and click on **Open**.

2. Edit the file, adding the following XML code:

```xml
<?xml version="1.0" encoding="utf-8"?>
<CodeSnippets
xmlns="http://schemas.microsoft.com/VisualStudio/2005/
CodeSnippet">
  <CodeSnippet Format="1.0.0.">
    <Header>
      <Title>Wrap text in a span</Title>
      <Shortcut>spanned</Shortcut>
      <SnippetTypes>
        <SnippetType>Expansion</SnippetType>
        <SnippetType>SurroundsWith</SnippetType>
      </SnippetTypes>
    </Header>
    <Snippet>
```

```
<Declarations>
  <Literal>
    <ID>id</ID>
    <Default>elementId</Default>
  </Literal>
</Declarations>
<Code Language="HTML">
  <![CDATA[<span id="$id$">$selected$</span> is now
  in a span!]]>
</Code>
    </Snippet>
  </CodeSnippet>
</CodeSnippets>
```

3. Save the file as `spanned text.snippet` in your `Documents` folder.

4. From the menu, select **Tools | Code Snippets Manager** (shortcut *Ctrl+K, Ctrl+B*).

 If you are using VS Express for Windows and cannot locate the **Code Snippets Manager** on your menu, enable **Expert Settings** via **Tools | Settings | Expert Settings**.

5. Click on the **Import** button. Select the file you saved in *Step 3*, and click on **Open**.

6. Leave the location as **My HTML Snippets**, as suggested, and click on **Finish**, as shown in the following screenshot:

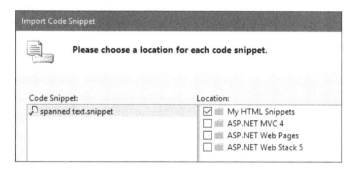

7. The snippet file will be automatically copied to the appropriate location in `Documents\Visual Studio 2015\Code Snippets`.

8. In the **Code Snippets Manager**, change the **Language** to **HTML**, and expand the My HTML Snippets location to confirm your snippet has been loaded. After confirming this, click on **OK** to close the dialog:

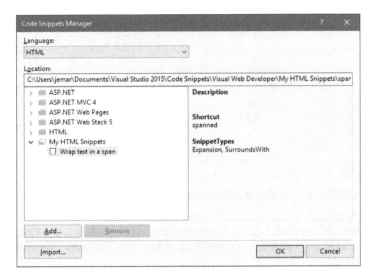

9. From the menu, select **File | New | File**, select **General | HTML Page**, and click on **Open**.

10. In the contents of the body tag, enter `<p>this is some text</p>`.

11. Select the words is some. Right-click on the selection, choose **Surround With**, then **My HTML Snippets | Wrap text in a span**, and hit *Enter* as shown in the following screenshot:

```
<html lang="en" xmlns="http://www.w3.org/1999/xhtml">
<head>
    <meta charset="utf-8" />
    <title></title>
</head>
<body>
    <p>this is some Surround With: My HTML Snippets  > |
</body>                                        Wrap text in a span
</html>                          Shortcut: spanned
```

12. The snippet will be expanded, and the contents of the id attribute for the span will be selected. Enter the text myId to replace the highlighted elementId placeholder and hit *Enter*. The cursor will move to the end of the closing span tag.

How it works...

The `Header` section is where the display title of the snippet, a shortcut name (in this case, `spanned`), the human-friendly description, and the type of snippet is being defined. Our example is in the `Expansion` and `SurroundsWith` categories. This means our snippet can be used with the selected text (`SurroundsWith`) or at the cursor's current position in the editor (`Expansion`).

The `Snippet` section is where the bulk of the work is done. Visual Studio automatically scans the code body of the snippet for an identifier placeholder of `$id$` so that it can populate it with the default value and prompt you for your own value.

By declaring the snippet as a `SurroundsWith` snippet, the selected text is passed to the `$selected$` placeholder in the body. Since `Expansion` is also supported, if you enter the snippet on a blank line, Visual Studio will still just generate the following text:

```
<span id="elementId"></span> is now in a span!
```

There's more...

There is a **Snippet Designer** project on GitHub (`https://github.com/mmanela/snippetdesigner`) from Matthew Manela that provides a GUI tool to make creating of snippets much easier. It also enables you to select a section of code and export that as a snippet so that you have an easy starting point for making your own custom snippets.

Remember that snippets are more than just a simple text entry/replacement mechanism, and it's worth spending a little time looking through the full schema reference for snippets on MSDN at `https://msdn.microsoft.com/en-us/library/ms171418(v=vs.140).aspx` to get a better idea of what they can do for you.

Index

UWP app development
enabling, on Windows 10 31-33
UWP app performance
analyzing 62-65
UWP app simulator
fresh app install 52
network properties, changing 51
remote debugging 52
resizing 51
resolution 51
screenshots, capturing 52
using 45-51

V

variable values
finding 174
Visual Studio
code, searching quickly 22-24
Python, integrating into 309-313
searching and navigating 21, 22
using, for Node.js development 108-113
Visual Studio 2013 (VS2013) 1
Visual Studio 2015
about 82
Linux, targeting with 316-320
settings, synchronizing 2-4
Visual Studio add-ins
creating 338-341
Visual Studio commands
searching 18-20
Visual Studio extensions
creating 338-341
Visual Studio Gallery
reference 316
Visual Studio Graphics Diagnostics
using 243-247
Visual Studio Online (VSO) 250

Visual Studio Team Services (VSTS) 250
VS2015 IDE
CodeLens 11-13
Code Maps 13, 14
notifications 7, 8
Peek Definition 10, 11
scroll bar thumbnail 9, 10
Send Feedback menu 6
touring 4-6
user account 8

W

web applications
asynchrony, using with 199-202
Windows 10
UWP app development, enabling 31-33
**Windows Communication
Foundation (WCF) 116**
Windows Metadata (WinMD) 38
Windows Runtime (WinRT) 30, 192
Windows Store
UWP apps, submitting to 335-337
UWP app, submitting 74-76
Windows Store app
validating 71-73
work
managing 259-265
work items 259

X

XAML
using, with C++ 210-214
XAML toolbar 215
XAML toolset
with Update 2 214
XCopy 323

www.ingramcontent.com/pod-product-compliance
Lightning Source LLC
Chambersburg PA
CBHW062051050326
40690CB00016B/3050